10/26/22

Go Bearcats!

"Reading *Both/And Thinking* has changed how I see myself and the world around me. Through their rigorous research and vulnerable voices, Professors Smith and Lewis gently guide us toward promising possibilities we may not have imagined in our either/or minds."

—**DOLLY CHUGH,** professor, NYU Stern School of Business; author, *The Person You Mean to Be* and *A More Just Future*

"We need to move beyond our reductionist, dichotomous thinking to embrace more holistic, integrative approaches. Smith and Lewis show us how we can all work together to do just that."

—**ZITA COBB,** founder and CEO, Shorefast; innkeeper, Fogo Island Inn

"Is life a zero sum game? Does wanting more X mean we have to settle for less Y? Nowhere is this question clearer than in business and finance. Which is why this book is so important for today's decision makers. By posing the alternative 'both/and' to the traditional 'either/or,' Wendy Smith and Marianne Lewis explore the current relevance of the work-life balance debate in top-level employee management. A must-read for all senior executives."

—**SIR STELIOS HAI-IOANNOU,** founder, easyJet; owner, easyGroup; and Chairman, Stelios Philanthropic Foundation

"This book is a must-read for anyone who wants creative and sustainable new insights to address our world's greatest problems. Smith and Lewis have integrated compelling research to show us how to engage in a revolutionary new way of thinking. Our world would be a better place if everyone read this book and adopted the tools for both/and thinking."

—**JEREMY HOCKENSTEIN,** founder and CEO, Digital Divide Data (DDD)

"We experience paradoxes everywhere, in business and in our personal lives. As leaders, the more we can identify paradoxes and know how to deal with them while avoiding the trap of solving for one issue, the more effective we can be. Wendy Smith and Marianne Lewis's book offers new insights into the many paradoxes we all face, along with a road map for addressing them. I highly recommend this book to all leaders."

—**TERRI KELLY,** former CEO, W. L. Gore & Associates (Gore)

"Part of being human is the internal tension we experience from competing demands across our personal and professional lives. Oh, the hours we spend in mental anguish! Both/and thinking replaces win/lose solutions with problem-solving that collaborates with alternative choices and allows for creative possibilities. There are many people, including myself, who will sleep better after reading this brilliant book."

—**BETSY MYERS,** author, *Take the Lead*; former Executive Director, Center for Public Leadership, Harvard Kennedy School

"Both/and thinking is mandatory for leaders today, as they must transcend the binary world of either/or and adopt a more holistic and transformative approach. Having spent decades studying how leaders do this, Smith and Lewis bring us the wisdom necessary for all leaders—and for all of us—living in this complex world."

—**ANTHONY SILARD,** author, *Screened In* and *The Connection*; professor of leadership and Director, the Center for Sustainable Leadership, Luiss Business School, Rome

"To navigate the increasing complexities of work, we need to abandon either/or thinking and embrace a both/and mindset. Smith and Lewis, the world's leading authorities on paradoxes, have given us the guidebook to do exactly that and tackle our most difficult problems."

—**SCOTT SONENSHEIN,** Henry Gardiner Symonds Professor of Management, Rice University; bestselling author, *Stretch* and coauthor, *Joy at Work*

"Wendy Smith and Marianne Lewis are giving their readers the gifts of critical thinking, discipline, and perspective as we learn to overcome life's daily dilemmas in a more thoughtful, satisfying, and time-efficient manner."

—**MARTY WIKSTROM,** founding partner, Atelier Fund

BOTH/AND THINKING

BOTH/AND THINKING

Embracing Creative Tensions
to Solve Your Toughest Problems

WENDY K. SMITH
MARIANNE W. LEWIS

HARVARD BUSINESS REVIEW PRESS

BOSTON, MASSACHUSETTS

The web addresses referenced in this book were live and correct at the time of the book's publication but may be subject to change.

Library of Congress Cataloging-in-Publication Data

Names: Smith, Wendy K., author. | Lewis, Marianne W., author.
Title: Both/and thinking : embracing creative tensions to solve your toughest problems / Wendy K. Smith, Marianne W. Lewis.
Description: Boston, Massachusetts : Harvard Business Review Press, [2022] | Includes bibliographical references and index. | Provided by publisher.
Identifiers: LCCN 2021062002 (print) | LCCN 2021062003 (ebook) | ISBN 9781647821043 (hardcover) | ISBN 9781647821050 (epub)
Subjects: LCSH: Multiple criteria decision making. | Creative ability in business. | Choice (Psychology) | Problem solving. | Success in business.
Classification: LCC BF448 .S64 2022 (print) | LCC BF448 (ebook) | DDC 658.4/03—dc23/eng/20220211
LC record available at https://lccn.loc.gov/2021062002
LC ebook record available at https://lccn.loc.gov/2021062003

ISBN: 978-1-64782-104-3
eISBN: 978-1-64782-105-0

The paper used in this publication meets the requirements of the American National Standard for Permanence of Paper for Publications and Documents in Libraries and Archives Z39.48-1992.

Wendy
To Michael
for being the yin of my yang

Marianne
To my father, Steve Wheelwright,
for modeling the way

CONTENTS

FOREWORD

The Power of Both/And Thinking
in a Vexing World

Opportunities to shift from either/or thinking to both/and thinking have never been more present than they are today in our increasingly complex, uncertain, and tenuous world. Seemingly intractable conflicts and unsolvable challenges are ubiquitous. The path forward often lies in identifying and integrating different perspectives. Wendy Smith and Marianne Lewis, whom I have known for many years, set out to unpack the thorny paradoxes lurking behind our greatest challenges and to illuminate a path forward. Building on their innovative research, these two talented researchers present the value of tensions—even as we resist their pulling us in opposing directions—as a crucial mindset shift in helping people find novel, lasting, and creative solutions.

Why Both/And Thinking Matters Now

A brief scan of headlines over recent years reminds us that tensions are the norm. We grapple daily with persistent and rising conflicts at all levels—societal, organizational, and personal. For starters, a global pandemic disrupted nations around the world, affecting physical, mental, and economic life in widely varying ways. Work-life tensions boiled over as the pandemic progressed, triggering what some call the *great resignation*—people's departure from employers in large numbers, seeking better wages, greater flexibility, or deeper meaning. Pivotal incidents—from natural disasters to the murder of a Minneapolis citizen named George Floyd—sparked vital conversations on shared humanitarian and planetary challenges. Yet rather than bringing us together, these incidents instead widened political divides. Ensuring the sustainability of our habitat while ensuring justice and fairness in society and economic opportunity for all often seem like impossible dreams. Yet thoughtful business leaders, notably Paul Polman, former CEO of Unilever (featured in this book), have called on businesses to support rather than denigrate our fragile environment. Nonetheless, progress is slow. The problems we face remain vexing, wicked, complicated . . . and diverse.

Wendy and Marianne argue that understanding paradoxes, which they define as persistent interdependent contradictions, is vital to solving such problems. As you read their ideas, you are likely to start seeing paradoxes everywhere. You will discover conflicting demands that pull in opposing directions: tensions between today and tomorrow, between ourselves and others, or between keeping things stable and wanting them to change. Whether you are a national leader seeking to respond to a pandemic, an organizational leader trying to be agile in a shifting market, or a person struggling with the next move in your career, you are encouraged to embrace tensions. Doing so, Wendy and Marianne suggest, fosters creativity and thriving amid all these challenges.

Like Wendy and Marianne, I have learned in my own research—which has focused on learning and teaming in organizations—to appreciate the challenge of crossing boundaries. Success in knowledge- and expertise-intensive environments depends on constant learning and, increasingly, on constant teaming—communicating and coordinating with people across boundaries of expertise, status, and distance.[1] Learning and teaming are both fraught with tensions. Learning requires us to honor what we know today, while also letting go in order to develop new insights for tomorrow. Teaming depends on strong individual contributions, while being willing to subsume individual needs and preferences for collective gain. These paradoxes make learning and teaming both powerful and challenging. It's difficult to navigate them without a safe interpersonal context in which candor seems feasible. My research, extended by the research of dozens of other scholars and practitioners, shows that psychological safety—a climate in which people are comfortable expressing and being themselves—allows teams to more effectively learn.[2] Yet even the concept of psychological safety encompasses paradoxical tensions: it takes courage to be vulnerable. I think of courage and psychological safety as two sides of the same precious coin. On one side, psychological safety describes an environment that lowers interpersonal risk; on the other, the individuals who must take those risks must be courageous because they cannot fully know, in advance, that what they do and say will be well received. An individual who wants to contribute an idea but who fears it will be rejected by others is, in effect, in a bind. When you are in a bind, I have found, it's helpful to name it. To call attention to the tension! In that way, you invite others into the conversation to help navigate the tension and find a way forward.

What makes Wendy and Marianne's book so compelling is that they go beyond labeling the paradoxes we face. They also offer ways to navigate them, turning seemingly vexing puzzles into wellsprings of creativity and possibility. Drawing from more than twenty-five years of research, they present tools and show how these tools work together in an integrated system. Given the power and elegance of their ideas, I believe that their paradox system will be widely used in leadership development courses for years to come.

Why I'm Excited That Wendy and Marianne Wrote This Book

I first met Wendy when she was a doctoral student at Harvard Business School, where I had the privilege to be part of her dissertation committee. She arrived at the idea of paradox in her research by studying how IBM's top leaders pursued innovation at the same times that they maintained the company's existing products and services. They recognized the need to steward the revenues of the present while developing the revenues of the future. A focus on paradoxes made sense in her research but doing so was also risky. Even though ideas about paradoxes date back thousands of years, and influential management academics like Charles Perrow, Andy

Van de Ven, Marshall Scott Poole, Bob Quinn, and Kim Cameron had explored paradox in organization theory in the 1970s and 1980s, this stream had largely remained silent for some years.[3] Yet Wendy persisted.

Fortunately for Wendy, Marianne was also boldly paving the way to explore paradox in business research. And fortunately for me, I also met Marianne many years ago—introduced by her father, who had been a treasured senior colleague at Harvard Business School. Marianne wrote a groundbreaking paper on paradox, stitching together long-standing insights from philosophy and psychology along with a rising but still limited set of publications in our shared field of organizational behavior. That paper won the best article of the year in a top journal and was soon opening broader academic conversations.

Working together on these ideas, Wendy and Marianne made a formidable team. They first pursued the concepts intellectually, together writing an important paper that laid out the foundations of paradox and became the most cited in a particularly prestigious scholarly journal over the last decade. They then conducted research experiments to expand on and test fundamental knowledge about paradoxes and how we navigate them. Consistent with their own philosophy, Wendy and Marianne also built communities that connected academics, business leaders, and individuals interested in paradox, organizing conferences and symposia for academics in the field. In the last 10 years, we have seen extensive research building on ideas about the nature of management of paradoxes from scholars across the globe. Wendy and Marianne also worked with corporate leaders, middle managers, and frontline employees to both learn from them and help them use these ideas to further their own work. In sum, Wendy and Marianne have pushed forward paradox as a concept that will have a critical impact on research and practice, an impact that is greatly needed at this time.

Ultimately, Wendy and Marianne highlight the capacity for both/and thinking as a way to enable more creative and sustainable solutions to individual challenges and global problems alike. As already noted, whenever we dig deeper into dilemmas, we discover persistent contradictions. Paradoxes can thus vex and paralyze, but if we embrace these creative tensions they present, they also can spark energy and innovation. The tools and illustrations in this book serve as a valuable guide to doing just that. Enjoy reading about them.

Amy C. Edmondson
Novartis Professor of
Leadership and Management
Harvard Business School

Why Some Problems Are So Challenging

I (Wendy) was consistently interrupted as I wrote the first draft of this introduction. It was the heart of the Covid-19 pandemic. Our house was abuzz as the five of us in my family tried to manage work and school while being in lockdown.

As I was writing, my then nine-year-old son was sitting across the dining room table, repeatedly needing my help or asking me questions. He couldn't find the right Zoom password. His headphones were not working well. He wanted to tell me all about China because his class was studying Chinese culture and he knew I lived there for four months when I was around his age. I wanted to engage with him but also felt pressure to get a draft of this introduction finished. Any boundaries I previously constructed between work and life had totally collapsed.

I could feel the frustration rising. My writing was messy (this chapter was rewritten several times). My son missed at least one Zoom class (I was appalled; he was fine!). I felt as if I were standing in the middle of the ultimate tug-of-war, feeling pulled between my own work needs and my son's school needs.

Meanwhile, isolated in a different city, I (Marianne) struggled as I got off the phone with a valued supporter of my business school. He was not happy. A decade before, when I was then associate dean, I had partnered with him to build a new honors program. We now had three such honors programs, each initially designed to serve different needs.

Yet the programs had morphed over time, their once distinct purposes blurred. We needed to innovate to meet rapidly changing business and student demands, while addressing brand confusion and internal inefficiencies.

Now as the dean of the business school, I faced intense pressures. Results of a six-month strategic planning process identified considerable benefits to combining the strengths of each program into an integrated single offering. Yet students, alumni, and supporters cherished their respective programs. I felt torn between innovating for the future and honoring our traditions. Emotions were running high—mine included.

People say that academics study the things that personally challenge them most—that research is "me-search" (or, in our case, "we-search"). We believe this observation is true. Over years of academic collaboration and friendship, we have shared with one another the many problems we face in our work, in our lives, and in the intersection of the two. We've also stayed up late at night wondering about the bigger issues that plague our world including issues of political polarization, climate change, racial inequities, economic justice, and others. These issues—both personal and global— raise tensions. We know we are not alone in these experiences. Tensions make us human; and they help connect us with one another. Reading ancient and modern texts in literature, philosophy, psychology, sociology, organizational theory, and so forth reminds us that ongoing tensions are part of the perpetual human condition.

Think about it for a moment. Consider a difficult problem that you faced. Maybe, like us, you confronted parenting issues during the pandemic. Or maybe you struggled with how to maintain healthy physical distancing while in the global lockdown without feeling socially isolated. Likewise, perhaps you had to decide whether to take a new job, or to lay off an employee, or to spend resources on a new initiative. Or maybe, like us, you struggled with leading a group, a business unit, or an organization through a difficult strategic decision. We imagine that it won't take you much effort to identify a problem that you faced. It doesn't matter whether you're the

CEO of a *Fortune* 500 company, an entrepreneur, a manager, a parent, a student, or someone else: we all face tough problems, sometimes daily—from personal issues to collective organizational challenges to the greatest and most intractable global crises. These vexing problems take up a large amount of our emotional and mental energy.

Now, ask yourself, why was the issue so difficult? When all of us look back at our challenges, we often remember our anxiety, our doubt, and our second guessing. In some cases, we may remember the play-by-play details of how we came to a solution. But we rarely understand why those issues caused us so much trouble.

This driving question has motivated our research for decades: *What underlies our toughest problems, and how can we deal with it?* We feel particularly driven by this question because the challenges we all face in our personal lives and in the broader world are extensive. If we all have better approaches to address our problems, then we can develop more effective, creative, and sustainable solutions.

In the research that we conducted over the past twenty-five years, the two of us noticed significant differences in how people understand and respond to their toughest problems. Our own quest has explored corporate behemoths such as IBM and LEGO, startups and social enterprises, as well as nonprofits and government agencies. This research has taken us to places like Greece, Cambodia, and an island at one of the four corners of the flat world. We've learned from all kinds of leaders as they grapple with some of their most difficult organizational challenges. We have also studied people struggling with personal concerns, from mundane issues to life-changing decisions.

Regardless of context, such messy problems are difficult because they present us with dilemmas—choices between alternatives. Do I stick with the comfort of my current career path or make a bold jump to a new opportunity? Do I do what's best for my company overall or what's best for individual employees? Do I spend my time focusing on my own needs or put those needs aside to be there for others? We feel tension—the experience of opposition. It feels like an inner tug-of-war, and it begs us for a response.

FIGURE I-1

The language of tensions

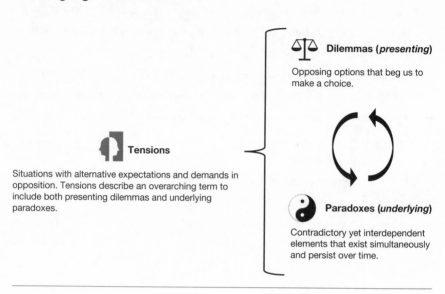

Dilemmas (*presenting*)

Opposing options that beg us to make a choice.

Tensions

Situations with alternative expectations and demands in opposition. Tensions describe an overarching term to include both presenting dilemmas and underlying paradoxes.

Paradoxes (*underlying*)

Contradictory yet interdependent elements that exist simultaneously and persist over time.

Lots of books offer important suggestions about how to make clear and compelling choices in response to these kinds of problems. But before making a choice, we must all first look deeper to understand the nature of the problem. We need to examine the core topics that have animated the research done for this book. We need to understand tensions, dilemmas, and, most vitally, paradoxes. Let's start by defining these terms.

- Tensions include all types of situations where alternative expectations and demands are in opposition. We feel an internal tug-of-war. The word tensions offers an overarching term to describe both presenting dilemmas and their underlying paradoxes. Tensions are neither good nor bad; they can drive creativity and sustainability or lead to defensiveness and destruction. Their impact depends on how we respond.

- Dilemmas present opposing alternatives, each option offering a logical solution on its own. Our problems and challenges often show up for us as a dilemma, where we feel pressure to choose between alternative options. Yet as we try weighing the advantages and disadvantages of each, we find ourselves stuck. The pros of one option define the cons of the other, and vice versa. We chase our tails looking for the clear, right, and lasting solution, but it often doesn't appear. Moreover, when we decide between options, we can, over time, become stuck in a rut that leads to a vicious cycle.

- Paradoxes are interdependent, persistent contradictions that lurk within our presenting dilemmas. Diving into a dilemma, exploring the options at a deeper level, we find opposing forces interlocked in a circular ebb and flow. Paradoxes may seem absurd at first as they integrate contradictions, yet a more thorough investigation can unveil a logic to the holistic synergies of competing demands. Other researchers use words like polarity or dialectics in similar ways. In our own studies, we adopt the word paradox to align with a rich research tradition, and to reflect their often complex and mysterious ways.

Consider the dilemmas we noted at the opening of this introduction. I (Wendy) struggled with how to get my own work done while also pay attention to my son. Underlying this dilemma lies the paradoxes of work and life, self and other, discipline and spontaneity, giving and taking. How could I support my son, be spontaneous and engaging to give him what he needed, but also maintain discipline and hold boundaries so that I could focus on what I needed? I (Marianne) grappled with the challenge of enabling important strategic innovation for the school while supporting valued donors and alumni. This dilemma created alternative options between whether or not to change our honors programs. Yet underlying this dilemma were paradoxes between past and future, stability and change, centralization and decentralization. How could I address market opportunities and operational needs while also honoring treasured traditions and identities?

Tensions pull us in opposite directions. In doing so, they create discomfort and anxiety. We often experience these tensions as dilemmas between alternative options, and we feel forced to make a choice. But the paradoxes underlying these dilemmas are not just oppositional. They are also interdependent. The opposing forces of paradoxes define and reinforce one another. Consider the paradox between focusing on ourselves and focusing on others. The healthier we are, the more effectively we can engage with and support others. The more we are supported by others, the healthier we are. Similarly, organizations with a strong centralized core can better empower distinct decentralized units, and vice versa. These competing demands reinforce one another.

Or consider how the paradox of stability and change underlies so many of our life challenges. Do we stay the course or try something new? We reach for stability to keep us grounded and focused. Yet we seek change for novelty, adventure, and growth. Even as they oppose one another, stability and change are also intertwined. Looking to make change in yourself or your organization? The best place to start is with valuing who and what already exists. Want to reach for greater stability? You might need to do so by making some changes. To live and thrive in the long run depends on embracing the interactions between stability and change.

Oppositional yet interdependent relationships never go away; they persist. No matter how many times you face conflicting forces between self and other, past and future, stability and change, the tension will reemerge. While the details of the presenting dilemma may change, the underlying paradoxes remain. The moment that I (Wendy) sat across from my 9-year old at the dining room table represented one of hundreds of similar moments that I faced as a working parent. The nuance of these experiences changed over time, yet all these situations pointed to the same underlying paradoxes between work and life, self and other, and giving and taking. While a presenting dilemma presses us for a solution, the underlying paradoxes can never be resolved.

From Either/Or Thinking to Both/And Thinking

Developing both/and thinking begins by starting to notice the paradoxes that lurk beneath our presenting dilemmas. The next step involves us learning to more effectively navigate these paradoxes.

Navigating paradoxes begins with understanding that tensions are double-edged swords—they can drag us down a negative path or catapult us toward a more positive one. In the same way that waves are a form of transmitting energy that can be both productive or destructive, so too can tensions be unleashed for destruction and detriment or harnessed for creativity and opportunity. Pioneering scholar and activist Mary Parker Follett stresses that tensions reflect natural, unavoidable, and even valuable conflict—differences between goals, demands, interests, and views. She describes these conflicts by exploring the nature of friction:

> Instead of condemning [friction], we should set it to work for us. Why not? What does the mechanical engineer do with friction? Of course, his chief job is to eliminate friction, but it is true that he also capitalizes on friction. The transmission of power by belts depends on friction between the belt and the pulley. The friction between the driving wheel of the locomotive and the track is necessary to haul the train. All polishing is done by friction. The music of the violin we get by friction.[1]

Tensions, however, foster anxiety. As we experience dilemmas, they present us with alternative options. The unanswered questions that arise as we face these options introduce uncertainty. Faced with uncertainty, we often want to run and reclaim more certain, stable ground. We narrow our approach and focus in on the question, applying more binary either/or thinking, evaluating alternative options, and choosing between them. Making a clear choice removes the uncertainty and therefore can minimize anxiety in the short term, but it can also limit creativity and diminish more sustainable possibilities. We tend to apply this kind of either/or thinking for all kinds of challenges in our lives, from something as mundane as where to go for dinner (pizza parlor or local bar?) to something as grand as what to do with our lives (marry our partner or break up?). Leaders adopt either/or thinking in response to their strategic dilemmas (move into a global market or stay domestic?) just as parents use this approach to choose between options for their kids (daycare or home care?). These dilemmas can feel mutually exclusive to us; picking one option means rejecting the other.

At times, either/or thinking is really useful. We may seek a clear choice when the consequences of the decision are minimal and it's not worth the time or effort to explore an issue further. We don't necessarily need to dig deeper into paradoxes to decide what to eat for dinner or which book on our nightstand to read next. We also may want to make a specific and final choice if we believe that the issue won't reoccur. As I (Wendy) like to tell my students, sometimes it is useful to make an either/or decision to break up from a bad relationship.

Yet most of the time, either/or thinking can result in responses to dilemmas that are limited at best and detrimental at worst. Tensions spark defensiveness that leads us to want to make a decision. But making a choice can add to our problems. Psychology studies show us again and again how we prefer stability and consistency over uncertainty and change. Once we make a choice, we often want to maintain consistency. We then become so engrained in how we do something that we become stuck in a rut. We stay where we are until something drastic forces us to change. This tendency usually leads us to overcorrect, swinging the pendulum to the opposite alternative and triggering an ongoing vicious cycle. If you are a dieter, you might have experienced these pendulum swings between dieting and indulging and then dieting again. Organizations often face swings between too much and not enough innovation. In politics, we see these swings between more conservative and more liberal policies. Ultimately, this kind of either/or thinking can lead us down a vicious cycle that shifts between alternative options—a long and windy road, with lots of chaos along the way.

What if we think about our dilemmas differently? What if, instead of trying to choose between the mutually exclusive options, we start by surfacing the paradoxes that lurk beneath our dilemmas and recognize that those paradoxes cannot be solved? Instead of choosing between alternative poles of a paradox, what if we ask a different question: how might we engage both poles simultaneously? How might we accommodate competing demands over time? Doing so invites us into both/and thinking, embracing tensions to enable more creative, effective, and sustainable solutions. In doing so, we start to see the holistic integration that moves us beyond the binaries. Both/and thinking can open up dialogue and fuel virtuous cycles.

Over the last twenty-five years, the two of us have worked with CEOs, senior teams, middle managers, colleagues, students, and friends navigating paradoxes. Many of these people first identified the paradoxes that informed their dilemmas and then applied both/and thinking. For example:

- Zita Cobb sought to help re-energize Fogo Island, Newfoundland, the island of her birth. As happens with many rural communities, Fogo Island's main resource—cod—had started to decline. Cobb had left the island in her twenties along with so many others. She returned in her forties after her leadership role at JDS Uniphase Corporation earned her the title of the second-highest-paid female executive in Canada. She wanted to support economic development efforts so that the Fogo Island community did not dry up like the cod. Yet Cobb struggled with how to link the local community to the global economy while maintaining what is unique about their heritage and culture. She felt the pull to focus on the past while changing for the present, the desire to maintain tradition while ensuring modernization, the advantage of connecting globally while valuing local ties.

- Terri Kelly took over as CEO of W. L. Gore & Associates as the company approached its fiftieth anniversary. The organization was built on the "power of small teams," with a strong culture of local decision making distributed across empowered leaders. But as the company grew, the dispersed approach lacked a strong core, pulling the organization into small, fractured bits. Kelly confronted dilemmas about how to grow large in a culture that valued being small. To address this dilemma, she knew she had to face paradoxes of centralization and decentralization and of growth and intimacy.

- Greg Mullen, chief of police in Charleston, South Carolina, was devastated by the racially motivated killing of nine Black people at the Mother Emanuel African Methodist Episcopal (AME) Church. He wanted to move the community forward to a safer place. Yet doing so meant addressing the deep fissures and distrust between the community and the police. Underlying his challenges were ongoing paradoxes between trust and mistrust, citizens and officers, inclusion and exclusion. Mullen then worked to break down barriers between opposing groups so that they could work together toward a common goal.

- Ella Franke (a pseudonym) was finally leading her dream team as a hospital fundraiser, when she was offered a new and bigger role in a different hospital. She faced a dilemma—should she stay and lead her current team through their major capital campaign, or should she leave to take on a more challenging opportunity? On the one hand, she valued loyalty to her team and wanted to complete the current campaign. On the other hand, she wanted to grow in her career and was intrigued by starting something new. To address this work dilemma, Franke first had to unpack the underlying paradoxes between her loyalty to her job and her desire to expand her own career.

These people leveraged paradoxes to solve their most challenging problems. They went beyond the presenting dilemmas to identify the underlying paradoxes. Doing so allowed them to find new, alternative approaches to their toughest problems. In this book, we share their stories and those of so many others who navigated paradoxes in their professional and personal lives. While varied in their circumstances and challenges, these stories have one thing in common. Both/and thinking brought underlying paradoxes to light and opened new, more creative, and longer-lasting possibilities.

Timing Is Everything

Paradox is not a new concept. These ideas emerged at the dawn of intellectual thought more than twenty-five hundred years ago. In our own explorations, we are constantly learning from ancient insights. We draw from Eastern philosophy such as that set forth by Lao Tzu in the *Tao Te Ching* and from Western philosophy, including that of Greek philosopher Heraclitus. Intriguingly, these insights emerged in the same era, but in different parts of the globe with limited communication or connections. Over time, however, our societies have lost touch with the paradoxes that underlie our challenges as we have become more focused on rational and linear thinking.

The challenges that all of us currently face both personally and globally call for paradox insights so that we can apply both/and thinking to address our toughest problems. In our own research, we identified three conditions that make underlying paradoxes more salient—change, scarcity, and plurality.[2] The greater the rate of change, the quicker the future becomes the present, and the more we must grapple with tensions between today and tomorrow. The scarcer the resources, the more we fight for our slice of the pie, revealing tensions between self and other, between competition and cooperation. The more voices, ideas, and insights, the more that conflicting approaches are raised to address a common issue and the more that we experience tensions between a unified global view and distinct local views. Given accelerating technological change, waning natural resources, and expansive globalization, the world we are living in today feels like the perfect paradox storm.

For example, beyond our daily problems, we see paradoxes underlying our most wicked and intractable societal challenges. Climate concerns expose paradoxes between system-level and individual-level change, between the short term and the long term. Similarly, issues of diversity and racial justice are infused with paradoxes of inclusion and exclusion, personal relationships and systemic change.

As challenges intensify, people are increasingly using the language of paradox and calling out the interwoven opposites in these situations. For example, we have seen world leaders—from opposing political sides—call for both/and thinking. When author and scholar Brené Brown interviewed Barack Obama, the former American president talked about the paradoxes he navigated:

It is both possible and necessary to see the paradoxes, the ambigui-
ties, the gray areas, the absurdities sometimes, of life, but not be
paralyzed by them. . . . [M]y job is to look out for the safety of
American citizens as the American President. On the other hand,
there is a universal interest in peace and fairness and justice
outside our borders, and how do I reconcile those things, but then
still be able to act as Commander in Chief and still be able to make
a decision?

Or a matter of dealing with the economic crisis, being able to
reconcile the fact that our free market system creates enormous
efficiencies and wealth, and that's not a system that we should want
to just tear down on a whim, because a lot of people are relying on
us making good decisions about the economy. On the other hand,
there are parts of the economy that don't work and are unjust and
get people frustrated and angry. . . . Both things are true, and you
then still have to make a decision.[3]

Senator John McCain, President Obama's own campaign opponent,
shared a similar sentiment. In 2018, McCain knew he was dying of a brain
tumor. He wrote a farewell message in which he urged us all to move beyond
the "tribal rivalries that have sown resentment and hatred and violence in
all the corners of the globe." Instead he called for unity and a chance to
find a both/and that connects us. "We weaken [our greatness] when we hide
behind walls, rather than tear them down, when we doubt the power of
our ideals, rather than trust them to be the great force for change they have
always been."[4] Both leaders knew that we needed to honor the complexity
in our world by understanding, appreciating, and embracing the vital opposing forces that fuel our political systems. Though political opponents,
Obama and McCain agreed with one another that to solve our greatest problems, we need to fight the increasing political polarization and find ways
to reconnect across our disparate ideologies and values.

Organizational leaders are also using both/and language to communi-
cate their organizations' goals and missions. Barclays unveiled a campaign
it called AND—stressing that the 300-plus-year-old bank would only sur-

vive the next century by being relevant to shareholders *and* stakeholders and by making sure that it focused on markets *and* mission. The CEO of Starbucks recently responded to a question about whether the company was trying to offer customers a convenient, quick cup of coffee or build a space for gathering community. He explained, "But we don't believe there needs to be this type of a tradeoff. . . . [O]ur third place can and will continue to unite *both* experiences."[5] Yale University's marketing campaign also adopted such language: "Yale University is best defined by the word AND" explained one brochure. The university described an approach to education that is both big and small, inside and outside the classroom, advancing diversity and community. More recently, political staffer Huma Abedin titled her memoir about living across disparate worlds *Both/And.*[6] Look around. Examples abound.

What's Next? What's New?

Both/and is becoming a mantra. Using the language of paradoxes is a good start. It helps us see the interwoven opposites that lurk within our dilemmas and highlights the importance of bringing together conflicting forces.

But the real power lies in moving from a label to an approach. How will we understand the deeper paradoxes in our dilemmas? How will we draw on both/and thinking to effectively navigate these paradoxes for positive and lasting impact?

That's why we wrote this book—to help all of us tackle our toughest problems personally and societally by unleashing both/and thinking. As academics, we spent over two decades studying paradox. We not only worked to specify the nature of paradoxes but also studied *how* people effectively respond by adopting both/and thinking. Our goal now is to translate that research, offering empirical evidence, theoretical insights, and practical tools to see and navigate paradoxes.

Applying both/and thinking begins with understanding the nature of paradoxes while also identifying the pitfalls that can keep pulling us back to either/or thinking. In part 1, we tackle these foundational ideas. In part 2, we unpack approaches to enable both/and thinking. These approaches impact how we think and feel about paradoxes. They require us to surround ourselves with an environment that both provides stable structures and enables dynamic change. We identify sets of tools to do so and introduce them in what we call the *paradox system*. And finally, with this tool kit in hand, we examine applications—how to put this system into practice so that you can engage both/and thinking in a variety of dilemmas. Part 3 dives into step-by-step processes—essentially the owner's manual to the paradox system. We examine the application of this system to an individual decision, an interpersonal conflict between groups, and an organizational strategy to accommodate competing demands.

For millennia, paradoxes have mystified, frustrated, and delighted philosophers, psychologists, theologians, and scholars. Now they increasingly surface in our personal and organizational challenges.

Ignoring paradoxes will only cause them to come back stronger. A better approach, we think, is to effectively engage them. Embracing creative tensions will allow you to better grapple with your own challenges while more purposefully working with others to address global problems. Doing so is an ongoing journey of growing and learning. We hope this book will inspire you to join us in working toward a world that can develop more creative, sustainable solutions to humanity's toughest problems.

PART ONE

FOUNDATIONS: THE PROMISE AND PERILS OF PARADOX

O ur world rests on a razor's edge, as we continually feel pulled in opposing directions, whether by everyday concerns or global challenges. Do we focus on the needs of today or tomorrow, of ourselves or others, of stability or change? Competing demands surround us. Yet lurking within these dilemmas are paradoxes—contradictory, yet interdependent tensions. To effectively respond, we first must understand more about the nature of paradoxes.

For millennia, paradoxes have energized and mystified philosophers, scientists, and psychologists. These contradictory yet interdependent tensions are double-edged swords. They contain possibilities for novel, creative, and lasting insights. Yet they also trigger tremendous frustration. Overwhelmed by their irrationality and absurdity, we can find ourselves down a dead-end path. In this part of the book, we explore the foundations of both/and thinking. Embracing tensions requires a deeper understanding of paradoxes; both the good and the bad, the valuable and the challenging. We examine definitions, characteristics, and types of paradoxes. We offer warnings about what can get us stuck and headed toward a vicious cycle. These foundations allow us to "stand on the shoulders of giants," benefiting from more than twenty-five hundred years of insights to inform how we can best navigate paradoxes today.

1

Experiencing Tensions

Why Paradox? Why Now?

Onward through the fog.

—Traditional saying in Newfoundland, Canada

Zita Cobb was torn. She had recently stepped down from an executive role and wanted to use her business acumen to help advance the local economy of Fogo Island, Newfoundland, the place where she grew up. Yet as an eighth-generation Fogo Islander, she also wanted to honor the island's distinctiveness—its customs, its beauty, its ways of knowing. This was no small task.

Cobb had seen many changes over the years on Fogo Island. As part of her "feral" youth, kids were free to explore the remote and wild terrain. On the island and its surrounding waters far north in the Atlantic, they picked partridgeberries, followed trails of caribou, spotted puffins out at sea, evaded icebergs, and spent hours at the craggy shores helping the fishermen unload from their small wooden boats their daily catch of the island's main resource—cod.[1] Growing up, Cobb felt empowered by the tight-knit community that worked together for its very survival.

But in the 1970s, international factory fleets launched large trawling boats to collect cod in the deep waters, depleting the inshore stocks. A good portion of Newfoundlanders made their livelihoods fishing, yet they started returning from a day at sea with empty boats. As local fishing stocks dwindled, people grew hungry, frustrated, and discouraged. As happens with any small town that loses its main resource, people started to leave. In an effort to replenish the fish stocks, the provincial government put a moratorium on inshore fishing, encouraging fishers to move on and take manufacturing jobs. The Fogo Island population started declining. As it did, the province cut back the ferry schedule and other services like waste removal. Medical care was limited, and day care nonexistent. Cut from their lives and livelihoods, more people left. Cobb eventually moved to Ottawa to study business at Carleton University.

Cobb eventually became the chief strategy officer of fiber-optic company JDS Uniphase and a prominent woman business leader in Canada. Yet Fogo Island beckoned. She returned to the island in 2006, living part time in the saltbox house inherited from her uncle Art. She was in her forties and among the community's younger generation.

Cobb, like so many Fogo Islanders, treasured the island's unique ways of knowing and being. The islanders valued their understanding of woodworking and fishing, their culture of hospitality, their honor and respect for the North Atlantic waters, and their resilience to thrive in a demanding climate. These ways of knowing were gifts passed down to them, and they wanted to continue passing them to future generations. But they now felt that the only way to sustain their traditions would be to change them. The world had moved on. No longer could they find a subsistence in inshore fishing. No longer could they ignore the call from the global economy. They would, as Cobb said, need to find "new ways with old things." Moreover, they knew that survival in their local economy depended on how they could connect with the global community.

The task was daunting. How could they honor the past while moving into the future? How could the islanders connect with a global economy without losing what was unique and valuable about their local community? To stay the same, they needed to change. To value their uniqueness, they had to be open to broader perspectives.

Cobb, along with her brothers Alan and Tony, first decided that the best way to support Fogo Island was to create a scholarship for students to attend college. Many of the people on the island had never traveled beyond Gander—the first town across the harbor. Empowering the youth to expand their worldviews and skills could help infuse Fogo Island with new opportunities. But community members quickly pointed out the unintended consequences of this idea. Scholarships would only hasten the island's brain drain. Students would go to college, appreciate the allure of the new opportunities, and never come back. Cobb scrapped that plan.

Her next experiment was to build things that would bring people with new perspectives to Fogo Island. Who better to do so than avant-garde artists? She had four artist studios built, and set up a residency program that invited writers, painters, sculptures, and the like to develop their work surrounded by the natural beauty of Fogo Island. The hope was that the artists would connect with local residents, sharing their creative and worldly perspectives, while learning about the island's unique gifts and helping promote them in the global community. While artists came, bringing along new insights, the advances were slow to be realized, and the need for change was growing more imminent. If Fogo Islanders wanted to build their economy and replenish their population, they needed more than four artists in residence every few months.

What else could Cobb do to rebuild Fogo Island? The easiest route might be to start a company or factory. But a manufacturing plant would ruin the wild, natural culture and communal vibe that sustained the island for centuries, not to mention devastate the natural landscape.

Cobb was at a crossroads. She felt the tensions—between the old and the new, tradition and modernization, local distinctions and global connections, and between slow advances and imminent needs. Essentially, Cobb was grappling with paradoxes.

Understanding Paradox

Paradoxes are everywhere. That's what the two of us told each other the first time we met. I (Marianne) had just completed a manuscript that involved a deep exploration of the philosophy, psychology, and history of paradox. The more I read, the more I could see interwoven opposites embedded in every challenge in our lives—big and small. The more I wrote, the more I felt energized. Yet I also felt a bit anxious and overwhelmed by how to cope with these pervasive and puzzling irrationalities. I was relieved that when I described these ideas and feelings to Wendy, she just kept nodding vigorously. She too saw paradoxes around every corner and felt the mixed emotions evoked by their mysterious complexities.

I (Wendy) was a doctoral student at the time. I was studying how leaders in large corporations innovated while simultaneously managing their existing products in the marketplace. My first conversation with Marianne helped crystalize my thinking. The leaders in my study were facing competing demands between today and tomorrow. The idea of paradoxes helped me understand their most pressing challenges. Yet I too felt the anxiety. How could these business leaders move forward to embrace both the past and the present at the same time?

As we talk to broader audiences about paradox, we see others also toggle between clarity and confusion. What feels like an idea that elucidates our greatest challenges can easily turn fuzzy. What feels like a powerful insight can quickly be reduced to the absurd.

Management scholar William Starbuck once recognized just how absurd paradoxes can seem to us. As he suggests, it may be the limitations of our human cognition that lead us to think of paradox as so irrational and confusing. "We may be like chimpanzees swinging about in the rafters of the New York Stock Exchange and trying to articulate its laws. The paradoxes that we see may look illogical to creatures with our limited reasoning capacities and our form of logic, yet they might make sense to creatures with more complex brains or with brains that employ a different form of logic."[2]

As Starbuck suggests, paradoxes might push the boundaries of human cognition. Yet we believe that even within our own cognitive capabilities, we can find patterns and insight to more effectively understand and grapple with paradoxes. To cut through this fog, we have, over the years, turned to our academic tool kit to be more precise: What is paradox? Why is it important? How do we manage it?

FIGURE 1-1

Yin-yang: an image of paradox

- **Contradiction:** Black and white portions reflect opposing dualities.

- **Interdependence:** Black and white portions define and mutually reinforce one another, together forming a perfect, circular whole.

- **Persistence:** Black and white portions consistently flow from smaller to larger, while the opposing dots within each portion convey how one force seeds its opposite, suggesting ongoing movement.

We started with clarifying the definition. People have many ways of defining these illogical and unsolvable loops between opposing forces. In our own work, we build from scholars both ancient and modern to define paradox as *contradictory, yet interdependent elements that exist simultaneously and persist over time.*[3]

The sidebar "Paradox: Millennia in the Making" discusses the early roots of paradox thinking. The yin-yang symbol, introduced by Eastern philosophers, depicts the three core features of paradoxes: contradiction, interdependence, and persistence (figure 1-1).

The liar's paradox offers a classic example of these persistent interdependent contradictions. Greek philosophers conceptualized this paradox thousands of years ago, and it has been vexing logicians ever since. It can be simplified to the statement "I am lying." The statement presents the opposing nature between truth and falsehood. These contradictions exist in an absurd, interdependent loop. If I say I am lying, and I'm telling the truth, then I am lying. If I say I am lying, and I'm lying, then I'm telling the truth. Despite multiple efforts toward a logical and philosophical

Paradox: Millennia in the Making

Insights about interwoven opposites emerged around the fifth century BCE—well over twenty-five hundred years ago. Karl Jaspers, a modern Swiss-German scholar, described that period as the "Axial Age."[a] Given the transformative ideas that emerged during that time, it seemed as if the world pivoted on its axis, resetting the foundations of civilization. It was during this time that societies first grappled with ideas of paradox.

These ideas emerged across the globe. As examples, we focus on the insights from Eastern philosophy (from China) and from Western philosophy (from Greece). Intriguingly, different philosophers in distinct geographies generated similar understandings of the paradoxical nature of our world. Their insights share two features: dualism and dynamism.

First, both philosophies emphasized the unity of opposites—that a holistic harmony depends on the integration of dualities. For example, China's Lao Tzu presents the synergy of being and non-being in *Tao Te Ching*: "All things are born of being. Being is born of nonbeing."[b] Greek philosopher Heraclitus offers a more direct assertion of the same idea: "What opposes unites, and the finest attunement stems from things bearing in opposite directions, and all things come about by strife."[c]

Second, these philosophers described life as dynamic and in a constant state of flux. Heraclitus is famous for the line often repeated

resolution, the statement creates a tension between truth and falsehood that never goes away—it persists over time.[4]

The paradoxes in our lives operate in a similar way to this logical puzzle. Consider the challenges facing Fogo Island. The residents faced a number of presenting dilemmas—alternative options that beg for a solu-

today as: "No person ever steps in the same river twice." The flowing river changes from moment to moment; so too does the person. Similarly, Lao Tzu says, "True steadfastness seems changeable." Even more profoundly, these philosophers noted that duality fuels dynamism; constant change emerges as opposites continually crash against and shift one another. Lao Tzu expands on this idea: "If you want to shrink something, you must first allow it to expand. If you want to get rid of something, you must first allow it to flourish. If you want to take something, you must first allow it to be given. This is called the subtle perception of the way things are."[d]

These features of dualism and dynamics form the foundations of paradoxical thought that remain today more than twenty-five hundred years later. Modern-day paradox thinkers are building on ideas that are millennia in the making.

---

a. Jaspers (1953).

b. Lao Tzu, *Tao Te Ching*, verse 40. All quotes from *Tao Te Ching* come from Mitchell (1988).

c. As an undergraduate in the University of Oklahoma, Randy Hoyt realized that there were intriguing insights in the work of Heraclitus but that these fragments were largely inaccessible to the broader public. He created a website to post the Greek fragments, their transliteration to English, their translation to English, and some textual notes. See Randy Hoyt, compiler, "The Fragments of Heraclitus," accessed July 2020, http://www.heraclitusfragments.com/files/e.html. The fragment quoted in the text is B9. Graham (2019) also offers more analysis of the fragments.

d. Tzu, *Tao Te Ching*, verse 36, in Mitchell (1988).

tion. For example, they grappled with the dilemma of what kinds of programs and opportunities to invest in in order to rebuild the population of the island. But underneath those dilemmas were paradoxes. Trying to sustain the people, livelihoods, culture, and knowledge of Fogo Islanders meant that the community ultimately had to change. Seeking to honor local communities meant finding support from the global economy. Lurking beneath the presenting dilemmas were paradoxes of stability and change, old and new, tradition and modernization, local and global: they felt pressures to choose between these poles, to focus on either the past or the present. To maintain their local culture or allow global forces to come rushing into their community. Yet Cobb recognized that choosing between these alternative poles would lead to limited and detrimental solutions. It was this kind of reductionist thinking, failing to see the more holistic picture, that got Fogo Island into the problem in the first place. Provincial efforts to close the fisheries and move the islanders to manufacturing towns focused on short-term economic challenges and completely overlooked what was so valuable about place and community. The islanders needed a different approach to get themselves out of the problem.

As another example, perhaps one closer to home, consider the paradoxes that underlie relationships between significant others. Partners often remember their similarities as the things that brought them together. Yet as the adage goes—opposites attract. It is often our complementary differences that encourage us to engage with one another, providing sparks and enabling synergies. Over time, those opposing approaches can also be the source of ongoing debate. In some cases, these differences are mild; in others, they become heated. They show up in everything, including daily chores, vacation choices, and financial decisions. These moments where the debates arise around opposing approaches are the presenting dilemmas. But beneath the dilemmas are persistent dynamic dualities—the underlying paradoxes.

Presenting dilemmas are like symptoms of the common cold. We feel drawn to take care of the symptoms, often missing what lies beneath them. We might, for example, decide where to go on our next holiday by weighing options between an organized tour or an unstructured stay on a beach, between a staycation or an exotic adventure, between spending time with extended family or ticking off a bucket-list destination. Yet no matter how we choose between the alternatives in a particular moment, the underlying paradoxes remain between opposing desires to be planned or spontaneous, frugal or extravagant, self-focused or other-focused. These interwoven and persistent opposites pose vexing challenges that can leave us paralyzed and frustrated. But they are also ripe with opportunities for learning, growth, and creativity. We can tap into these possibilities if we value our shared, overarching goals and the complementary differences that fuel connection, deepening bonds and mutual support.

Four Types of Paradoxes

We are not alone in seeing interwoven opposites everywhere. From early history to modern times, philosophers and others have grappled with these issues (see the sidebar "The Long and Winding Road of Paradoxical Thought"). Increasingly, people are writing about tensions in all kinds of domains. Examples of paradoxes abound: knowing and unknowing, power and vulnerability, good and evil, stability and change, love and hate, advancement and retreat, centralization and decentralization, work and life, discipline and pleasure. We experience paradoxes in our psyche, in groups, in organizations, and in broader systems.

Psychologists and psychoanalysts point to paradoxes in our psyche. Paradoxes infuse the writing of psychoanalyst Carl Jung—mind and matter, virtues and vices, spirit and body, life and death, good and evil, truth and falsehood, unity and multiplicity, and so on. More recently, psychologist Kirk Schneider described such paradoxes in his book *The Paradoxical Self*.[5] Drawing on ideas from philosopher Søren Kierkegaard, he argues, that the human psyche exists on a continuum between more constrictive, reserved, and withdrawn aspects and more expansive, adventurous, and outgoing ones. Human dysfunctions arise when we veer too far toward either pole, habits that can result in depression at one end and mania at the other. The challenge is to live with these tensions, continually seeking points of intersection. Author and scholar Brené Brown further reminds us how our own strengths depend on our ability to embrace our vulnerabilities. If we can accept our fears, they can no longer take hold of us.[6]

Paradoxes define our groups and teams, as we grapple with the individual and the collective, collaboration and competition, self and other.

The Long and Winding Road of Paradoxical Thought

Shared insights about paradoxes emerged in both the East and the West. Yet these ideas developed along different paths in each geography. Lao Tzu, a scholar and an adviser to the ruling class, informed the thinking of Confucius and traditions that would become an expansive Chinese mindset. In contrast, the ideas of Heraclitus, a loner viewed as abstract and absurd, were challenged by his contemporary, Parmenides, a charismatic speaker praised as clear and logical. Parmenides won the day, and over centuries the differences between Eastern and Western philosophies became increasingly nuanced and pronounced. As psychologists Kaiping Peng and Richard Nisbett explain, a Western proclivity to linear, rational thought informed rigorous methods that fueled significant scientific developments. Likewise, Eastern civilizations leaning toward dualism, harmony, and cyclicality fostered forms of mysticism that significantly advanced human capacity for mindfulness and transcendental thinking.[a]

Today, as ideas cross geographic divides in nanoseconds, these alternative intellectual worlds are converging. Take, for instance, the field of physics. The linear physics of Isaac Newton fostered deeper understanding of gravity, advancing thinking across such fields as astronomy and fluid dynamics. Yet in the late 1800s, scientists like Michael Faraday and James Clerk Maxwell and, later, Albert Einstein and Niels Bohr started to conceptualize the push and pull between opposing forces at subatomic levels—insights that came to inform quantum physics. In his book *The Tao of Physics*, scientist Fritjof Capra details how these breakthroughs came to value and reflect Eastern philosophical approaches, embracing the unification of opposing forces and engaging more cyclical and spiritual ideas.[b]

Whereas the field of physics introduced paradox insights to the material world, the field of psychoanalysis did so to the human psyche. Launched by scholars such as Sigmund Freud and Carl Jung, psychoanalysis started to conceptualize human experiences as the integration of deeply dualistic internal instincts and motivations. Jung, in particular, advanced a paradoxical theory of human nature. He suggested that the Age of Enlightenment left Western culture to overvalue logic and reason, which he depicted as one-sided, lacking the value of feeling and intuition. As he famously stated, "Only the paradox comes anywhere near to comprehending the fullness of life," describing paradox as "one of our most valuable spiritual possessions."[c] For example, Jung believed that the self was an integration of both the positive reflections of our expressed self along with the negative desires of our repressed "shadow" self. He argued that our efforts to avoid or diminish the shadow self can trigger detrimental behaviors in our expressed self. He defined narcissism, for example, as a preoccupation with how others view us. In hopes of avoiding and distancing themselves from their shadow, narcissists project their shadow traits onto others. Jung proposed that individuals grow by accepting and integrating, rather than rejecting and repressing, shadow traits.

This brief history highlights an interesting and repeated pattern. What began as convergent thoughts in geographically distant locations soon diverged, only to eventually converge again thousands of years later. So is paradox an age-old concept bringing fundamental insights to light or a new approach brought to bear on the complexity of our world? Well, paradoxically . . . it is both.

---

a. Nisbett (2010); Spencer-Rodgers et al. (2004); Spencer-Rodgers et al. (2009). To explore broader cultural and philosophical approaches to paradox, dualities, and dialectics, see Hampden-Turner (1981).

b. Capra (1975) offers a deeper dive into the paradoxical nature of Eastern traditions of Hinduism, Buddhism, Taoism, Zen, and broader Chinese philosophy and explores how these ideas relate to the science of physics.

c. Jung (1953), paragraph 18.

Kenwyn Smith and David Berg point to these tensions in their book *Paradoxes of Group Life*. For example, as they note, high-performing teams need individuals to give their best and distinctive efforts. Doing so often fosters competition between team members, but it also requires collaboration to prioritize the collective.[7] Moreover, paradoxes persist as groups and teams want to grow, learn, and adapt. In her book *Teaming*, Amy Edmondson reminds us that the only way for groups, teams, and organizations to perform well is to be constantly learning. Learning requires us to experiment, try new things, make mistakes, and fail—all in service of enabling ourselves to thrive and succeed. Her work explores how building a culture of psychological safety in teams enables us to learn for the future while performing in the present.[8]

Challenges of leadership are further mired in paradoxes. Scholars consistently point to opposing yet interwoven demands that leaders face, such as tensions between authenticity and transparency, technical skills and emotional intelligence, and learning and performing. In their book *Being the Boss*, Linda Hill and Kent Lineback note that grappling with paradoxes is a vital leadership skill.[9] Leaders must develop their people while managing the larger context beyond the group.

Paradoxical tensions are also pervasive in organizations. In her studies of product development, Dorothy Leonard found that organizations build core capabilities as they strengthen their technical capabilities, shared values, and current products. Resulting successes lead to efforts that, in turn, further bolster these strengths but also trigger a downside. Core capabilities become core rigidities that inhibit innovation.[10] Leonard's insights have since been repeated in other studies, illustrating paradoxically that what fuels an organization's success often leads to its failure.[11] Kim Cameron and Robert Quinn further suggest that organizational success depends on engaging paradoxes. Their "competing values framework" identifies alternative and opposing organizational values—collaborating, creating, controlling, and competing. Organizational effectiveness depends on drawing from across these varied values.[12]

These examples are broad and diverse. As we present them to audiences, we get mixed reactions—similar to our own responses. People feel inspired

FIGURE 1-2

Four types of paradoxes

Performing paradoxes

Tensions of outcomes
Why?

Work and life
Ends and means
Instrumental and normative
Mission and market

Belonging paradoxes

Tensions of identity
Who?

Whole and part
Global and local
Insider and outsider
We and they

Learning paradoxes

Tensions of time
When?

Short-term and long-term
Traditional and modern
Today and tomorrow
Stability and change

Organizing paradoxes

Tensions of processes
How?

Control and flexibility
Centralization and decentralization
Emerging and planning
Democratic and authoritative

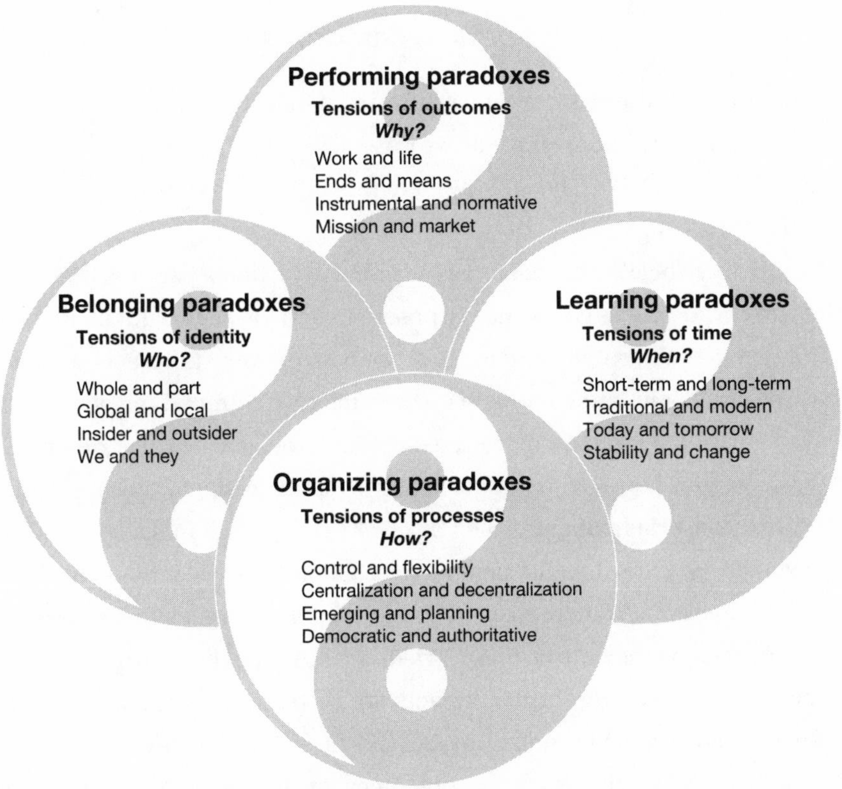

but overwhelmed. To tap into the amazement while also breaking through some of the fog, we compare and catalog the varied paradoxes. In our research, we identified four types of paradoxes: performing, learning, organizing, and belonging (figure 1-2).[13] These paradoxes emerge across many levels. For example, the paradox of today and tomorrow might underlie a dilemma around the next steps of a person's career and simultaneously infuse challenges that the person faces as a leader of a large organization.

Knowing exactly how to categorize a paradox is not critical to being able to navigate its tensions. The strategies presented in this book work across categories, and most paradoxes overlap categories. Rather, the value of this typology lies in helping us see the widely varying ways that paradoxes affect our world and our lives.

Performing paradoxes

Performing paradoxes involve competing demands in our goals, outcomes, and expectations. They surface as we raise *why* questions: Why am I choosing this life path? Why should I invest in this initiative? Why are we adopting this strategy?

Corporate social responsibility is a classic performing paradox. Debates about a corporation's goals and purposes started long ago, with increased attention in the twenty-first century as we hold organizations accountable for issues like climate change, economic instability, racial injustice, and environmental degradation. On the one hand, the goal of corporations is to make money for their shareholders. In 1970, University of Chicago economist Milton Friedman published a *New York Times* op-ed that became the standard-bearer for this perspective. Titled "The Social Responsibility of Business Is to Increase Its Profits," the piece argues for leaders to keep focused on the bottom line.[14] Friedman stressed that concerns about social issues or environmental impacts are better left to nonprofit organizations or government regulations. Yet this laser focus on profits can lead to bad behaviors and destructive outcomes, as evidenced by the crash of organizations like Enron, WorldCom, and Tyco in the late 1990s.

As an alternative to the shareholder focus, people have been calling on organizations to engage in multiple goals simultaneously, adopting a double or triple bottom line. Ben Cohen and Jerry Greenfield became some of the early leaders of this approach when they founded Ben & Jerry's in 1978. Over the years, the call has grown louder for leaders to focus on profits and passion, mission and market, stakeholders and shareholders— embedding performing paradoxes into their organization's strategy. Our colleagues and professors Tobias Hahn, Lutz Preuss, Jonatan Pinske, and Frank Figge make a strong case for how adopting both/and thinking that values the complex interactions between social missions and financial outcomes leads to long-term organizational sustainability.[15] More recently, organizational scholars Ed Freeman, Kirsten Martin, and Bidhan Parmar explore new approaches to corporate engagement in their book *The Power of And*. Drawing on extensive research, they find that leaders develop more impactful, profitable and sustainable business solutions by building on five core ideas:

1. the importance of purpose, values and ethics as well as profits

2. the centrality of creating value for stakeholders, as well as shareholders

3. seeing business as a societal institution as well as a market institution

4. recognizing the full humanity of people, as well as their economic interests

5. integrating "business" and "ethics" into more holistic business models[16]

Performing paradoxes emerge in people's personal lives as well. We might struggle with social and financial outcomes in our personal decisions about what to buy and from whom. National big-box supplier or local store? Cheaper goods or goods more sustainably made? We also face conflicting expectations of multiple bosses at work, must resolve professional and personal demands, and have to negotiate between discipline and flexibility in meeting our own goals and needs. If we looked through our New Year's resolutions each year, we might see budding performing paradoxes starting the tug-of-war between commitment and abandonment.

Learning paradoxes

Learning paradoxes create challenges for how we grow from the past to the future. These paradoxes involve tensions across time such as those between today and tomorrow, new and old, stability and change, tradition and modernization. Such paradoxes raise questions of when: When do we shift from our current reality to a new one?

Issues of innovation and change highlight core learning paradoxes. When we talk with organizational leaders, they often note rising demands for agility and constant adaptation. Yet great companies grow so large and structured that they are like oil tankers in the ocean; they can't turn easily when the winds change. Consider how companies are spending less and less time on the *Fortune* 500 list. The late James March, an organizational scholar, has articulated the challenge: innovating takes different skills, approaches and perspectives than managing the core business. He describes these two modes as *exploring* new opportunities and *exploiting* the current realities.[17] Given this challenge, research launched by Michael Tushman and Charles O'Reilly shows that organizations need to be ambidextrous—to learn to both explore and exploit at the same time. That is, they need to embrace learning paradoxes. Rather than choose between today and tomorrow, they need to develop ways to focus on both and find the synergies. How could today's successes support tomorrow's growth? How could tomorrow's innovation reenergize today's successes?

Imagine the same challenges between today and tomorrow at the individual level. I (Wendy) have a friend who wanted to return to law school but was afraid to give up his current role and salary in financial services. He spent ten years debating whether to take this leap—and then decided it was too late. Change happens around us. Are we agile enough to respond? Can we explore new skills and possibilities even before the world around us shifts? And are we able to navigate these changes while still exploiting the successes of our current world?

Belonging paradoxes

Belonging paradoxes raise questions of *who* we are, highlighting tensions in our roles, identities, values, and personalities. For many of us, engaging with multiple, competing identities is challenging. We can go to great lengths to ensure a unified presentation of ourselves. Early psychology experiments by Leon Festinger and James Carlsmith emphasized the human drive for consistency. When subjects spent an hour engaging in a boring task for little financial pay, they had to figure out how to justify their time spent. So, when asked, they said that they thought the experiment was interesting and exciting. Festinger and Carlsmith labeled this phenomenon *cognitive dissonance*, suggesting that we will change our sense of self to be consistent with the objective reality.[18]

Work-life tensions often emerge in questions of how to allocate our time; yet at the heart of these dilemmas are identity challenges. Am I a committed organizational leader or a good parent? Am I available to others, or am I focused on my own needs? Such dilemmas run even deeper, however, because our sense of self often involves multiple, contradictory identities. We grapple with whether we are an insider or an outsider, an inventor or an implementer, a lover or a fighter, a leader or a follower, a giver or a taker, a unique individual or committed team member. Yet depending on the day, time, context, and issue, we often switch identities—we are both. Our sense of self is embroiled in interwoven opposites. American poet Walt Whitman captured this idea in his "Song of Myself":

> Do I contradict myself?
> Very well, then, I contradict myself;
> (I am large, I contain multitudes.)[19]

Many of us feel these multitudes when taking personality tests. We may lean to one side or the other in our automatic preferences (introvert or extrovert, intuitive or rational, leader or follower) yet find ourselves drawing on other tools, skills, preferences, and identities when in different situations, or seeking to integrate both at the same time. Putting ourselves into one box or another can too easily cut off the vital multitudes and synergies of our identities. More recently, the late professor, author, and activist Gloria Jean Watkins, better known by her pen name bell hooks, reminded us to be more holistic about our multiple social identities: "If we move away from either/or thinking, . . . we think, okay, every day of my life that I walk out of my house I am a combination of race, gender, class, sexual preference and religion or what have you."[20]

Organizations also face the challenges of complex, interwoven identities underlying their strategies. I (Wendy) recently worked with an insurance company with more than a hundred years of history and traditions. The new CEO recognized that to survive the next century, the company needed to be more innovative and agile. Doing so involved moving from its disciplined, methodical, and risk-averse identity to include a more experimental and accountable approach to the bottom line. The greatest challenge was helping the employees see the value of a new culture and identity, and appreciate that it could build from the existing one.

Organizing paradoxes

Organizing paradoxes address questions of *how* we structure our lives and organizations. How do I get something done? These paradoxes include tensions such as those between spontaneity and planning, risk taking and risk avoidance, control and flexibility.

Leaders consistently grapple with these challenges when considering organizational structure. How much decision making happens centrally and globally, and how much is more nuanced and local? How much autonomy do we give to employees compared with how much leadership control is needed? Looking back, we can see these tensions play out historically in the development of organizations. From the Industrial Revolution onward, we have witnessed the rapid growth of organizational life. With it, we also saw a movement toward increased centralized control. In the late 1800s, Max Weber, Henri Fayol, and other European theorists detailed ways that leaders need to assert control over their organizations. These ideas took on a whole new level with Fredrick Taylor in the United States when he introduced scientific management, methods of timing and incentivizing people toward increasingly more efficient work. The efficiencies were obvious, but so too was the degradation of human rights, as people felt treated like machines. The response was the human relations movement. Launched by Harvard professors Elton Mayo, Fritz Roethlisberger, and others, this movement placed human motivation, needs, and desires at the heart of employee management. In the 1950s, Douglas McGregor became the champion for these ideas, suggesting that individuals need carrots over sticks. People do not need overt controls to drive performance but rather conditions that allow them to grow, learn, and feel impactful and purposeful.

Our shifting economy has brought back into focus many of these debates between centralized control and decentralized autonomy. As organizations started reopening their doors after the pandemic lockdown, leaders were asking how they could manage virtual or hybrid work arrangements. The same question emerges as we see more workers moving toward the gig economy. Employees gravitate to that work, allured in part by the high levels of personal decision making, yet they often find even more subtle forms of control in use in the gig world.[21]

We experience organizing paradoxes in our personal lives as well. Struggles between autonomy and control, for example, are central to every parenting relationship. I (Wendy) just experienced this struggle the other night as my husband and I debated how to navigate the expectation of doing the dishes. Our daughter hates doing the dishes, yet it's part of her chore rotation every three weeks. How much autonomy do we give her? Does she get to decide when she does the dishes? Does that mean that the plates and cups can stack up for days until she feels like getting them done? Until we have to eat off paper plates? Until we start to see flies? How much control do we assert? The questions are endless when it comes to parenting and other issues in our personal lives. How flexible are we with our own boundaries? How disciplined?

Knotted and Nested Paradoxes

Underlying the presenting dilemmas facing the residents of Fogo Island are paradoxes across each of the four types just described. The community's goal to preserve the island's past by advancing the community into the future reflect learning paradoxes, experienced as tensions between the past and present, tradition and modernization. Addressing these challenges points to performing paradoxes. The residents' goal was to sustain the culture of the island, but achieving this social mission depended on outcomes to build economic resilience—tensions between mission and market, economic growth and community development. Belonging paradoxes also abounded. The islanders have strong language to differentiate insiders from outsiders, known as the "come-from-aways." Yet rebuilding the island would require insiders and outsiders working together. And these tensions sparked all kinds of organizing paradoxes—particularly as the community wanted to democratically integrate members' diverse and sometimes opposing perspectives without creating arduous processes that would stall progress. Because the tensions were interwoven, attempts to address one paradox would introduce others, raising *knotted paradoxes*.[22] Seeing the tensions in this way does not necessarily help you isolate your tensions, but rather it helps you recognize their complexity.

Not only are paradoxes knotted, but the same paradoxes show up at different levels—from the individual to the group, organization and society. We describe these as *nested paradoxes*.[23] The same challenges facing organizations are reflected in the tensions of its members. Fogo Islanders individually grappled with the new and the old, mission and market, and tradition and modernization in their lives. Should they stay on the island to try to help it regrow, or should they move away in search of better economic and social opportunities? Moreover, tensions felt at the organizational level are also experienced at the more macro, societal levels. These challenges on Fogo Island are a microcosm of universal questions of how to support distinct local communities to advance within the world economy rather than be swallowed up by it.

The Paradox System: Enabling Both/And Thinking

Through decades of research, we identified tools to help navigate paradoxes. We pull these ideas together in what we call the *paradox system*— integrated sets of tools to enable both/and thinking. The system includes tools that shift how we think (assumptions) and how we feel (comfort) when navigating paradoxes. They further address how we approach situations by building static structures (boundaries) while enabling adaptive practices (dynamics) (figure 1-3).

FIGURE 1-3

The paradox system

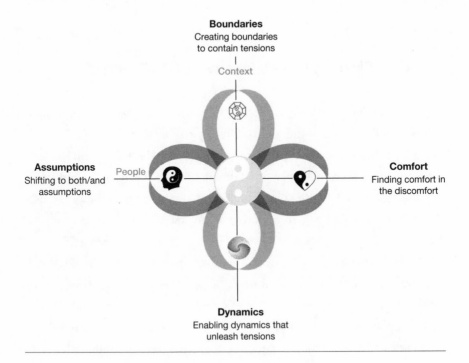

Boundaries
Creating boundaries
to contain tensions

Context

Assumptions
Shifting to both/and
assumptions

People

Comfort
Finding comfort in
the discomfort

Dynamics
Enabling dynamics that
unleash tensions

Two important insights emerged as we studied people applying these tools. First, we use the label of a paradox system because the most effective both/and thinkers don't just pick one set of tools. They engage with all these tools, enabling them to work together. They adopt both/and mindsets while also managing their emotions to become comfortable with the discomfort. They set static boundaries to guide their response to tensions while staying flexible to learn, adapt, and change over time.

Second, navigating paradoxes is paradoxical. Tensions are embedded in the foundations of the paradox system. As shown in figure 1-3, across the horizontal (people) axis are tools to engage the heart and mind. Often in conflict, heart and mind can also reinforce one another. The vertical (context) axis in the figure represents tools that help frame a particular situation, fostering stable boundaries and enabling changing dynamics. Again, stability and change pull in opposite directions but also foster synergies.

Together, these tools support both/and thinking that addresses paradoxes both personally (assumptions and comfort) and contextually (boundaries and dynamism).

Finding New Ways with Old Things

Zita Cobb understood the paradoxes that lurked on Fogo Island. In fact, she argued that most islanders lived in paradox as they continually experienced the liminal spaces of the craggy shoreline where land and sea confront one another. As she once proclaimed, "The best way, or the only way, to experience life is to be comfortable with death. Fogo Islanders understand that. The only way to experience any sense of control is to let go. And so it's this lovely ability to live in the seeming contradiction."[24]

She knew that if the community were to thrive going forward, the islanders would need to draw on both/and thinking. They could not afford reductionist thinking; they needed a holistic approach. In response, Cobb and two of her brothers—Alan and Tony—created Shorefast, a registered Canadian charity, to help rebuild economic resilience and community integration. A shorefast is the line that connects the fishing boat to the pier. Similarly, the organization sought to be a link, helping connect the community's initiatives with one another and linking the community with the broader economy. "We exist in relationship to the whole: The whole planet, the whole humanity, the whole existence," Cobb says on the company's website. "It is our job to find ways to belong to the whole while upholding the specificity of people and place."[25]

The world, as Cobb argues, benefits from being a "global network of intensely local places," an interconnected web valuing unique contributions. To this end, Shorefast built the Fogo Island Inn, a twenty-nine-room inn that honors the local culture while building an economic engine for growth. The inn draws on the culture of unbounded hospitality inherent to Fogo Island and, more broadly, Newfoundland. The endeavor revitalized islanders' skills to fill the inn. Woodworkers who once built wooden boats created artistically designed wood furniture for the inn. Quilters, who honed their skills through decades of sewing fabric scraps into blankets for the harsh subarctic winters, stitched beautiful quilts for each of its beds. Foragers, whose skills became moot as people started buying canned fruits and vegetables, now lead trips through the island's wilderness in search of its natural delicacies. As Cobb expected, these practices have helped "find new ways with old things."

The inn brings outsiders—and revenue—to the island. Guests also introduce new ideas that can help expand the vision and possibilities for community members. That relationship, however, is reciprocal. Cobb set up a community host program in which the islanders pick up guests from the inn and take them on a tour. Stops can include their favorite hiking spots, the local watering holes, and even the hosts' own homes for a home-cooked dinner. Guests experience Fogo Island through the eyes of its people, feeling the deep connection to the land, the reverence for cod, the soulfulness of the ballads influenced by Celtic fiddling, and the deep value of what it means to treasure a place and its people. The authentic interactions spur tremendous connections, some of which last long after the guests leave the island.

Cobb viewed the sustainability of the inn and the local community as tightly interwoven. The inn could not advance the economic resilience of the island without advancing other aspects of the community. Shorefast worked with the local community to rebuild a fish cooperative, supporting people who wanted to get back to fishing. The organization helped launch a wood and craft shop, allowing the woodworkers and quilters to continue their work and create a market for their goods. Impressively, the success of the Fogo Island Inn and advances in the community have slowly attracted people back to live on the island.

For Cobb, community and economy ideally exist in a virtuous cycle. Strong communities enable the local economy to thrive, just as strong local economies nurture vibrant communities. Yet the cycle isn't only at the local level. She stresses that local successes serve as engines of global sustainability, just as connecting with global resources allows for local successes. The problem, as Cobb suggests, is that we tend to use too narrow a lens. We overemphasize corporate success in a global world, neglecting the critical role of local organizations and local communities. Or we stay focused and insular locally, hoping to avoid the threats but also missing the opportunities posed by the broader world.

Cobb transcended divergent paths, honoring tradition and building community while modernizing practices and enabling global connections. Yet the Shorefast organization needs to sustain that complexity over time. How does it do so? We explore that question in the rest of the book.

 **CHAPTER TAKEAWAYS**

- **Tensions pull us in opposing directions.** Beneath the presenting dilemmas lurk paradoxes. We tend to adopt an either/or approach to choose between alternatives. Yet coping with our most challenging problems depends on understanding the messy, complex paradoxes that fuel them.

- **Paradoxes—contradictory yet interdependent elements that exist simultaneously and persist over time—are everywhere.** We can differentiate between four types of paradoxes—performing, learning, belonging, and organizing.

- **Paradoxes are often knotted such that multiple tensions reinforce one another, and are nested, with similar tensions emerging at different levels.**

- **Paradoxes have been studied for millennia.** Yet we experience tensions increasingly in our world today, as paradoxes become more salient in situations marked by greater change, plurality, and scarcity.

- **Navigating paradoxes is paradoxical.** The tools that we use to take advantage of a paradox are themselves opposing and interwoven.

2

Getting Caught in Vicious Cycles

Rabbit Holes, Wrecking Balls, and Trench Warfare

We should never allow ourselves to be bullied by an "either-or."
There is often the possibility of something better
than either of two given alternatives.

—Mary Parker Follett

Master carpenter Ole Kirk Christiansen founded LEGO in 1932. Since then, the company maintained a sharp focus on its brilliant product, the interlocking brick. In the early 1990s, this strategy paid off. The organization experienced a meteoric rise. Far outpacing rivals, LEGO controlled nearly 80 percent of the construction toy market globally.

At the time, LEGO was well known for its rigorous quality control and strong shared values. Leaders took seriously any innovation decision. For example, it took nearly a decade for the leaders to finally add a fifth color—green—to its mix of bricks. Likewise, senior leaders experienced

painstaking internal debates over whether to partner with other companies. In response to a proposal from Lucasfilm, one vice president proclaimed, "Over my dead body will LEGO ever introduce *Star Wars*." As
another vice president stated, "LEGO didn't trust outside partners. . . . [T]he
thinking was always 'We'll do it our way. We can do it better.'" For more
than six decades, this approach worked. In 2000, LEGO was proclaimed
"toy of the century."[1]

Yet by the late 1990s, competitors started to challenge their position in
the market. As digital and computerized toys emerged, LEGO found itself
stagnant and flat-footed. Sales plateaued and then fell—a first in the firm's
long history. To remain the industry leader in the twenty-first century, the
company would need to make significant changes.

In 2001, Lotte Lüscher, then a doctoral student in Denmark, reached out
to me (Marianne). Lüscher was studying the change efforts at LEGO. Leaders found themselves and the firm to be complacent, insular, and out of
step with rapidly changing markets and competition. Pressures were
intense, as the firm was restructured to remove whole layers of management in search of agility and savings. The remaining middle managers were
swimming in tensions between innovation and efficiency, modernization
and traditions, flexibility and control. Lüscher wanted to know more about
research on paradox and how these ideas informed what she was seeing
at LEGO.

LEGO's is a familiar story—a great empire on the verge of failure. We
see it in the rise and fall of the Roman Empire, the British Empire, and the
Soviet Union. We also see it in the lifecycles of great businesses, not to mention the vicissitudes of our own careers, our marriages, and so on.[2] The
universal pattern playing out in LEGO reflected an age-old, vicious cycle,
where success led to complacency and ultimately downfall. When the
LEGO leaders focused narrowly on one approach that had served as its
greatest strength and fueled past successes, the storied ruler of the toy
industry held itself back from learning and changing. LEGO leaders were
caught in a pattern of either/or thinking—either they held on to their long-
successful strengths or they shifted to new ventures, risking all that they
had worked to create. It was this either/or thinking that was the actual risk.

Perils of Either/Or Thinking

Either/or thinking is limited at best, detrimental at worst. The danger lies in overemphasizing one side of a paradox to the neglect of the other. As the LEGO story suggests, holding too tightly to current successes without simultaneously innovating means that when the future becomes the present, the organization is stuck in the past. Yet this is a typical response when presented with a dilemma. Indecision or even staying flexible leaves us feeling anxious with uncertainty. Either/or thinking can provide a sense of relief to these emotions as we weigh the alternatives and make a clear choice. We also feel anxious when we are inconsistent.[3] Therefore we try to align our decisions with our previous commitments. Over time, however, our repeated commitments to a particular course of action intensify. Once we start down a particular path, we tend to want to stay on that path, which results in our becoming stuck.

Society reinforces this logical yet limiting either/or approach to addressing dilemmas. Consider, for example, Robert Frost's poem "The Road Not Taken." In the first two lines, he states:

Two roads diverged in a yellow wood,
And sorry I could not travel both.[4]

Frost wrote the poem for his British friend Edward Thomas in 1914. Thomas confronted an agonizing decision between joining the army as the United Kingdom prepared to enter World War I or moving to the United States to be with Frost. Thomas faced a dilemma—stay or go? As difficult as it is to enter war, staying in the United Kingdom was the more conventional path and therefore the easier option to choose. Relocating to the United States felt more novel, unconventional, and riskier. In this poem, Frost encouraged his friend, and years of readers afterward, to take the riskier path:

I took the road less travelled by,
And that has made all the difference.

Despite Frost's encouragement, Thomas chose the more conventional approach. He joined the army and, sadly, was killed in the war.

Frost's poem has inspired many to take risks, be bold, and try new things. But what if the problem is not that we are too conventional in our choices? What if the problem is not about choosing novelty or convention? What if the problem is that we are too narrow in how we frame the problem? We see two roads and think that those are our only options, rather than diving deeper, asking why we feel forced to make that choice to begin with.

Ruts: Stuck in Our Either/Or Choices

Stressing only one side of a paradox oversimplifies and narrows our options. The tricky thing is that picking one side usually offers us short-term success—comfort, respect, rewards, efficiency, joy. Success motivates us to stick with that option, until we get stuck in a rut. The greater the success of those either/or choices, the deeper the ruts. LEGO leaders learned this all too well as their commitment to the organization's greatest strengths nearly led to their downfall.

In his book *The Second Curve*, Charles Handy builds from decades of research about how such ruts develop. He uses the mathematical representation of the sigmoid curve, or S curve, to depict how choices lead us from progress to stagnation and, ultimately, decline. The curve has been used to illustrate a similar path that emerges across many phenomena, including learning, product innovation, evolution, and career progression.[5] In our own work, we've seen this curve also represent the path associated with progress in our personal identities, team development, and organizational governance.

Progress starts slowly. Performance improves with time, thanks to trial and error, hard work, and focused investments. Gradually and then more rapidly, we develop strengths and the confidence to achieve mastery. The upward trajectory feels exhilarating. As performance improves, learning quickens, and acclaim builds. That rising curve of progress, however, eventually stagnates, flattening and turning downward. We sometimes believe

FIGURE 2-1

The S curve of resources and performance

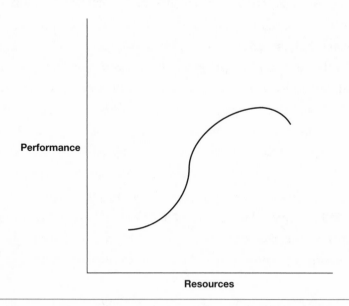

Performance

Resources

we can avoid this downturn, but it is inevitable—and the downward slope is slippery! As our strengths grow and related challenges decrease, so comes complacency, rigidity, and even arrogance. We start to miss changes in the external environment or weaknesses in internal competencies. New problems come up, and we lack the tools to address them.

The S curve highlights the paradox of success and failure (figure 2-1). Stay committed to the path of your success, and you will ultimately find yourself a failure.

I (Marianne) lived this experience in my own career. Completing a doctoral program, I had my dissertation in hand but no career momentum. My PhD years had been more reproductive than productive. I welcomed three beautiful children into the world, but my research remained a distant priority. I was still at the bottom of the career S curve. Shocking many people, particularly my parents and parents-in-law, my husband gladly took the family reins, becoming "Mr. Mom" so we could fully invest in my career. I went all in—arriving to work by 5 a.m. so that I could be home by 5 p.m. to relieve him and enjoy the kids.

My dissertation was about tensions raised by technological change. These tensions became my obsession. I read everything I could find about these contradictions, competing demands, and, ultimately, paradoxes. I was convinced that paradox could significantly inform the thinking of organizational scholars—an idea mostly overlooked until that time. I wrote a paper for the *Academy of Management Review*, one of the top journals in our field. When that paper won the journal's Best Paper Award for 2000, my husband and I joked that I was now famous to five people.

Yet my relative anonymity was changing quickly. As my knowledge and visibility grew, so did related opportunities. Researchers started to contact me from around the globe to learn more about these ideas. Within a few years, my research had progressed and my publications multiplied. I could feel the upward trajectory of my career S curve. But I could also feel myself getting stuck. I began to worry that my cutting-edge research would became commonplace and that my energy and excitement would wane.

The key to continued progress is to start the next curve while still in the successful upward trajectory (point A) of the first curve (figure 2-2). Reenergizing through creative exploration, bold innovation, and radical change is vital to sustain progress.

There are several key challenges to this recommendation, though. First, we don't always know when we are at point A. Moreover, at point A, when we are finally experiencing the thrill of success, there is no motivation to change. After all, as the saying goes, if it ain't broke, don't fix it. Only when we hit point B and start to see the downward trajectory do we feel the pull toward change. By then, however, it may be too late. We don't have the same resources to reenergize and change. You might know the shrewd observation that it's easier to get a job while you have a job (at point A) than it is when you don't have a job (at point B). Likewise, a company can fuel innovation far better when it is thriving (at point A) then when it is struggling (at point B). As Handy summarizes, "The nasty and often fatal snag is that the Second Curve has to start before the first curve peaks. Only then are there enough resources—of money, time, and energy—to cover that first dip, the investment period."[6]

FIGURE 2-2

The double S curve of resources and performance

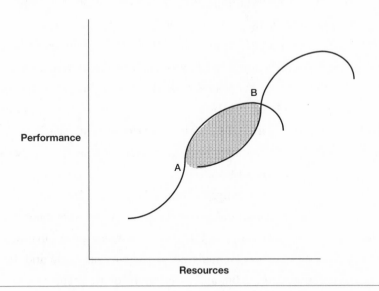

In his book *The Icarus Paradox*, Danny Miller, an expert on innovation and change, offers examples of how the S curve plays out for organizations. He details how the greatest trigger for organizational failure is success. The most successful organizations start to oversimply processes; become proud, insular, and immune to feedback; and lack the motivation or resources to change. Once highly effective processes, organizations, and leaders start to fail when faced with new technologies and shifting market trends.

Miller named this challenge the *Icarus paradox*, after the Greek god. Icarus became so enamored with the flight enabled by his wax wings that he flew too close to the sun, melting the wings and falling to his death.[7] Miller offers eye-opening examples of market leaders rising in the markets, becoming so enamored by their own success that they fail to take precautions and then falling swiftly down their S curves.

Consider Texas Instruments. The company's greatest strengths stemmed from high-tech designs and sophisticated engineering. When the market demanded products more basic and user-friendly, Texas Instruments could not deliver. Its embedded skills and overconfidence inhibited a shift. Likewise, Apple came to excel at finding the next big breakthrough. Acclaimed for its bold, award-winning designs, Apple pushed ever further. Increasingly, however, designers in the organization were creating mind-blowing and elegant yet commercially useless new products.

How do we know when we are at point A—the tipping point between success and failure, the point where we need to shift between what we've been doing for our past success and what we need to do for the future? When all is going well, there is no reason for us to believe that our upward trajectory will ever change. The trick, therefore, is to always believe that you are at point A, to constantly scan the horizon for the next curve, even while enjoying your current success.

Essentially, we must always be doing both—leaning into our well-developed skills, insights, and products while also experimenting and exploring to develop new opportunities. Yet engaging our current skills while building new ones is challenging, as the current world and the new world are not only different but also often contradictory. The new may disrupt and overturn the old. This is why we need to live in paradox. As Charles Handy advises, "Wise are they who start the second curve at point A, because that is the pathway through paradox, the way to build a new future while maintaining the present."[8]

In my own career, I (Marianne) was lucky to see the signs that my career S curve had started to peak and I needed to make a change. I was starting to burn out. Feeling depleted and exhausted was not fun, but it did provide a valuable signal that I might be approaching point B. Thankfully, academia has a tradition of sabbatical to deal with this exact problem. My family and I headed to England. This time away helped me out of my rut, offering the opportunity for much-needed, if sometimes uncomfortable, reflection on what was next. I did not want to give up the research, but I also needed a new challenge to fuel my focus and energy. Eager to start moving to a new curve, I returned to the University of Cincinnati with the vision that I needed to practice what I professed and start embracing competing demands. I became an associate dean. This decision again shocked many people, as I had not yet earned tenure. In academia, earning tenure depends so heavily on research productivity that professors rarely take significant leadership roles prior to doing so. Yet given my own burnout, I found that I needed to move into new responsibilities, even as I continued to advance my research. Embracing tensions of past and the future, theory and practice sparked my energy.

As the S curve illustrates, when we find ourselves stuck in ruts of our own creation, we have choices. If we continue to apply either/or thinking, as tensions mount, we will face another dilemma: Do we intensify our current efforts or make a radical change? The resulting responses, however, will deepen the current trap or create a new one. Ultimately these traps lead us into vicious cycles. In our research, we identifying three patterns of vicious cycles: rabbit holes (intensification), wrecking balls (overcorrection), and trench warfare (polarization).

Rabbit Holes: Intensification

Like Alice in Wonderland, we can enter a rabbit hole only to find ourselves falling deep and fast without even realizing it. What drives us farther down the hole, keeping us stuck in a narrow pattern of choices long after we realize the need to grow and change? Alternatively, why might friends, family members, leaders, businesses, and societies continue in ruts long after strengths have turned into liabilities, making bad situations even worse?

A vicious cycle of intensification develops because the more we respond to tensions in a certain way, particularly if the action benefits us initially, the more we overuse that response. We get better at, more comfortable with, and more automatic in that response. The response becomes a habit. Three traps fuel the vicious cycles of intensification. The ways we think (cognition), feel (emotion), and act (behavior) all advance our descent down a rabbit hole.[9]

Cognitive traps

Cognition, our mindset or way of thinking, traps us in a reinforcing cycle: we see what we expect to see. Acting as a mental lens, our existing assumptions inform how we frame both problems and responses. The more skilled and comfortable we become with our way of thinking, the more we take for granted our existing assumptions, our mental limits, and our biases. We become committed to a way of viewing the world and defensive when those views are challenged. This defensiveness, in turn, reinforces our existing assumptions. In his research, organizational psychologist Adam Grant stresses that we often aimlessly and continuously intensify our current mindset, as rethinking takes courage, humility, and curiosity.[10]

Experiences can trigger learning but also reinforce existing understandings. Psychologist and education researcher David Kolb described experiential learning: (1) experience—trying something new; (2) reflection—reviewing what happened; (3) theorizing—developing abstract ideas according to what happened; and (4) experimentation—finding ways to test the abstract ideas.[11] I (Marianne) am amazed how clearly I can observe this learning process play out by my one-year-old grandson. He might touch the front of my heated oven, jump back, and look from the stove to his hand to me. I say, "Hot," and I can see his little brain spinning. Is the kitchen dangerous? Do all large silver things burn? What does grandma mean? He toddles to the cabinet nearby, touches it, experiences nothing, registers that this is boring. He waddles to the stainless steel refrigerator, finding it cold. After dinner, he tests the stove again. Now it feels different. His actions introduce new experiences. He is reflecting, theorizing, and then experimenting with his theories. I try to explain, loving his openness, knowing he has so much of the world to explore and process, but also knowing how critically his own actions and reflections inform his learning process.

Among adults, experiential learning happens so quickly and automatically that we rarely question our assumptions, regardless of our experiences. People's developed assumptions frame their experiences, triggering a self-fulfilling prophecy. For example, if we know we are strong analytically but a peer criticizes our work, we question their mathematical skills or seek to clarify our presentation. Our colleague Jean Bartunek, professor of management at Boston College, argues that when confronting more direct contradictions and challenging dilemmas, we need to reframe the problem, moving to higher-order thinking to consider both/and alternatives.[12] Yet we are more likely to try to rationalize, seeking to make sense of the conflict using what we already know well. We try to create the familiar out of the strange, using past approaches to resolve the tension and move on. The results, however, reflect what renowned psychologist Gregory Bateson called a *double-bind*.[13] Staying within our current frame, we choose interpretations that support, rather than challenge, our mindset, narrowing our lens when we need it widened the most. The slight modifications we make to our thinking are more likely to reinforce than to change our view. And if we don't expand our thinking, we can't learn, adapt, or expand our options.

At LEGO, Lotte Lüscher sought to help middle managers navigate paradoxes. As senior leaders introduced significant strategic changes, production managers struggled to make sense of the changes through their current mental frameworks. These production managers had reached their positions through years of high performance, supervising employees to meet rising efficiency and quality targets. Yet given LEGO's financial strain, senior leaders raised those targets even higher. And now the production managers were also expected to build innovative self-managed teams that improved the production process. These managers knew how to increase production rates and all the ins and outs of supervising the production line. But the more they intensified their approach to advance production, the less time they had to coach their teams and encourage experimentation. And what did it even mean to manage a self-managed team?

Our mental limits and shortcuts tighten the trap, speeding our slide down the rabbit hole. Nobel Prize–winning economist Herbert Simon defined mental limits as bounded rationality.[14] Given our constrained capacity to digest complex, ever-changing information, we focus on what our existing mindset deems the most important. That selected information, however, is likely to support and intensify our existing way of thinking.

Tunnel vision develops as our ideas become increasingly narrow, stuck, and self-reinforcing. In his research, Clayton Christensen depicted the vicious cycle of intensification in his book *The Innovator's Dilemma*.[15] As leaders grapple with innovation paradoxes—needing to boldly innovate for tomorrow while addressing the operational needs of today—biases can push highly successful firms to further invest in and strengthen their core capabilities while neglecting the exploration of future possibilities. Ironically, leaders' biases are reinforced by their loyal customers. Christensen found that when asked what they wanted in new products, long-standing customers consistently called for less expensive, enhanced versions of past innovations.

Cognitive traps go beyond how we think, also intensifying our feelings and behavior in well-worn patterns. Famed Stanford psychologist Paul Watzlawick describes self-fulfilling prophecies as magical in their ability to create the reality we expect.[16] If an experience agrees with the prophecy and matches our expectations, we accept it as proof that we are correct. When we face a conflict or contradiction between our prophecy and our experiences, we ignore, reject, or rationalize the experiences. In their classic 1968 experiment, Robert Rosenthal and Lenore Jacobson demonstrated how these self-fulfilling prophecies played out in the classroom. The researchers randomly labeled a group of young students as "growth spurters" with high potential to learn quickly, irrespective of the students' abilities and performance. At the beginning of the school year, the researchers informed teachers of these labels and then observed both teachers and students. The labels impacted how teachers interacted with the students. The teachers set higher expectations and offered more praise to the students labeled as growth spurters. As a result, these growth spurters on average substantially outperformed the other students. Rosenthal and Jacobson labeled these self-fulfilling prophecies as the Pygmalion Effect as the actions of the students were molded by the expectations of the teachers. The Pygmalion Effect has been found to extend beyond school-aged kids to inform how managers interact with their employees.[17]

Emotional traps

Our emotions also create traps that keep us stuck in ruts. Our natural desire is to feel confident, certain, and secure; however, tensions raise uncertainty and insecurity. As we confront competing demands, we experience this uncertainty in our body—that feeling in the pit in our stomach or the racing of our heartbeat.

We naturally want to take actions to reduce the discomfort. To do so, we often avoid, reject, or move away from tensions. In their studies of paradoxes, Kenwyn Smith and David Berg found that when we embrace tensions and move into the fray of emotions, we can explore new options, and question and revise our existing approaches. Through practice engaging tensions, we can reduce anxiety at its source. Yet people often do not get to this point. Instead, our most immediate tendency is to reduce exposure to tensions and resist change. While doing so can minimize anxiety in the short term, it often leaves us with more emotional discomfort over time.[18]

Why do emotions spark such counterproductive defenses in response to tensions? According to psychoanalysis, tensions trigger anxiety that threatens the ego. Contradictions, competing demands, and conflicts surprise and confuse us, challenging beliefs in ourselves—throwing into question our existing mindsets, skills, identities, or relationships. Tensions also introduce uncertainty, leaving future possibilities unclear. Uncertainty triggers increased anxiety and discomfort. Like cognitive biases, our emotional defenses can lead us to ignore, reject, or reinterpret experiences and information. We seek conclusive outcomes that can minimize the uncertainty and discomfort. Rather than change, we may intensify our favored responses.

Defense mechanisms temporarily minimize our exposure to uncomfortable tensions. One defense mechanism is splitting, which involves efforts to separate opposing forces. When tensions rise in a meeting, for example, our minds might split people into two groups—those for and those against a particular issue. Doing so can help us to clarify where we stand on an issue, and identify our allies and opponents. This practice also makes us feel more content that we are not alone in our position. Yet such splitting intensifies we/they distinctions, while downplaying potential links between opposing views. Rather than generate new and integrative approaches, splitting fosters cliques and turf wars.

Likewise, we can temporarily avoid discomfort by blocking our awareness of tensions through repression or denial. We shift our attention away from anxiety-provoking matters to less perplexing issues. Doing so can help us to feel reenergized in the short term. Yet we can only kick the can down the road so far. Eventually, we need to confront the tensions and make a decision. To protect our sense of self, we can overemphasize our favored, comforting side of tension. By using these defense mechanisms, we end up leaning into our routines, intensifying uses of existing skills to showcase our capabilities and bolster our ego, even in light of evidence that new efforts are needed.[19]

Behavioral traps

The final trap that keeps us stuck in intensifying rabbit holes involves our behaviors. Creatures of habit, we tend to stick with existing routines rather than try new things. Though our habits can be powerful forces in our lives, helping us achieve our goals through consistent effort, they become problematic when they are too rigid or automatic.

We can see habits forming at all levels—individuals, groups, and organizations—which can help or hinder problem solving. In their classic book *A Behavioral Theory of the Firm*, Richard Cyert and James March map out this process.[20] As people develop routines that prove effective, the practices are rewarded, shared, and repeated. Habits move from individuals to groups and organizations through informal cultural norms and more formal standard operating procedures. While resulting norms and procedures enable better coordination and sharing of best practices that can benefit the firm, not all problems are standard. In fact, often new opportunities emerge when situations are most uncertain, complicated, and tenuous. Over time, our superpowers—such as LEGO's quality control and shared values—become our kryptonite, limiting bolder innovation and more critical self-examination in times of change.

Similar patterns of intensifying behaviors appear in studies of specialists, such as doctors, engineers, scientists and others. Reviewing decades of related research, management professor Erik Dane found that specialists gain accolades because of their deep knowledge, which inspires them to deepen, but also narrow, their expertise. Such patterns constrain their ability to think and respond differently to varying, novel problems. Specialists so capable in their current routines, found experimenting with radically new approaches both physically and mentally challenging.[21]

Behavioral traps become tightly interwoven, and reinforce our cognitive and emotional traps when our performance starts to decline. As our

S curve dips, rather than pull out of our behavioral ruts, we are more likely to double down. In his famous studies, organizational scholar Barry Staw asked why good leaders make poor decisions. Over nearly four decades, his and others' research found that once people invest their time and energy in a decision, they tend to stick with and grow that investment, regardless of contrary signals. Staw calls this tendency a pattern of *escalating commitment*, a bias in favor of our previous decisions and existing mindsets. Our habits and growing anxiety fuel this cognitive trap as we dive deeper into the hole. For example, entrepreneurs avoid pulling out of a struggling venture, sure that with a little more money, passion, and sweat, it will pay off. Our career feels stalled and lacks meaning, but if we only worked harder, we will triumph. The greater the sunk resources, the greater the desire for success and the tighter the blinders. We follow our preferred patterns of behavior even more strictly. Staw and colleagues go further to find a link between threats and rigidity. The more we experience a threat, the tighter we hold to our existing approaches, seeking to regain control over what has become uncontrollable.[22]

Wrecking Balls: Overcorrection

Seeking to break out of a deep rut of either/or thinking, we can overcorrect, reversing our either/or thinking too far in the opposite direction. Imagine Newtonian balls—a set of several balls that can be swung back and forth. When we pull the ball on one side and release, it comes crashing down on the other balls and transfers energy to the other side. The ball farthest on the other side rises up, but then comes crashing down again. The energy transfers back and forth repeatedly, but accomplishes nothing. In our research, we find that either/or thinking can follow this pattern, but also be much more destructive. Overcorrections can ultimately launch ourselves into a new rut. In this case the pendulum becomes a wrecking ball; an overly powerful swing in the opposing direction creates a new and even greater challenge.[23]

When the LEGO leaders recognized that their once successful strategy had led them into a rut, they overcorrected. Identifying the downsides of a single-minded approach to quality control and the resulting isolation, stagnation, and decline, they decided to go all in for radical innovation. In *Brick by Brick*, David Robertson and Bill Breen chronicled this overcorrection. Hiring the top innovation specialists globally, LEGO was applauded for textbook-perfect implementation of the era's seven best innovation practices. The mantra became "Creativity above all else." As the company cut costs in production and moved resources into R&D, new ideas and products began to flow from LEGO's new design centers in London, Milan, and San Francisco. The centers were focused, aligning structure, targets, and processes at all levels to one strategy: innovate, innovate, innovate.

LEGO's previous S curve had taken decades to plateau and dip. Its next curve accelerated far faster. New products, brand visibility, and sales skyrocketed. By 2002, LEGO leaders were expecting record profits. Instead, sales started to decline and inventories ballooned. What happened? The board asked Jørgen Vig Knudstorp, recently hired from McKinsey & Company consulting, to lead LEGO's strategy development and to investigate.

What Knudstorp found shocked him. Despite early successes, few of the innovations were actually profitable. Sales had plateaued, and R&D costs were excessive. Gauging the damage, he found that LEGO was on track for sales to decline by nearly 30 percent and to potentially default on its debt. Innovation drove LEGO to the brink of bankruptcy. Their innovation strategy had little discipline and became a wrecking ball that intensified complexity and chaos. Whereas it once took nearly a decade for LEGO to introduce the color green, within a few years the toy maker started making parts in 157 different colors. A once-tight supply chain now lacked cost, quality, and coordination controls. Longtime loyal customers questioned new offerings. Tensions mounted between the new and old guard of LEGO leaders, and retailers were overwhelmed by the "new product binge." In a memo to the board, Knudstorp summarized his findings by stating, "We are on a burning platform."[24]

Our colleague Barry Johnson developed a valuable tool, a polarity map, to depict vicious and virtuous cycles of paradox like the one that LEGO was facing (figure 2-3).[25] Each opposing alternative—or pole—has upsides

FIGURE 2-3

Polarity map: upsides and downsides of LEGO's strategy

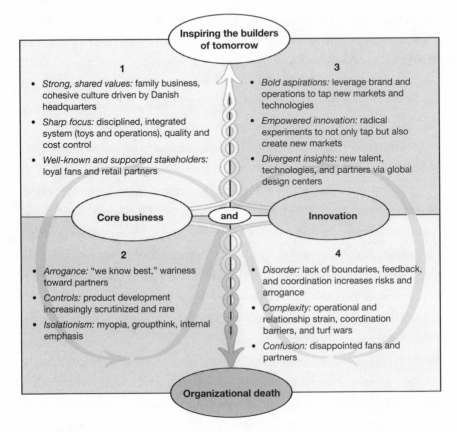

Source: Polarity map concept courtesy of Barry Johnson and Polarity Partnerships, LLC. ©2020.
All rights reserved.

and downsides that contrast almost diametrically with the other pole. Focusing too much on the upsides of only one pole eventually leads to its downsides—when the S curve dips. To escape the rabbit hole, we seek out the missing upsides. Swinging to the opposing option, we start a new S curve. Yet eventually that S curve declines as well and the pendulum swings again. The resulting swing forms the shape of an infinity loop; our goal is to reduce the extremes of our swings, keeping the loop more in the upsides of the map.

The decisions of the LEGO leaders, however, reflect a detrimental loop in the polarity map. LEGO leaders found themselves falling into the downside of each pole, with an infinity loop that dipped far into the lower quadrants. Initially, the leaders intensified their grip on their core product, drawing on their strong shared values, disciplined focus, and commitment to well-known fans (quadrant 1). When the market for toys started to shift, this approach led to significant downsides noted in quadrant 2. So the leaders decided to shift intensely toward innovation, quadrant 3, until that extreme response led to the downsides listed in quadrant 4.[26]

I (Marianne) also experienced this radical swing in my career. While on sabbatical, I realized that I had become so laser focused on my research that I had pushed myself to the brink. Rigorous and creative research enabled my theory building, resulting in a series of well-cited papers and traditional academic success. Yet I too was on a burning platform, and I was the one burning out. With such a deep focus on theory building, I started to question my relevance to a broader audience, wondering if I was having any impact on people's lives or on issues I cared about.

Luckily, studying inspiring individuals in my research, I saw the tremendous impact made possible by those who practice leadership. I thought about the potential for my own career. This realization, inspired by a break from my regular routine, invited me to consider a totally different path. I returned to Cincinnati determined to become an administrator at the university. Over the next ten years, I practiced leadership with the same drive and abandon as what I had shown in my research. The demands on my time were intense. Early on, mistakes—sometimes big and ugly—were my norm, and countless times during that first year, I questioned my decision to move into administration. Had I overcorrected from my burnout with research by now swinging too hard in the opposite direction? What had I done?!

I had wonderful mentors and colleagues to offer me constructive and critical feedback that could help as I painfully and slowly climbed the learning curve. Over time, it became easier. My confidence grew from my failures as well as my successes. I loved practicing innovation and leading remarkable teams. Yet I soon found myself in a familiar position. I was again laser focused, now on providing leadership at the college rather than theory building. This single-mindedness—or let's call it what it became, obsessiveness—again drove me to burnout. After helping lead a massive university project, I had lost my mojo. Worse, I was questioning my life. I had divorced, was hyper critical of my mothering, had become an empty nester, and had literally no hobbies. Luckily, enough time had gone by that I had earned another sabbatical. This time, I won a Fulbright award and headed to London, determined to stop the wrecking ball.

Trench Warfare: Polarization

The final warning of vicious cycles comes from patterns of polarization. Until now we have pointed out what happens when individuals, leaders, and organizations become stuck in their own either/or ruts. Yet what happens when an issue arises and people fall to opposing sides, each group stuck in its own rut and then confronting one another? Trench warfare.

Battles between those stuck in opposing ruts reinforce each other's "stuckness." Because our ruts run deep, affecting and affected by how we think, feel, and behave, responding to someone from an opposing camp may be the ultimate challenge. The more we feel challenged by the other side, the more we defend our own position. Ultimately, we end up in an intensifying and unending tug-of-war. I (Marianne) noticed this never-ending struggle while visiting the Imperial War Museum in London to see the exhibit on the hundredth anniversary of World War I. During the war, the two sides continued improving their trench warfare technologies, bettering their living and fighting sections, and enlisting more partners. Ultimately, the more each side worked to protect itself with trench warfare, the more the enemies prolonged the war, rather than finding a way to end it.

Years ago, a colleague, Chamu Sundaramurthy, approached me (Marianne), frustrated by an escalating debate among people who study and advise corporate boards. One side argued vehemently that boards should control and monitor executives, given the leaders' potential for mismanagement. Consequently, they recommended organizational structures that separated these roles. Others argued that boards could better serve their organizations by collaborating with top management. Collaboration, they encouraged, would help all the participants find new opportunities to improve and support the firm by learning from each other. Yet no matter who made the argument, those listening would either praise or criticize it, depending on their increasingly entrenched view.

Sundaramurthy and I began reviewing the research on corporate governance, trying to pull apart each approach and understand the different underlying assumptions and recommendations. We quickly learned that we needed to change the question. Rather than examine which approach was correct, we started to ask ourselves about the dangers of applying either approach in the extreme. Each approach relied on a different and singular view of human nature as a guide. The first group viewed human nature as problematic: because humans tend to prioritize their own self-interests over those of others and the firm. For this group, control mechanisms are necessary to overcome individual self-interest. In contrast, the second group emphasized humans' social nature, stressing that people want to feel part of a greater whole, seeking, benefiting from, and excelling at collaboration.

Taken too far, a control approach fostered reinforcing cycles swirling around distrust. Concerned about potential mismanagement, boards were vigilant in their monitoring of top leaders. Staying removed from managers, boards provided discipline and outside perspectives. When a firm performed well, this approach was confirmed, encouraging the board to apply more controls and to further separate itself from management. Yet this approach also fostered fissure between the board and the leaders. Both the board members and the company executives believed that success proved their own effectiveness rather than that of the other group, further narrowing their perspectives and commitment to the current firm strategy. But when an external shock occurred—new technologies, more innovative rivals, economic downturns, and so forth—and firm performance declined, those ruts became dangerous. Boards and managers turned to impression management, seeking face-saving rationalizations to explain the downturn and scapegoating the other group. Rather than learn together how to pull out of the downturn, the board members and executives intensified their turf wars, and boards applied even greater controls that challenged creative thinking, experimentation, and collaboration.

Collaborative approaches demonstrated the same pattern but in a different flavor. Boards and managers worked as a governing team. Often led by the CEO, who also served as the board chair, these teams focused on collective decision making, excelling at setting and achieving organizational goals. Working and learning together, the managers and boards could improve the organization and their mutual understandings, becoming increasingly committed to the organization and to each other. In high-performing times, the teams would attribute success to their strong collaboration and became adept at quickly reaching consensus. When the firm's S curve dipped, as it eventually would, they attributed failures to factors beyond their control. Rather than seek outside perspectives or shift their current strategy, they escalated their commitment to the current plan and to their collaboration. Although distrust fueled the previously described control approach, groupthink was core to extreme collaborative approaches.

Intriguingly, Sundaramurthy's and my experience publishing our findings reflected this same pattern of trench warfare. While we sought to offer an alternative that could bring together different perspectives, responses tended to be polarizing. The academics reviewing our paper came from one or the other camp. Throughout the process, reviewers too became entrenched in their own point of view. Sundaramurthy and I thought the prolonged anonymous review process would never end. Finally, the editor overrode the reviewers, stating that such a change in questioning—not asking whether one approach or the other was better but which parts of both approaches were important—was critical to get the opposing camps to rethink the debate and help organizations improve governance.[27]

We see reinforcing patterns of polarization across debates big and small. Opposing groups, each aligned in how they think about, feel about, and respond to a particular hot topic, dig in their heels. Like the governance example, underlying assumptions of each side typically focus on only part of a more complicated issue, such as the intricacies of human nature. But as the debate heats up, the arguments simplify, the groups polarize, the camps isolate into separate, supporting echo chambers, and arguments can turn personal, ugly, and even dehumanizing.

While leading a business school in London, I (Marianne) experienced just how uncomfortable these debates can become. Emotions ran high during and long after the Brexit vote. Cass Business School is an institution infused by diversity of students, alumni, faculty, and supporters from more than one hundred nations.[28] As dean of the school and as an expat new to the European Union and to Britain, I tried to learn quickly the nuances of this highly complicated issue. Views ranged widely but publicly seemed to have solidified into two opposing, simplified, and angry sides: the *remain* camp and the *leave* camp.

One evening soon after the vote, I hosted a Dean's Lecture with José Manuel Barroso, past president of the European Commission. He delivered an insightful and provocative keynote on global economics and the evolving roles of the European Union and Britain. Afterward, Barroso, two members of my board, and I all walked to the dining room for a private dinner. I had discussed Brexit with each of the board members separately, learning from their exceptionally thoughtful, strong, and opposing views. In that moment, one member railed against the vote, saying, in short, that those who voted to leave were uneducated and racist. My heart raced as I surreptitiously glanced at the dissenting board member. Without missing a beat, Barroso smiled and noted the vital intricacies of individuals' personal voting decisions. He continued, saying that, given the extensive negotiations remaining, now was the time to learn about others' deeper concerns and to seek the best future possible for all. Both board members smiled, taking the statesman's cue, and an exceptionally open and insightful dinner discussion ensued.

That night—after my heart rate slowed—I thought about how this pattern occurs in politics on both sides of the pond. Patterns to simplify, polarize, isolate, and dehumanize escalate into intractable conflict. Our biases, defenses, and habits march along on overdrive. As we seek the win for our side, our chances to listen to others, let alone discuss issues meaningfully, evaporate. In times of extreme polarity, I often think back to Barroso and his tactful ability to help those in the ruts step out and explore new, more creative, and more inclusive alternatives.

A Better Way

Are we doomed to repeat past mistakes, burrowing down the rabbit hole until our S curve peaks and declines? Maybe. Our natural tendencies are to overplay our strengths until they become liabilities. And when we do, we may overcorrect and frantically begin digging a new rut. Likewise, we may catch ourselves engaged in trench warfare, fueling intractable and polarizing conflicts.

Yet the pendulum that swings between alternatives does not need to become a wrecking ball, sapping the creative energy that emerges from opposing perspectives. Nor do opposing sides always need to stand in defense of their positions. There is a better way—a way of embracing a both/and mindset, to engage competing demands simultaneously. Organizational scholar Charles Hampden-Turner has long stressed the value of embracing opposites to advance our personal and professional pursuits. In his 1982 book *Maps of the Minds* he writes:

> It is in vain that we search for an essential difference between good and evil, for their constituents are the same. The crucial distinction lies in their structure, i.e., the manner in which the pieces are assembled. Evil is disintegration, an angry juxtaposition of alienated opposites, with parts always striving to repress other parts. Good is the synthesis and reconciliation of these same pieces.[29]

Reconsider LEGO. As Knudstorp prepared to pivot out of the innovation nosedive, he told the firm's leaders that they all had to use a "bifocal perspective" to become renowned for world-class and bold innovation as well as disciplined quality and financial control.[30] The effort would be hard, given the ongoing global changes, but LEGO survived two near disasters and could continue to learn and thrive. And he often reminded himself and others to review the eleven paradoxes that had hung on the walls of LEGO offices since the 1980s and that are showcased today in the LEGO museum:

- To be able to build a close relationship with one's staff, and to keep a suitable distance.

- To be able to lead, and to hold oneself in the background.

- To trust one's staff, and to keep an eye on what is happening.

- To be tolerant, and to know how you want things to function.

- To keep the goals of one's department in mind, and at the same time to be loyal to the whole firm.

- To do a good job of planning your own time, and to be flexible with your schedule.

- To freely express your view, and to be diplomatic.

- To be a visionary, and to keep one's feet on the ground.

- To try to win consensus, and to be able to cut through.

- To be dynamic, and to be reflective.

- To be sure of yourself, and to be humble.

In his 2020 report, LEGO Group CEO Niels Christiansen celebrated a year of record profit with a call to stay creative and disciplined: "Our industry, like many others, is being redrawn by digitalization and global socio-economic shifts. We're leveraging our strong financial foundation to invest in initiatives that will allow us to keep ahead of these trends and enable growth in the long term."[31]

Likewise, I (Marianne) have since jumped another curve. My experiences in London were exhilarating and challenging, pushing me far out of my previous rut. Following my personal infinity loop, I've again come full circle, returning to the University of Cincinnati as dean. Through subsequent curves, I've come to see that I can integrate my leadership, my research, and my life by shifting seamlessly between all of them set in the place I love, near those I love. It is an ongoing process of learning and growth. Onward.

 **CHAPTER TAKEAWAYS**

- **Either/or thinking is limiting at best, detrimental at worst.** Stressing only one side of a paradox oversimplifies and narrows our options and can trigger vicious cycles.

- **The ways we tend to think (cognition), feel (emotions), and act (behaviors) are self-reinforcing, intensifying our favored side.** The S curve illustrates how the initial benefits of intensification can turn negative in time as we overplay our strengths.

- **Three patterns lead to vicious cycles when navigating paradoxes:** rabbit holes (intensification), wrecking balls (overcorrection), and trench warfare (polarization). Always beware of mindsets, emotional states, and behaviors that spur these patterns.

  - *Rabbit holes:* Our favored and overused ways of responding to tensions keep us stuck in a rut. Overplaying our strengths hinders our ability to learn, grow, and change, even when we most need to expand our capabilities, understandings, and options (to move to a new S curve).

  - *Wrecking balls:* Intense pressure from a long-neglected side of a paradox can highlight our current ruts and trigger overcorrection. We swing the pendulum too far to the opposing side, a practice that leads us to descend rapidly down a new rabbit hole or to ping-pong erratically between opposing forces.

  - *Trench warfare:* When groups stress opposing sides of a paradox, polarization can lead them to dig in, deepening each rut as they vehemently defend their position. Intractable conflict develops as each side becomes more simplified, reactionary, and insular in its stance.

PART TWO

APPROACHES: THE PARADOX SYSTEM

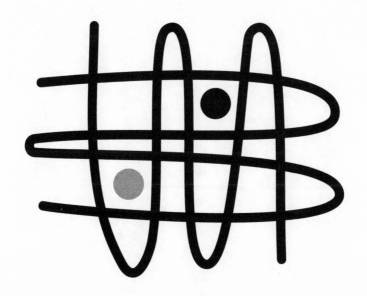

f paradoxes underlie our most vexing problems, then we need to more effectively navigate these contradictory and interdependent demands. We need tools that will rouse us from the allure of either/or thinking and inspire us to dance with the complexity of the absurd. We need tools that move us from being reductionist to exploring holistic options. We need tools that allow us to move beyond the label of both/and to engage deeply with the mysteries of paradoxes. But one tool won't do the job. We need sets of tools that work together toward creating a complete system.

In this part of the book, we introduce those tools. To set the stage, we explore how paradoxes can trigger generative virtuous cycles, identifying two different patterns that we call *mules* (creative integrations) and *tight-rope walkers* (consistent inconsistencies). We then introduce an overall system—the paradox system—with its sets of tools that we label as assumptions, boundaries, comfort, and dynamism (ABCD). We devote the subsequent chapters to each of these tool sets, providing extensive examples of how to operate these tools in real life.

3

Enabling Virtuous Cycles with the Paradox System

Mules and Tightrope Walkers

Well, the way of paradoxes is the way of truth.
To test reality we must see it on the tight rope.
When the verities become acrobats, we can judge them.

—Oscar Wilde

A while ago, I (Wendy) led a workshop on navigating paradoxes for mid-career executives at a large *Fortune* 500 company. Talking about paradox can get heady pretty quickly, so I started the workshop by asking people to identify dilemmas in their own lives. I suggested that they think about a problem they were grappling with at the moment and identify the competing demands associated with that problem. I encouraged them to identify issues at work; after all, the company was paying me to help address challenges in their workplace. However, to be as inclusive and as relevant as possible, I suggested that they also consider issues they grappled with outside work. I then invited volunteers to share their thoughts.

The first person that raised a hand said, "I'm struggling to not bring work home with me."

I saw a lot of heads nodding.

Someone else agreed: "I'm trying to not respond to work emails while I'm with my kids."

Another person added, "And, I also need to let go of all that is going on at home to be more focused at work."

I asked, "How many of you wrote down some challenge around balancing work and life?" Almost half the hands went up in the room. (And the response wasn't only women).

Balancing our professional lives with our personal lives is a constant juggling act. Many of us confront dilemmas between demands at work and demands in the rest of our lives—our spouses or partners, kids, parents, friends, school, hobbies, and so forth. The global pandemic made this issue more acute. During periods of lockdown, boundaries between work and life collapsed, intensifying the challenges of attending to both effectively. Yet we learned new ways to work from home, and many started to like it. These changes surfaced new issues about how workplaces can accommodate more hybrid and flexible work arrangements. As we write this chapter, both employees and company leaders are experimenting with what will become the new normal in terms of how we organize our work and our lives.

Much has been written about work-life challenges, offering wide ranging ideas about how to address the tensions. There is advice on how to achieve balance and advice about how to let go of achieving balance. Some insights stress ways to keep our work and life separate while others propose ways to find synergies between them. Our guess is that you have heard much of this already, even as a steady stream of new recommendations continues to emerge.

This prevailing, and often conflicting, guidance deals with presenting dilemmas—the day-to-day questions about how to address competing demands. It is important advice. Yet as we have been advocating in this book, we gain more powerful insights when we look beyond the dilemmas. The more valuable question is how can we identify and embrace the underlying paradoxes. To confront the stormy waves, we need to navigate the opposing forces that cause, and will always cause, the waves.

Balancing work and life is only one tension that people face. Yet its pervasive nature makes it a good example to help us introduce overarching approaches for both/and thinking. We start by describing how two patterns of navigating paradoxes can foster virtuous cycles. We label these patterns as mules (finding a creative integration) and tightrope walkers (enabling consistent inconsistencies). These approaches offer alternatives to the patterns of vicious cycles discussed in the previous chapter—rabbit holes, wrecking balls, and trench warfare. We then introduce the *paradox system*—an integrated set of tools that help us adopt these approaches.

Mules: Finding a Creative Integration

The first pattern of both/and thinking involves finding a mule—a creative integration. Mules are the offspring of female horses and male donkeys. Horses are strong and hardworking but can be impatient and bored. Donkeys are patient but can be stubborn and not particularly intelligent. When you put these two species together, you create a biological hybrid that is more patient, hardier, and longer-living than a horse and less stubborn and more intelligent than a donkey. Humans have been breeding mules to help carry heavy loads over long distances since as early as 3000 BCE (long before people started to uncover paradoxes!).

Finding a mule involves identifying a synergistic option that integrates the opposing sides of a paradox. In the late 1970s, psychiatrist Albert Rothenberg elucidated the potential and the process of finding mules when he noticed that creative geniuses usually developed their breakthrough ideas by bringing together opposing ideas. Rothenberg analyzed the diaries and letters of such people as Albert Einstein, Pablo Picasso, Wolfgang Amadeus Mozart, and Virginia Woolf. While their professional fields differed dramatically, he noticed remarkable similarities in their creative processes. Their big aha moments often started with noticing the opposing forces in their work. The tensions vexed and challenged them. Yet instead of deciding to focus on one side over the other, they explored how they could bring the oppositions together.

Einstein's theory of relativity emerged as a way to understand how an object could be both in motion and at rest at the same time. Picasso's paintings involved integrating light and dark into the same images. Mozart's music brought together harmony and discord. Woolf's novels depicted the interdependencies between life and death. Rothenberg labeled this creative process *Janusian thinking* after the two-faced Roman god Janus, who looks forward and backward at the same time.[1]

The good news is that you do not have to be a genius to find a mule. In their research, our colleagues Ella Miron-Spektor at INSEAD, Francesca Gino at Harvard Business School, and Linda Argote at Carnegie Mellon's Tepper School of Business found that they could encourage such creative integration when they brought students into a laboratory. All the researchers had to do was change the question they asked people—either encouraging them to consider alternative options as oppositional or to consider them as paradoxical, opposing yet interdependent. The people encouraged to think of the alternatives as paradoxical generated significantly more creative solutions to problems.[2]

In the early 1900s, Mary Parker Follett encouraged people to seek a creative integration when they experienced conflict with another individual or between groups. She identified three responses to conflict. Dominating involves an either/or choice, in which one side wins and the other loses—a win/lose. With a compromising option, both sides get some of what they want but also have to give something up. This option seems like a win/win, yet as Follett points out, it may be limited as both sides also lose something.

As an alternative, Follett explores the idea of a creative integration, in which both sides get what they want without having to give something up—a real win/win. As an example, she describes a disagreement she had while working at a library. She was sitting near a window in the library when another woman entered. The woman wanted to open the window next to Follett. Follett wanted the window shut. A dominating solution would mean that one woman would win; the window would either remain closed or be opened. Compromising might involve having the window opened only some of the time or perhaps opened only partway. Both sides would get some of what they needed but not all. Yet as Follett argues, when both sides can be clear about what they really need, they can explore the problem further to find an integration. When talking through the problem, they realized that the other woman wanted the window open to allow for airflow while Follett wanted the window closed so that the wind would not blow away her papers. They changed the question to ask how they could ensure airflow without the papers blowing away. They decided that they could open a window in an adjacent room of the library—a solution that both allowed for airflow but did not disrupt Follett's papers. Both sides got what they wanted without having to give anything up.[3]

More recently, Roger Martin has argued that this kind of integrative thinking is at the heart of successful leadership. In his book *The Opposable Mind*, he suggests that our capacity for holding opposing ideas in our mind at the same time is a human evolutionary advantage. As he argues,

> Human beings, it's well known, are distinguished from nearly every other creature by a physical feature known as the opposable thumb. Thanks to the tension we can create by opposing the thumb and finger, we can do marvelous things that no other creature can do—write, thread a needle, carve a diamond, paint a picture, guide a catheter up through an artery and unblock it. . . . Similarly, we were born with an opposable mind we can use to hold two conflicting ideas in constructive tension. We can use that tension to think our way through to a new and superior idea.[4]

Martin compares different modes of thinking. Unlike conventional thinking, integrative thinking makes more features of the problem salient to increase the potential connections across competing demands. Drawing on those various features, integrative thinkers then recognize more complex, multidirectional, and nonlinear relationships between competing demands. Further, they use those relationships to inform a more holistic view of the problem, even while narrowing in on specific, individual parts. Finally, integrative thinkers search for more creative options rather than settle for merely adequate trade-offs.

Consider how we might find a creative integration for work-life tensions. Imagine, for example, that we are at work and learn the dates of the next weekend strategy retreat. Senior executives ask us to take a leadership role at this retreat. We are excited about the opportunity. Then we look at our calendar. The dates conflict with a family member's wedding in a different city. We are presented with a dilemma, as we can't be in both places at the same time. Our first reaction may be that we have to make an either/or choice between the retreat and the wedding.

Before making that decision, what if we take a step back. First, we can identify the variety of interwoven paradoxes lurking within this presenting dilemma. Perhaps we really want to attend the work retreat but feel pressure from our family to be at the wedding (or vice versa!). Note the underlying paradox of self and other—doing something for ourselves and doing something for others, as well as the paradox of want and need—doing something we desire and fulfilling an obligation. We might know that the family wedding will fun and valued in the short term, while the work retreat will require effort benefiting our long-term career goals. Herein lies a temporal paradox between today and tomorrow.

What kind of mules could we find to navigate these paradoxes? How could we identify a solution that addresses our needs and other people's needs, a solution that enables both short- and long-term opportunities? Maybe there is a way that we could help organize the work retreat, demonstrating our leadership and commitment to the company, even if we are not there on the actual day. Perhaps the senior leaders wanted us to give a keynote at the retreat. Could we give the talk virtually, stepping away momentarily from wedding festivities? Or maybe we could prerecord the talk to be played at the retreat. Alternatively, we might notice that the most important demand of the wedding was supporting the bride and the groom. Maybe we could commit to spending quality time with the couple in advance of the wedding to help them prepare or afterward to hear their stories about the experience. New possibilities will emerge as we start changing the question that we ask. In each of these cases, we are able to find opportunities to accommodate the underlying paradoxes.

One thing is important to remember about mules. They are infertile. Mules do not produce mules. Rather, we have to breed horses and donkeys to produce new mules. This too is an important feature of navigating paradoxes. Creative integrations can provide effective yet temporary responses to our dilemmas. For example, even if we find a creative integration to address the dilemma between the work retreat and the family wedding, we will still face ongoing tensions between work and life, self and other, short term and long term, and so on. The paradoxes reemerge in new presenting dilemmas that require us to find new solutions. Although we can find solutions to our dilemmas, the underlying paradoxes are not resolvable. They persist over time.[5]

Tightrope Walkers: Living with Consistent Inconsistency

Looking for a win/win creative integration is valuable, but finding one is not always easy. Nor is it necessarily the best way to address every dilemma. Sometimes we need to shift between opposing alternatives in a process that we describe as tightrope walking.

I (Wendy) remember struggling to find a creative integration to my work-life dilemmas when my twins were about six months old. I was already back at work from my maternity leave. It was my first year in my job as an academic, and I was eager to get back to work and continue my research, knowing the short time frame I had before my colleagues made a decision about academic tenure. I had gotten used to the morning routine—wake up, nurse twins, hand the twins over to my husband, take a shower, get myself and the babies dressed for the day, hand the twins over to the nanny, and leave the house. Still, the routine felt frenzied and chaotic.

One morning, I was standing in my local coffee shop waiting for a double-shot coffee that could jolt my weary brain into productivity. I was feeling particularly magnanimous—even heroic—just for having made it out the door. As I was figuratively patting myself on the back, I looked down. Contrasting perfectly against my black sweater was a lovely white gob of spit that one of my twins had left me that morning as a parting gift. I could feel the holes start to emerge in my imaginary superwoman cape. Heroism deflated. Doom quickly filled the crevices in my mind laid bare by sleep deprivation. "This sucks!" I thought. "Why am I doing this? Why do I continue to try to respond to all these work demands while my kids are at home with a nanny? I'm barely alert at work. And what kind of parent am I? I'm probably scarring my kids . . . for life."

Then I thought, "I study paradox. Can't I figure out a better creative integration to this dilemma?" How could I still work but also spend more time with my kids and be less stressed and harried? As is the case with both/and thinking, this question launched me into considering new possibilities.

"Aha!" I thought. "I can make work and life the same thing." I could give up my academic career and open a day care center for my twins and other kids. Work would be life; life would be work. I could forgo the morning mayhem and have a slow, leisurely transition to the day. Likewise, there would be no unfinished items left at my desk while I rushed home for dinner. I even got as far as planning how my day care would look in the empty storefront next to the coffee shop.

Then my double shot arrived; the first sip shocked me back to reality. There are some people who would value this kind of win/win, serving as a professional childcare provider while raising their own children. I am not one of those people. I love my children, but I also love my academic job. I remembered why I had never considered childcare as a full-time profession in the first place. This creative integration was not going to be the solution to my dilemma.

Instead, I would focus on a different pattern to address these dilemmas, a kind of ongoing balancing. We call this the pattern of the *tightrope walker*, a person who engages with competing demands by being consistently inconsistent across dilemmas over time. You might be familiar with the famous picture of the French tightrope walker Philippe Petit as he successfully crossed between the Twin Towers in New York City on a thin wire in 1974. To do so, he had to skillfully balance on the cable. But he never achieved a static balance; rather he was constantly dynamically balancing. Without losing focus on his goal off in the distance, he would subtly and consistently maneuver his body to make microshifts to the left and right. These shifts were ever so slight; if he moved too far in either direction, he would fall.

We can navigate paradoxes by tightrope walking, making microshifts between alternative options to continue to move forward. We are not making big either/or choices that lead us to get stuck in the ruts described in chapter 2. Instead, these are small either/or choices that constantly move us back and forth between alternative poles, creating a pattern in the big picture that accommodates both options over time.

We realize that many people have never tried tightrope walking, and the metaphor may be a bit foreign. But we like this metaphor, in part, because it reminds us that navigating paradoxes is not easy. It can be risky, even a bit dangerous. The image also gives us a sense of the consequences of falling too far to one side or the other. Yet to be fair, not all paradoxes involve the level of danger and challenge of tightrope walking. Some of these tensions are easier to manage than others. If you want a metaphor that is a bit more widely accessible, think about sailing or even biking. Like tightrope walking, both of these activities require constant microshifts between opposing sides to move forward. At times, these shifts are so slight or so natural that we are not even conscious of them. Yet tilting too far to either direction will cause us to fall off the bike, or, in the case of sailing, lead us to capsize. Thankfully, such microshifting activities become easier and more natural with practice and experience. In fact, someone recently reminded us that even in the mundane act of standing we are never truly balanced, we are unconsciously making microshifts to enable ongoing balancing.

Addressing dilemmas that emerge from work-life tensions often involves tightrope walking. We might decide to stay at work late to finish a project and miss family dinner one night but make the opposite decision the next night. Consider again the dilemma of having both a work retreat and a family wedding on the same day. Being consistently inconsistent would mean that we consider this decision in a broader context rather than isolate our thinking to this one instance. Maybe we recently have been working really hard and have missed the last several family events. It might be time to shift the balance a bit and decide to make the family wedding a priority this time. Or vice versa—we might have had a significant amount of family time recently and need to focus on work. Whatever we decide, we can still leave ourselves open to a different decision for the next time we face a dilemma. This kind of oscillating decision making does not lead us into reinforcing vicious cycles. We are not overcorrecting. Rather, cycles become vicious when we make a choice and then get stuck in a rut that keeps us committed to one side or the other—for example, leading us toward work burnout on one end or to the inability to get work done on the other.

In his book *The Paradoxical Self,* psychologist Kirk Schneider explores how we tend to engage in such tightrope walking when navigating paradoxes in our internal psyche. Schneider draws on ideas from philosopher Søren Kierkegaard to describe a tug-of-war between being expansive (open, externally focused, adventurous, willing to try new things, risk-accepting) and being constrictive (disciplined, internally focused, bounded, reserved). People experience psychological distress when they go too far to either extreme. Psychologically healthy people are constantly balancing between expansion and constriction. Schneider explains:

> It appears that such people are healthier, or what existentialists call more "integrated," creative or hardy than ordinary people. This does not mean that life is geometrically balanced for them or what they practice is "moderation in all things" as the Greeks admonished. Far from it. It means however, that optimal people—especially within the limited sphere of their interests—dare to challenge and confront their constrictive and expansive capacities. They find the right (that is, most useful) blend of constriction and expansion to meet the relevant demands.[6]

Breeding Mules That Walk Tightropes

Breeding mules and walking tightropes offer two patterns of both/and thinking that can enable virtuous cycles. Yet these patterns are not isolated from one another. Over time, they are often intertwined. We may be walking a tightrope when a mule occasionally emerges. Or we might find a good mule that suddenly requires us to focus on one side or the other.

We first noticed how these patterns intertwine in our own research. I (Wendy) was studying how IBM's strategic business unit leaders grappled with innovation challenges. The need to maintain existing products in the marketplace while exploring new opportunities raised all kinds of dilemmas. How should they allocate resources? How should they structure their leadership team? How should they manage their time in senior team meetings? These leaders were trying to navigate the ongoing paradoxes between today and tomorrow, innovations and existing products.

When I started the research project, I assumed that the best leaders were those that could find a creative integration between innovation and existing products. But I observed something very different. The successful leadership teams would indeed find a creative integration every once in a while, identifying a solution to accommodate the needs of both their core product and their innovations. For example, they could find ways to leverage existing customers and relationships to sell the new innovation. Yet these creative integrations were rare. In fact, the most successful leaders realized that trying to respond to each dilemma with such an integration was futile. Rather, those leaders more often engaged in tightrope walking, more subtly, frequently and purposefully shifting their focus and support.[7]

Consider how these patterns might intertwine to enable virtuous cycles that embrace our work-life tensions. We might mostly shift our attention between work and life but then have moments of integration. For example, our work might spill over into a productive conversation at the dinner table and enable learning and connection within the family. Or working through our parenting challenges might inform our broader interpersonal skills, helping us become a better leader. Similarly, we might be focused on a creative integration, only to note that we sometimes need to make more consistently inconsistent decisions.

The pandemic lockdown highlighted the challenges and opportunities of work-life paradoxes for me (Wendy). The lockdown often forced me to integrate work and family demands. I mostly figured out how I could sit with my then nine-year-old son at our dining room table doing my work while he was in virtual school—an integration of both his needs and mine. Yet I knew that I also needed some focused work time. Luckily, my husband is also an academic with a similar level of work flexibility. We quickly devised a schedule in which, for each day, we identified which parent was on duty and available to be interrupted—spending the day tightrope walking—and which parent had uninterrupted work time.

The Paradox System: Integrated Tools for Both/And Thinking

What enables people to find the mules and to walk the tightropes that will lead to virtuous cycles of navigating paradoxes? Doing so depends on our ability to engage both/and thinking. The notion of both/and has become a bit of a buzzword. But we've found that successful people know how to go beyond the buzz and truly engage with this approach. Drawing on our research and that of others, we identified four sets of tools that work together to support both/and thinking. To make these ideas sticky, we used an easy mnemonic to name the tools—ABCD: (A) assumptions, (B) boundaries, (C) comfort, and (D) dynamics (figure 3-1). Importantly, successful people do not choose between these sets; they engage all of them so that the tools reinforce each other. We bring them together in what we call the paradox system.

Both/and thinking begins with *assumptions*, mindsets and underlying beliefs that enable us to cognitively hold two opposing forces at the same

FIGURE 3-1

The paradox system: four sets of tools

Creating boundaries to contain tensions
- Linking to a higher purpose
- Separating and connecting
- Building guardrails to avoid going too far

Shifting to both/and assumptions
- Accepting knowledge as containing multiple truths
- Framing resources as abundant
- Problem solving as coping

Finding comfort in the discomfort
- Building in a pause
- Accepting the discomfort
- Broadening our perspective

Enabling dynamics that unleash tensions
- Experimenting using measured steps
- Preparing for serendipity
- Learning to unlearn

time. The first step in shifting our approach is changing how we frame the problem. Rather than asking, "Should I choose A or B?" both/and thinkers ask, "How can I accommodate A and B?" This revised questioning is what the geniuses in Rothenberg's study did. Rather than asking if an object was in motion *or* at rest, Einstein wondered if an object could be both in motion *and* at rest at the same time. Changing the question shifts our view. Mindsets matter. They affect how we think about and respond to challenges. Rather than assume that the world is consistent, linear, and static, both/and thinking assumes that the world is contradictory, circular, and dynamic.

Boundaries involve the structures that we build around us to support our mindsets, emotions, and behaviors as we confront paradoxes. Competing demands can lead us into a rut if we pick a side and then stubbornly defend it until we get stuck in a vicious cycle. Boundaries help keep us from falling into that rut in the first place. We describe the value

of a higher purpose—an overarching vision that motivates and unites—
to help remind us why and how we engage with paradoxes in the first
place. We identify the benefit of creating structures that both separate
competing demands—pulling them apart and valuing each one—and
connect them, finding synergies and integration. We also examine the
role of guardrails that keep us from going too far into a rut with each side
of the paradoxes.

Comfort focuses on our emotions. These practices allow us to both
honor our initial emotional discomfort with paradoxes and find ways to
be comfortable with the discomfort. Paradoxes trigger deep emotions.
On the one hand, tensions spark anxiety and defensiveness, which can
trap us in either/or thinking. On the other hand, the unleashing of
new and creative options to address tough problems can be exciting
and energizing.

Finally, *dynamism* involves actions that enable continuous learning and change, encouraging shifts between competing demands. Paradoxes involve dualism and dynamism—as two opposing forces constantly
crash against and shift one another. Dynamic actions allow us to capture the constant that is change, keeping us from getting stuck in an
either/or rut.

The next four chapters dive deeper into each category, describing specific tools to navigate paradoxes more effectively in our personal lives
and in our organizations. These sets of tools are not independent; they
reinforce one another. The more that we change our assumptions and
mindsets, the more that we can build supporting boundaries, scaffolding,
and guardrails. The more that we create such boundaries, the more that
they reinforce our assumptions and emotions. Note, however, that the
paradox system is itself paradoxical. The system involves tools that have
an impact on both people and contexts. The tools require people to attend
to hearts and minds and to nurture contexts that enable both change and
stability. People and contexts, hearts and minds, change and stability—
the paradox system helps us embrace these tensions. As our colleagues
Kim Cameron and Bob Quinn note, navigating paradoxes is paradoxical.[8]
We agree.

 **CHAPTER TAKEAWAYS**

- **Intertwined patterns help us navigate paradoxes toward more virtuous cycles:**

  - Breeding a mule (creative integration) involves finding a synergy that accommodates opposing sides simultaneously;

  - Tightrope walking (consistent inconsistency) involves making choices that enable ongoing microshifts between opposing sides.

- **The paradox system includes four sets of tools that work together to support both/and thinking:** assumptions, boundaries, comfort, and dynamism (ABCD).

- **The tools in the paradox system are paradoxical, comprising opposing yet interwoven elements.** Navigating paradoxes is paradoxical.

4

Shifting to Both/And Assumptions

Toward a Paradox Mindset

If you cannot make a change, change the way you have been thinking. You might find a new solution.

—Maya Angelou

In 2000, Jeremy Hockenstein boarded a plane from Boston to Hong Kong. He felt confused and frustrated about his work and his career. He was hoping that if he got far enough away from his work, he would be able to have some clarity about what to do when he returned.

Six months earlier, Hockenstein had graduated with an MBA from MIT and an impressive résumé, including a Harvard undergraduate degree and work experience at both McKinsey and Mercer Management Consulting. His credentials could have opened doors to lucrative jobs in banking, consulting, and industry—jobs coveted by so many of his classmates. But Hockenstein had other ideas.

Since early childhood, Hockenstein had focused on making a positive impact on the world. His mother was a Holocaust survivor, born in a displaced-persons camp at the end of World War II. That legacy left him both grateful for his life and obliged to give back. In elementary school, he organized the neighborhood kids to run a fundraising carnival each Labor Day for the Jerry Lewis telethon. In high school, he won a public speaking contest for his speech "How One Person Can Make a Difference." In college, he organized students to collect the discarded disposable cups across all the dining halls. By demonstrating the mountain of waste created daily, they pressured school administrators to buy reusable cups.

After college, he worked at McKinsey, joining their newly formed environmental policy team. But when it came to considering a job after his MBA, he dreamed of making a more direct impact. In the 1990s, the social responsibility movement was starting to take hold in large *Fortune* 500 companies. Yet these initiatives still remained peripheral to the core business; most companies viewed corporate social responsibility as a philanthropic unit to manage corporate donations or to organize employee volunteer days. Wanting to do more, Hockenstein looked toward nonprofits. He accepted an opportunity with a Harvard student organization. Hoping to draw on his MBA training and consulting skills, he would manage strategic innovation that could help students find community and forge connections.

After only six months in this position, Hockenstein was frustrated. Eager to make a difference, he had suggested a number of new initiatives. Unfortunately, he found the pace of work very different from his previous consulting culture. It seemed as if he were just running in place, rather than really having an impact. He felt trapped. It felt like he could either work at a fast-paced, innovative consulting firm or a mission-driven, but much slower-moving, nonprofit. It seemed like a no-win situation.

Mission or money? Profits or passion? Do good or do well? Underlying Hockenstein's tensions are what we describe as *performing paradoxes*—competing demands in our goals, outcomes, and expectations. Like his "nonprofit or for-profit" dilemma, our career decisions can reveal tensions between making a difference and making a salary. We might feel the same conflict when we spend money; a simple decision of how and where to buy toilet paper can raise questions of whether we buy what is convenient and cheap or what aligns better with our values. Mission and market tensions emerge in companies as well, particularly as we face mounting complex, systemic challenges across the globe. Leaders increasingly grapple with questions about how business can address these problems while also managing their bottom line—whether they are introducing corporate social responsibility into a for-profit organization or creating social enterprises. Performing paradoxes show up in other ways too. We can often spot them lurking beneath intergroup conflict, as opposing groups strive for their own contradictory, yet interdependent goals.

For Hockenstein, the performing paradoxes felt paralyzing. He traveled to Asia in search of an answer. While there, however, he found a different question that led him down a new path.

Shifting to Both/And Assumptions

Mindsets matter. As psychologist Paul Watzlawick once argued, the problem is not the problem; the problem is how we think about the problem.[1] Research repeatedly demonstrates that how we think influences how we act.[2] Our first set of tools to navigate paradox involves shifting our assumptions, as described earlier, adopting mindsets and underlying beliefs that enable us to cognitively hold two opposing forces at the same time.

Shifting our assumptions is not easy. Engaging with paradox often brings us to the limits of our rational thought. We can feel queasy peering over the edge toward the absurd or the illogical. Such uncertainty and irrationality drive our anxiety. We pull back toward more clarity. But learning to value and accept tensions helps us avoid oversimplifying our presenting dilemmas and instead to explore more creative alternatives. That is, we need to move from more dichotomous mindsets that foster either/or thinking to paradox mindsets that empower both/and thinking. First, we have to clarify the nature of paradoxes (see the sidebar "Paradox: Is It All in Our Minds?").

In our own research with colleagues Ella Miron-Spektor, Josh Keller, and Amy Ingram, we studied different approaches to competing demands and how these approaches affect creativity, performance, and job satisfaction. We surveyed more than three thousand people from the United States, China, and Israel. We found that people differ on two interwoven factors: the extent to which individuals experience tensions and the extent to which they adopt a paradox mindset.

First, people differ in how much they experience tensions. Such differences can stem from varying situations, as some environments are filled with more tensions than others. As our Israeli team member likes to point out—living with ongoing regional conflict in the Middle East creates tensions very different from those felt by, say, someone living on a sheep farm in rural New Zealand. Similarly, an emergency room physician might be surrounded by more tensions than a yoga instructor. The context can have a great impact on our experience of tensions.

As we noted previously, our own research suggests that people experience increased tensions in settings with (1) faster change, (2) greater plurality, or (3) more scarcity. The faster the pace of change, the more we experience tensions between what is and what will be. In terms of plurality, the more voices and perspectives from different people and stakeholders, the more we experience tensions between varied goals, roles, and values. And finally, the more that people experience a scarcity of resources, the more competition there will be over how the resources should be shared.[3]

Even as the nature of tensions in our environment varies, it is also the case that some people are more attuned to tensions than others. Tensions swirl all around us. Some people seek them out, purposefully surfacing tensions to enable more creativity. Others may avoid or ignore them to minimize potential conflicts. Yet even two people in the same situation can experience varying degrees of tension. In our own research, we found that people who all had the same job and worked in the same organization reported different levels of tensions.

Second, people vary in how they understand the relationship between opposing forces. People with a more dichotomous mindset narrow their thinking to frame alternatives as a binary choice and then choose between them. A paradox mindset instead involves appreciating contradictions

FIGURE 4-1

Paradox mindset inventory: zones of navigating paradoxes

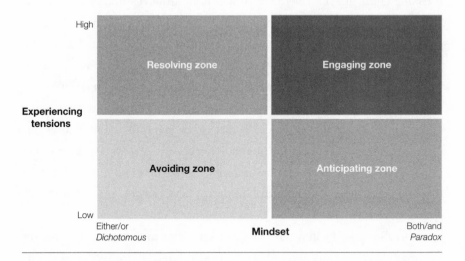

between opposing forces and recognizing how they are mutually reinforcing. Those with a high paradox mindset tend to accept tensions as natural, valuable, and energizing. Rather than asking if they should choose option A or option B when confronting dilemmas, they ask, "How can I accommodate A and B at the same time?" Just changing the question introduces new options and invites both/and thinking.

In combination, the extent to which we experience tensions and the mindsets we adopt determine the different zones of navigating paradoxes (figure 4-1; for further discussion see appendix). In the *avoiding zone*, we experience limited tensions and adopt a dichotomous mindset of either/or thinking. We may blissfully be in a stress-free environment. Or we may live or work in a stressful environment but blissfully ignore the tensions swirling around us. Of course, blissful ignorance is sometimes valuable. We don't have the time and energy to address every tension that arises. For example, we might be actively ignoring a recurring question about our professional achievement and social impact at work because other life factors need us to postpone a major career change. Sometimes, we need to pick our battles.

While we can avoid tensions sometimes, we can't always ignore them. At some point, those subtle work tensions may burst forward, posing a pressing challenge. Or one day, we will find ourselves in a new situation with more overt and trying pressures. For example, work might be relatively stress-free until we get a new boss and stuff really starts hitting the fan. What happens when those tensions rear their heads? Do we have the tools to navigate them? When we adopt a dichotomous mindset, the uncertainty of the decision may leave us feeling uncomfortable, and we want to quickly make an either/or choice. We are in the *resolving zone*. The either/or decisions that we make in the resolving zone might lead us to a sense of relief in the short term, but watch out. As we detailed in chapter 2, in the long term, those decisions are limited at best and detrimental at worst, sparking vicious cycles.

On the flip side, we may tend to adopt a paradox mindset, ready to simultaneously engage interdependent contradictions. "Paradox?" you might think. "Bring it on!" In the *anticipating zone*, we draw on a paradox mindset but experience few tensions. We are all dressed up with nowhere to go. Again, we might be in a low-stress situation. Yet once the context changes, we will be poised for both/and thinking. However, we can also start uncovering the tensions that exist around us. Rather than sweep them under the cognitive rug, we can bring them out in the open to deal with them. Many of the leaders profiled in this book do just that. Outfitted with the tools of both/and thinking, they seek out underlying paradoxes to address them head-on and to generate solutions that are more creative and sustainable. Doing so moves us into the *engaging zone*—where we both experience tensions and adopt a paradox mindset.

In our research, we explored how these zones impact people at work. We found that the people in the engaging zone performed better at work. They were seen as more innovative and productive by their managers. Not only that, but they were also more satisfied with their jobs.[4] As it turns out, if we are going to adopt a dichotomous mindset, we perform better in situations that involve a lower degree of tensions. That is, if we are immersed in either/or thinking, it's better to have fewer tensions or avoid the ones that come our way, given that our approaches to addressing them are limited. Once we experience more tensions, a paradox mindset offers us the tools to more effectively respond.

From our research, we developed the paradox mindset inventory to assess the extent to which people experience tensions and adopt a paradox mindset. We included the inventory in the appendix and added a link to an online version—you too can test your mindset, share it with your friends, or use it in your organization.[5]

In our discussion of zones, we assume that people can be in different zones at different times. You can shift the extent to which you experience tensions just by changing your environments or by becoming more aware of tensions. You can also shift the extent to which you adopt a paradox mindset. Within the paradox system, we identify three tools to help us shift our underlying assumptions toward a paradox mindset. These tools involve reexamining our underlying views of knowledge, resources, and problem solving (figure 4-2).

FIGURE 4-2

The paradox system: assumptions

Creating **boundaries** to
contain tensions

- Linking to a higher purpose
- Separating and connecting
- Building guardrails to avoid going too far

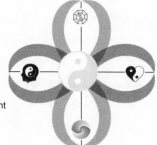

**Shifting to both/and
assumptions**

- Accepting knowledge as
  containing multiple truths
- Framing resources as abundant
- Problem solving as coping

Finding **comfort** in
the discomfort

- Building in a pause
- Accepting the discomfort
- Broadening our perspective

Enabling **dynamics** that
unleash tensions

- Experimenting using measured steps
- Preparing for serendipity
- Learning to unlearn

Paradox: Is It All in Our Minds?

Are paradoxes simply fabricated in our minds? Some people argue that our own mental templates about how we understand and interact with the world create a sense of interwoven opposites. We create the cognitive frames that reveal paradoxes. Underlying this view is the philosophy of social constructivism—the belief that reality is created through our shared collective interpretations.[a] As Fredrick Nietzsche summarized, "Facts do not exist, only interpretations."

Others argue that intertwined opposing forces are part of the inherent fabric of our world. Early philosophers like Lao Tzu in the East and Heraclitus in the West believe this to be the case. They describe the world as built on dynamic dualities—opposing forces swirling in a constant dance with one another. Scientists like Michael Faraday and Niels Bohr depict our physical world as embedded with paradox, while psychoanalysts like Carl Jung and Alfred Adler describe our human psyche as imbued with interdependent contradictions.[b] More recently, Barry Johnson described paradoxes as "gifts of nature, a natural phenomenon like gravity or sunshine."[c]

Socially constructed or inherent, interpreted or real? This debate has raged for centuries and continues today. The question seems to be the paradox version of the tree in the woods: If the tree falls in an empty woods, does it make a sound? Is sound a function of the tree or of the listener? Is paradox a function of our world or constructed by the observers of the world?

By this point in the book, you may have already recognized that the question is framed as an either/or: socially constructed or inherent? What if we changed it to a both/and question? How are the properties of paradox both socially constructed and inherent? How does our social construction influence the inherent nature of paradox? How is the inherent nature of paradox refracted through our social construction?

In our own writing, we have argued that paradoxes are latent features of a system that become salient through our social construction. That is, paradoxes lurk within our presenting dilemmas, but it is our own understanding that helps bring the underlying paradoxes to light.[d] Our colleagues and friends Tobias Hahn, professor at Esade Business School in Spain, and Eric Knight, dean of Macquarie Business School in Australia, took this argument a step further. They propose that paradoxes operate in ways similar to our understanding of matter in the universe. As quantum theory suggests, we don't know if matter is a particle or a wave. We can try to measure matter to answer this question, but the actual measurement interferes with the system so that the way matter shows up is partly a feature of the matter and partly a feature of the measurement. Hahn and Knight argue that the same may be true about our experiences of paradox. Complex interdependencies between opposing features may underlie the structure of a system, but how these interdependencies show up as paradoxes depends on our experience and social construction of reality. Social construction, they argue, does not just reveal latent paradoxes but also helps construct the complex underlying reality into paradoxes.[e]

Whether you believe that paradoxes are inherent, socially constructed, or an integration of both, they will swirl around us. And we still benefit by understanding the underlying sets of tools to effectively navigate these absurd irrationalities.

-----

a. Several colleagues have offered insights about the socially constructed nature of paradox. In an early depiction of paradoxes in organizational life, Marshall Scott Poole and Andrew Van de Ven differentiated between logical paradoxes and social paradoxes. Logical paradoxes reflect inherently contradictory statements, like the liar's paradox: "I am lying." The researchers suggest that social paradoxes, such as the tension felt by organizational leaders between managing for today and innovating for tomorrow, are constructed both by our own mental framing and also informed by how our social structures juxtapose opposites. If these paradoxes are created by how we understand time and space, they can be resolved by using time and space to pull poles apart (see Poole and Van de Ven, 1989). Linda Putnam and Gail Fairhurst further emphasize how our language and discourse foist opposites into relationships, creating double binds (see Putnam, Fairhurst, and Banghart, 2016; Fairhurst and Putnam, 2019; see also Bateson, 1979). More recently, Marco Berti and Ace Simpson expanded on these ideas by examining how our institutionalized systems create power dynamics that foist paradoxes upon us (see Berti and Simpson, 2021).

b. Scientists such as Faraday and James Clerk Maxwell in the 1800s, followed by Bohr and Albert Einstein in the 1900s, introduced insights that have informed what we now know as quantum theory. Interdependent opposites underlie much of this theory, with insight about how a particle can be both a wave and a point and can both exist and not exist. In the 1970s, scientist Fritjof Capra expounded on the connections between modern physics and Eastern mysticism in his book *The Tao of Physics* (Capra, 1975). In doing so, he identifies the highly paradoxical nature of modern physics.

c. Johnson (2020), 111.

d. Smith and Lewis (2011).

e. Smith and Lewis (2011); Hahn and Knight (2021).

Accepting Knowledge as Containing Multiple Truths (Not One Truth)

Many of us believe that truth is ubiquitous—that if something is true, its opposite must be false.[6] But as Nobel Prize–winning physicist Niels Bohr purportedly reflected, "There are trivial truths and there are great truths. The opposite of a trivial truth is plainly false. The opposite of a great truth is also true." Great truths involve complex webs of understanding, refracted through opposing lenses. We may only perceive contradictory fragments rather than grasp the totality of these intricate truths. Yet if we are so committed to a single truth that we reject its contradictions, we may miss deeper, more holistic insights. We may also trigger intractable conflicts with others committed to their single truth.

Early philosophers depicted this idea in the parable of the blind people and the elephant: A group of blind people approached an elephant and wanted to identify this unknown being before them. To do so, they all placed their hands on it to see what it felt like. The first person, whose hand landed on the trunk, suggested that the being seemed like a thick snake. The second person's hand reached the ear, and this person noted that it seemed like a kind of fan. Another person, whose hand ended up on a leg, thought that this being was like a tree trunk. Another person touched the elephant's tail, describing it as a rope. The last person felt its tusk, stating that the creature was like a spear. Each was sure that they were right about what they felt and equally sure that the others were wrong. None was willing to concede to the others or explore their points of view. The result was an enduring conflict.[7]

In the 1800s, John Godfrey Saxe summarized the lesson in his poem "The Blind Men and the Elephant":

> And so these men of Indostan
> Disputed loud and long
> Each in his own opinion
> Exceeding stiff and strong,
> Though each was partly in the right
> And all were in the wrong![8]

By assuming that everyone else had the same experience as they had, each blind person believed that their own experience reflected the total situation. But what if they had assumed the opposite—that their observation was only one of many, that they experienced part of the truth and so too did the others, and that, together, their disparate and opposing experiences held a deeper truth? Perhaps then they could have listened more openly to the reality of others. They could have questioned their own knowledge, explored alternatives, been open-minded listeners, and learned and generated new insights. Such open-minded assumptions underlie both/and thinking. To understand that knowledge is contradictory, we must assume that multiple truths can coexist.

From elephants to gorillas

One reason that we all see different parts of the elephant is that our brains can only take in so much information in a particular situation. Dan Simons, professor of psychology at the University of Illinois, and Christopher Chabris, professor and director of the Behavioral and Decision Sciences Program at Geisinger Health System, powerfully demonstrate how we can limit our focus, minimizing other information in a situation. They describe the phenomena as *inattention blindness.*

Simons and Chabris conducted a now-famous study at Harvard, described as a selective-attention test. The research involves a video of six students: three in white shirts and three in black shirts. The three students in white shirts are passing a basketball between them. The three students in black shirts are also passing a basketball between them. Simons and Chabris tell the viewer to count the number of times the people in the white shirts pass the basketball between them.

If you haven't seen the video yet and want to, now is a good time to put down the book and go watch it. If you have already seen it (spoiler alert: we are about to share the aha of the video), you will know that in the selective-attention test, the people in white shirts passed the ball fifteen times between them. However, the most important part of the video is not whether you counted the right number of passes but whether you noticed something strange that happened. In the middle of the teams passing the basketball, a person in a black gorilla suit steps into view. The gorilla walks right through the game, stands there, bangs on its chest, and walks off.

Here's the fascinating part. More than 50 percent of the people tested were so focused on counting the number of passes between the people in the white shirts that they totally missed the person in the gorilla costume. Focusing on one area means that we often miss others. If you already watched that video before or if you think that you, of course, would have seen the gorilla, you can consider watching another one of their videos, "The Monkey Business Illusion." It has a similar aha, but we won't spoil that here.[9]

These experiments suggest that we take in limited information and fail to see the full picture. We scan the environment, identifying information that is relevant while leaving other information behind. Psychologists call this tendency the *confirmation bias*.[10] Politics is a great example. It's not so much that people with different politics disagree on a fact; it's that they are starting with very different facts. In our politically polarized world, we focus on information that confirms what we already believe. We consume different news, talk with different groups of people, and focus on different issues.[11] As a result, we miss key insights that others are keenly focused on. Intensely focused on our own point of view, we get stuck in a rabbit hole. As soon as someone challenges us, the situation becomes trench warfare—we defensively hunker down.[12]

A paradox mindset, in contrast, starts with the assumption that multiple points of view coexist and that we often don't see or appreciate the other views. Starting with this assumption then invites us to be open to learning from others' perspectives.

Adventures in screen time

Just recently, I (Wendy) could feel an elephant-sized fight about to erupt in my own house. It reminded me that, no matter how often we talk about embracing competing demands, we can easily slip into assumptions of knowledge as singular truths that lead us into narrow arguments between right and wrong. I was falling into a familiar debate with my husband, and we were each focused on our own slices of information and our own experiences of truth. The topic: screen time. This was not the first time we had had this discussion. Nor would it be the last.

On this day, I was super busy. I stopped my work for a moment, went upstairs to check on my kids, and found my youngest son vegged out in front of his computer. He wasn't watching the full reruns of *The Office* for the second time like his older sister. He wasn't playing video games like his older brother. Those activities in excess already annoyed me to no end. But my youngest son's activities sent me over the edge. He was spending hours watching videos of other people playing video games. This is a thing—not actually playing the games yourself but watching as other people play the games. You may enjoy this hobby yourself, and if so, I honor your passion. For my son, however, I was beside myself.

My deepest fears started to bubble up. "I am the worst parent," I told myself. "Who lets their kids watch hours of videos of other people playing video games?" (Apparently, the answer is that a lot of people do, given the number of hits on these videos.) Then, because I didn't really want to call myself a terrible parent, I did what any unreasonable partner would do. I blamed my husband. If it wasn't my fault, then I'd figure out some reason that it must be his.

"We need him off screens," I told my husband.

"And which one of us is going to monitor that?" he responded.

My husband and I can both be rather competitive people, so when we each take a stand, we can really hold our positions. Dukes up!

Yet we had already had this discussion so many times, we didn't need to go through the details. Each of us knew where the other stood. We knew the other's arguments. And in moments like this, when our emotions were running hot, both of us believed that we were right and the other was wrong. I would argue that responsible parenting meant more discipline about screen time. The lack of discipline was just wrong. Not only did I want my husband to agree with me, but I was also, at that moment, asking him to provide the discipline to get my son off the computer.

He also believed in screen-time discipline but knew how hard it was to implement it. Both of us were swamped. We were having this conversation during a global pandemic, with three kids doing school from home while we parents were trying to manage our careers. My husband agreed that our kids should have more discipline around screen time, but knowing that he wasn't going to provide it, he wasn't asking it of me, either. A bit of a kinder stance than mine, I'd say!

We both stated our positions. But we knew this fight inside and out, so we just left it there. No need to rehash the same arguments.

Who was right? Both of us. I was right that our kids needed more discipline about screen time, and he was right that both of us had limited time and resources to apply that discipline, particularly at that moment. If we had started from that assumption, we could more easily and openly listen to one another, exploring alternative options and drawing on our best both/and thinking for a more creative and sustainable solution.

Later, when our emotions cooled and we weren't so crunched for time, we reminded ourselves that we were on the same team, trying to do what was best for our family, and we started to brainstorm. In our ideal world, our kids would manage their own discipline. They would have enough other activities that would draw them away from the allure of the screens. We could also set up a system for them to be more responsible for themselves. In the meantime, we knew that we needed to clamp down with a bit more external discipline from us.

What we found, though, was that getting there required some time and investment. This solution required us to help our kids engage in other activities and to support them as they did so. Finding new solutions to this challenge also depended on the age and maturity of our kids. While our teenagers were more responsible to manage their own screen time, our younger child needed much more hands-on discipline. My husband and I knew that we would consistently confront the debate over screen time. The important thing, however, was that we confront it together, honoring our different perspectives in doing so.

Yes, and

Sometimes we need to act our way into our beliefs, literally. To change our underlying assumptions, we need to start behaving in ways that reflect what we want to believe. Aristotle knew this when he exclaimed, "We are what we repeatedly do." The acting profession and, more specifically, improv actors have a suggestion about how we can act our way into both/and assumptions. They start by saying, "Yes, and." This core practice in improv can help us be open to, and build on, opposing points of view.

Improvisational theater is unplanned and unscripted. Everything looks free-flowing and spontaneous, but there are guidelines that performers follow to provide structure and prevent chaos. Early pioneers of improv created what they called the *kitchen rules*, rules that emerged as they sat around their kitchen table exploring what did and did not work from their scenes. The most famous kitchen rule is to never deny reality. Improvisers practice this skill of going along with teammates' established realities by using "Yes, and," which means that an improviser has to accept the ideas others assert in a scene (*yes*) and then figure out ways to run with and build on these ideas (*and*).[13]

In improv, the actors usually ask for suggestions from the audience to set the scene. Imagine that an audience member suggests that the scene should be an interaction between a mother and son at the playground. You are picked to play the mom.

You start thinking through a scene in your mind, imagining yourself as a young mom pushing your gleeful toddler on the swings. Your scene partner who was picked to play the child then jumps in and says, "Mom, I'm so glad you met me here, because I have something important to tell you. I've impregnated my girlfriend." Well, that doesn't quite fit the image of the swings. The youthful, joyful scene in your mind just turned mature and potentially tragic if we assume that the pregnancy was not planned and not initially desired.

One option could be for you to reject this assumption and assert your own. "Honey," you could say, "you can't actually get a girl pregnant at age three . . . And how do you know the word *impregnated* at your age, anyway?" You've just said to your partner, "No, but." Your partner asserted something, and you took control and reasserted something else.

What does your scene partner do then? The likely place to go next would be for you and your partner to debate whose assumptions to use. That won't really progress the scene. And it probably won't be that funny.

Yet this is what usually happens in reality. Someone asserts something. If it's different from what we imagined or assumed, we might immediately reject it, challenge it, or reassert our own reality. Where do we then go from there? "No, but" responses only set us up for a conflict over who is right and who is wrong—either/or thinking. Consider conversations that you have had recently. How often do these conversations involve a conflict over basic assumptions?

Instead, what if you said yes to the scene dynamics and then figured out ways to build on it. In the playground scene, you could say something like, "Oh, honey, I can't believe the day is finally here! I've been waiting for this moment since you moved in with your girlfriend twenty-five years ago. I might finally become a grandma before I die." In this scenario, you have agreed that your son is of an age to have a child (*yes*) and then you have built on this response to say that this son has been old enough to have a child for many years (*and*). You have figured out a way to honor your part- ner's assumptions and then used agility and surprise to transform tragedy into comedy.

Note that "Yes, and" is not the same as being so permissive that any- thing goes. As improv researcher Clay Drinko clarifies, "Agreement is actually going along with the reality being established in the scene, not necessarily literally saying yes to everything." The "Yes, and" approach works when people are building on each other's realities and not when one person is dominating the scene and the other is a pushover.[14]

The power of the "Yes, and" rule reaches far beyond the world of enter- tainment. Therapists see the value of teaching this approach to help patients address issues that leave them feeling stuck and to help couples find more opportunities to deepen their relationship. Coaches and trainers adopt "Yes, and" approaches to help organizational leaders become more creative and more connected. Research shows how this kind of improv training leads to greater innovation, increased psychological well-being, and more toler- ance of uncertainty.[15]

More to our point, "Yes, and" offers some specific practices for how we can navigate paradox. "Yes, and" reminds us that there are multiple truths and that we therefore do not have to simply reject someone when they challenge our assumptions. Imagine that we have an assumption about something, and someone tells us the opposite. Rather than reject that idea, we could start with yes; we could honor that person's reality. Importantly, honoring someone else's reality does not mean that we have to agree with it. It means that we recognize and respect their reality. We can then learn from and expand on this reality.

We encourage you to try this out the next time you are in a conversation. See what happens when someone says something that might challenge your ideas. In that moment, pause and check in with what you are thinking and feeling. You might be feeling a bit threatened, even angry. You might be thinking of the defensive arguments that you would make to challenge their perspective. Instead, try responding with "Yes, and." What if you started by truly honoring their position? Then, rather than reject it, see how you could build on it in light of your own insights. Then check back with yourself. How has this "Yes, and" informed your own mindset? Has it allowed you to see multiple perspectives? How has it changed the nature of the conversation?

"Yes, and" approaches are not only useful when people express different perspectives. They can also be helpful when you encounter resistance to your own ideas. As we noted in chapter 1, paradoxes show up at all levels—within ourselves, in relationships with others, in groups, and so forth. Consider our internal paradoxes. What if we adopted a "Yes, and" approach to these? For example, we may think of ourselves as a generally responsible and dependable person, and yet we mismanaged a deadline and let someone down. Our first reaction might be to berate ourselves. But what if we instead started with acceptance? Yes, we are responsible. Yes, what we did was not responsible. Yes, that happens. *And*, we will keep learning from the experience to minimize its happening in the future.

Framing Resources as Abundant (Not Scarce)

A paradox mindset also involves assumptions about resources, shifting from a focus on scarcity to a focus on abundance. Resources—time, space, money—drive most of our dilemmas. Alternative demands compete for resources. Challenges between work and life often boil down to questions about how to spend our time. Issues about which candidates to hire in an organization emerge because we have limited finances and have to make choices. In one of my (Marianne's) research projects, I studied product design firms. These firms struggled with tensions between enhancing their existing products and investing in radical innovation. At the heart of this tension was a question of resources. How much of the firms' resources—their people, their time, their office space—could they commit to radical innovations when they needed their bread-and-butter products to help pay their bills? One of the most important leadership challenges is resource allocation.

Many people approach these kinds of problems by looking for more effective ways to allocate resources—how to better slice the pie. This approach reflects a dichotomous mindset. It starts with the assumption that resources are scarce—that there are finite resources and, once we use them, they're gone. For example, we may have a limited number of dollars for a project. If we spend those dollars on one expense, we cannot then spend them on something else. It is this zero-sum thinking that leads us to feel as if we have to choose between alternatives; it therefore triggers significant conflict about accessing these limited resources.

A paradox mindset challenges this assumption about resources. What if resources are not zero-sum? What if we don't have to be constrained by resources? What if we can expand their value? Rather than assuming that values are scarce, a paradox mindset involves assumptions about resources as abundant—we can expand their value through their use. There are a variety of ways to expand the value of resources. We could recognize the multiple dimensions of a resource and realize that the value is not universally shared: what is valuable to one person is not necessarily valuable to others. We can use technology and innovation to generate new value. We can explore varied and multiple approaches to expanding value, knowing that such explorations create new opportunities for navigating paradoxes.

Splitting pizza

Good negotiators recognize that resources often have more value than we first assume. A successful win/win negotiation depends on the parties' ability to recognize the multiple dimensions of a resource, then grow its value.

Usually people view resources as a single dimension—and try to decide who gets more or less of that dimension. If we have a pot of money, we need to decide who gets more of that pot. If we have a chunk of time, we must decide what activities get more minutes. This kind of negotiation involves claiming value. The assumption is that these resources are scarce—and that we have to decide how to split them. Max Bazerman, Harvard Business School professor and negotiations expert, describes the scarcity assumption as the "mythical fixed pie."[16] In contrast, creating value assumes abundance, encouraging negotiators to expand the pie before splitting it.

Let's consider an actual pie—a pizza pie. Imagine that you and I go out for pizza together. We decide to buy a whole pie and split it. We each pay for half of the pizza pie. How should we split it?

We might say that we should split the pie exactly in half. If there are eight slices in the pie, I get four and you get four. That sounds fair, given that we each paid for half the pie. However, we might start to negotiate. Maybe we just came from work, where I skipped lunch to help you finish a project that was due that day. For this reason, maybe I'm feeling extra hungry, so I push to get five slices, while you only get three. Alternatively, maybe you noticed that you have been the one paying for the pizza the last couple of times and think that you should get more pizza this time. We could keep negotiating back and forth until we figure out a way to split the pie so that both of us are happy.

Notice our underlying assumption in this negotiation. We are assuming that there is one dimension to the pie—slices—and that resource is fixed. There are eight slices. Therefore, our negotiation is about how many slices we each get.

But is there a way to extract more value from that pizza without actually changing the size of the pie? Can we consider other dimensions of the pizza? Doing so will allow us to grow the value of the pie without changing the amount of the resource itself.

Let's say you and I started talking about pizza on our way to the restaurant. Maybe we realized that you really like the inside of the pizza—the sauce, the cheese, the toppings. You always leave the crust behind. (You give a nod to a low-carb diet, but your preference is truly just a layover from your nine-year-old self.) Let's say I'm not a toppings person at all; I'm vegan and won't eat the cheese or meat anyway. I usually just pick it all off and eat the bread (I give a nod to French cuisine, but again, it's a layover from my nine-year-old self.) From that information, we could think of a different way to split the pie; you get all the middle, and I get all the crust. Rather than each of us having four slices and only half the pie, we now each have a whole pie's worth of the parts that we like to eat. Bazerman describes this approach as "growing the pie."

In this approach, we move from thinking about resources as unidimensional (i.e., the slices of pizza) to considering other dimensions (i.e., our preferences for the different aspects of the pie). We can then rethink how we allocate the resource according to its multiple dimensions.

Consider time. We only have twenty-four hours that we can allocate in one day. Many tensions arise around how to divvy up those hours. If we just think of the dimension of time, then we are stuck in a zero-sum, scarcity approach. All we can do is consider whether to spend more of that time on one activity or another. But not all hours are equal as far as our productivity is concerned. The amount of work we can complete at nine in the morning is often very different from what we could get done at nine in the evening, especially if we are early risers or if we are night owls. The order in which we do things also shifts our efficiency in getting things done. Time management gurus often use the metaphor of a jar of stones and sand to describe how order matters in the work we do. If we first put the sand into the jar and then the small stones, we often have no room left for the big stones. But if we first put the big stones into the jar and then the small stones, most of the sand will fit around the stones. If we work on our big projects first, we can then figure out how to get the little tasks done in smaller periods of time. Allocating time to competing demands is not just about how much time to give to different projects but also about when to do so and in what order.

One person's trash

Some people have a knack for expanding the value in resources. Scott Sonenshein, professor of management at Rice University, describes these people as stretchers: people who figure out how to do more from less. One way to do so is to seek value in what others consider to have little value. As the adage goes, one person's trash is another's treasure. Stretchers can find treasure in someone else's trash—sometimes literally.[17]

Russell Maier, a Canadian artist stranded in the Philippines, found his life changed by trash. In 2010, he and his girlfriend at the time traveled from Paris to the Philippines to meet her family. Maier, an artist, had little in common with his girlfriend's father, a top executive of a big corporation in Manila. In fact, the meeting went so poorly that at the end of the trip, his girlfriend dumped him. She returned to Paris. Maier continued traveling through the Philippines—hiding from his pain and seeking inspiration for his art from indigenous wisdom. During his travels, he happened on a remote village among the Igorot people. But there his pain and depression took over. He was both heartbroken and financially broke, without motivation or destination. The villagers took him in. It took some time (years), but eventually he started to reclaim his own creative spark.

One thing that intrigued Maier was that the local language had no word for trash. The Igorot people believed that everything had value. Even when something was no longer used for one purpose, it could be transformed to be used for another. In fact, they had a word—*ayyew*—which defined how well an item was recycled into something else. Maier was fascinated by this notion, but he also saw plenty of trash—particularly plastics—around the community. Plastic bottles and other plastic material were polluting the village and were being thrown into the local river. He started to wonder how they could repurpose the plastic. One day he decided to stuff smaller plastic materials into larger plastic bottles. He realized that he could use this plastic-stuffed bottle as a building brick to create his own garden. The idea was so simple—communities had tons of plastic trash and plastic bottles creating waste, while they also desperately needed building materials to improve their homes, schools, and gardens.

Maier shared the idea with a local school and had the students create hundreds of these plastic bottle ecobricks. The local school superintendent picked up on the innovation, mandating more than two hundred schools to create ecobricks with their trash. The practice soon spread to thousands of area schools.

An idea that started in a remote Philippine village became a movement. Maier wrote a manual on how to make ecobricks. In 2013, he created the website ecobricks.org to share the story more broadly. He heard from others around the world—people who had independently created bottle bricks. Andreas Froese, a German inventor, also realized that plastic bottles can serve as building material. Filling the bottles with earth and sand, Froese built large projects with the bottle bricks—homes, a conference center, a water tank, and other structures. Maier connected with ecobrickers in South Africa, North America, and South America. Together they created the Global Ecobrick Alliance, sparking hundreds of thousands of ecobrickers from the United States, the United Kingdom, South Africa, Singapore, and beyond.

I (Wendy) was introduced to the idea of ecobricks by a neighbor in 2016. Since then, I've worked with our community to transform hundreds of pounds of trash into building material. We've delivered bricks to a school, a camp, and a local nature center, seeking uses to frame a garden, build benches, and create walls. We found ways to create value out of our own trash, expanding resources to be more abundant and to enable us to engage in more both/and thinking.[18]

Ladders to the top of the tree

One way to achieve abundance is to find new technologies to gain access to otherwise inaccessible resources. Peter Diamandis and Steven Kotler explore these many technologies in their book *Abundance*. Their thesis is simple yet provocative: there are plenty of resources in the world to feed, clothe, and shelter all the people around us, if only we have the ways to access the resources. They give the example of an orange tree. We can pick oranges off a tree to eat them. But what happens when we have picked all the oranges at the bottom of the tree? The tree is still full of oranges, but it isn't until we bring a ladder that we can reach them. New technologies can serve as ladders to make previously inaccessible resources more easily accessible.

Diamandis and Kotler offer several examples throughout their book. For example, they highlight the significant challenge of water. More than a billion people in the world lack access to clean drinking water, a problem that leads to more than two million childhood deaths a year. The problem is not that the planet has no water but that we need new ways to ensure that the water is clean and accessible. Similarly, worldwide hunger is not a function of a lack of food. In the United States, an estimated 40 percent of food produced is wasted. The challenge therefore is finding new approaches to effectively distribute the food and eliminate the food waste.[19]

So, too, we can find new ladders to gain accessibility to our own limited resources. New technology can help shift our view of resources from either/or to both/and thinking. Rather than seeking a way to slice our pie of time, money, and energy, we can explore novel options that grow the pie. For example, consider the technology around video conferencing, a technology that has transformed our ability to connect with people while minimizing the time and expense of travel. We can now attend a conference, deliver a speech, connect with a colleague, or join a party all from our living room. Technology can offer us new opportunities to stretch our resources and our thinking.

Virtuous cycles of give-and-take

An abundance approach not only allows us to expand resources before we allocate them between competing demands but also helps us see how those resources can benefit one another.

In his book *Give and Take*, Adam Grant argues for the virtuous cycle between taking what we need for ourselves and giving to others. We often see this tension as a dichotomy that involves distributing our resources. We assume that giving to others will take away from the time and energy that we need for ourselves. Grant turns this attitude around, showing instead how givers, people focused on helping others, gain personal benefits multifold in return.

Grant introduces the consummate giver, a nerdy computer programmer turned successful Silicon Valley serial entrepreneur named Adam Rifkin. People describe Rifkin as the person who always asks, "How can I help?" and then follows through. Because of his constant giving, Rifkin was named *Fortune*'s most networked person, and it was this network that allowed him to keep helping people by making connections with others. Through his exceptional practice of giving, he found his own sense of meaning, purpose, and fulfillment, not to mention the success of three entrepreneurial ventures. Resources spent giving to others came back to benefit Rifkin even more.[20]

When we face competing demands, scarcity raises tensions. The assumption of scarce resources pits one demand against another for access to these resources. In contrast, abundance thinking expands possibilities and recognizes how resources do not necessarily stand in the way but instead enable novel synergies.

Problem Solving as Coping (Not Controlling)

Finally, a paradox mindset shifts our assumptions about problem solving from controlling to coping. In general, people like to be in control. We prefer to have our feet on stable ground rather than caught in the swirl of constant change. We tend to choose clarity and certainty over absurdity and irrationality. When faced with ambiguity, change, and irrationality, we usually approach problem solving as a means to reclaim certainty and stability.

Confronting paradoxes is the perfect storm of ambiguity and change. Multiple, varying, and often conflicting options are spinning around one another. Opposing demands can offer creative friction and be energizing. But tensions often provoke anxiety, fear, and discontent. In those moments, we seek to minimize the uncertainty and enable stability by taking control of the situation. The easiest way to feel in control when facing paradoxes, at least temporarily, is to make a clear decision between options. We might also assert control over those around us—expecting our families, our work groups, and our organizations to act just as we do. If we have a dichotomous mindset, we view problem solving as a search for control.

Navigating paradoxes, however, requires a different approach to problem solving. Remember, paradoxes are both dynamic and persistent. They cannot be resolved, as the opposing forces remain. For example, in our quest to address work-life dilemmas, we never completely resolve the underlying paradoxes of doing for ourselves and doing for others, of planning and spontaneity. These paradoxes are constantly challenging and changing one another; they never go away. With a paradox mindset, we shift our approach from problem solving to coping. Coping means that we accept the uncertainty, honor the ambiguity, and find a way to move forward in the moment, knowing that we will need to revisit our decision. Colleague Lotte Lüscher and I (Marianne) describe this coping approach as finding a workable certainty. We may not grasp the totality of the situation, yet we have enough clarity to move forward, gaining the footing to make decisions and continuously learn and adapt.[21]

Coping involves finding a workable certainty. Rather than resisting the tensions, you accept them. Rather than resolving a persistent paradox, you are constantly solving smaller, more fluid problems. Throughout the book, we use language that reinforces this notion of coping, rather than controlling. We don't talk about resolving paradoxes but instead describe navigating, engaging with, or leveraging them. Rather than talk about minimizing or resisting tensions, we speak of accepting and embracing them. Language is a first step to changing any underlying assumptions. But first, all of us must also recognize how hard it is to let go of control.

Oh craps

Letting go of control can run counter to our instincts—or at least to our biases. Experiments by Ellen Langer, a Harvard psychologist, demonstrated this effect. She showed how we often assume we can control even the most random circumstances. Langer calls this bias the *illusion of control*.

Consider the game of craps. If you haven't spent significant time in a casino, craps is a dice-throwing game. People stand around the table and bet on the outcome of a dice roll. Then someone rolls the dice. People win or lose depending on how the outcome aligns with their bets. The people betting take turns rolling the dice. Assuming that the game is legal (and the dice are not weighted), then dice throwing is completely random—people have no control over the outcome. But Langer found that people believe they have control. People predominantly made larger and riskier bets when they knew that they would be rolling the dice themselves compared with when they expected other people to roll the dice.[22]

There are many situations that, like the roll of dice, we might want to control—or at least think we can control—but cannot. You might have a neighbor (hey, it might even be you) who believes that their sports team only wins when they wear their lucky shirt—and that the shirt can never be washed lest the luck fade. I (Wendy) remember being an undergraduate student at Yale and joining other students to walk across Yale's Old Campus to rub the foot of the Theodore Dwight Woolsey statue, as that was meant to ensure success on my upcoming test. Whether or not I believed that a quick foot rub would compensate for any lack of studying, this small act allowed me to assume a bit of control. Research finds that we frequently turn to such superstitions to believe that we are in control of a situation, and that the more we think we are in control, the riskier our decision making—whether it's in terms of our personal decisions or in terms of the strategic decisions in an organization.[23]

Leading through adaptive problems

If we seek to control things in situations where outcomes are random, imagine our desire for control when we feel responsibility. Consider problem solving in roles where the outcomes can be significant and when we are at the helm—as parents, team coaches, and organizational leaders.

Leaders are responsible for mobilizing a group of people toward a set of outcomes. With weighty expectations on their shoulders, people often seek control, finding ways to be assertive and bend the outcomes toward their will. However, research repeatedly finds that effectively achieving desired outcomes depends on leaders' ability to let go of control.[24]

Leaders' tasks are ambiguous and demanding, often becoming more chaotic and uncertain over time. In their book *The Practice of Adaptive Leadership*, Ronald Heifetz, Alexander Grashow, and Marty Linsky at the Harvard Kennedy School distinguish between two types of problems— technical problems and adaptive challenges: "While technical problems may be very complex and critically important (like replacing a faulty heart valve during cardiac surgery), they have known solutions that can be implemented with current knowledge. They can be resolved through the application of authoritative expertise and through the organization's current structures, procedures and ways of doing things."[25] To solve technical problems, we need to accurately diagnose the situation, have access to the solution, and know how to implement that solution. These steps may still be hard, but there is a road map. In contrast, adaptive challenges have no road map. They are messy, uncertain, emergent, and filled with competing demands. Adaptive challenges are paradoxical.

As Abraham Zaleznik, professor at Harvard Business School and a practicing psychoanalyst, argued in 1977, effectively addressing adaptive problems requires leaders to find innovation and inspiration amid the uncertainty. Great leaders, he argues, are like artists, staying open to multiple shifting possibilities, accepting and living in chaos. He contrasts leaders with managers, who often move quickly toward problem resolution in search of structure and stability. Managers seek control in the face of uncertainty; leaders learn to cope. Navigating paradoxes depends on the assumptions of leaders and artists who willingly live on the edge of chaos and enable developing insights with open possibilities, rather than seeking the refuge of certainty and resolution.

Hanging out on the balcony

Letting go of control and embracing uncertainty to cope, learn, and adjust is easier said than done. Heifetz, Grashow, and Linsky suggest that one way to do so is to "get on the balcony." Coping with complex situations can be taxing and messy. When we are in the fray, we want to escape it or clean it up. But we only have a limited view of our options. They compare the situation to being on a dance floor. Our focus narrows when we are dancing. We might be thinking about our own dance moves or worrying about stepping on others' toes. While dancing, we can't see who is moving on or off the dance floor. We can't see the patterns of how people respond when the music changes pace. We can't see how dancers engage with one another. To do that, we need to move up to the balcony. We need a broader perspective that takes in the bigger picture and moves beyond the present moment to consider shifts over time.

Assumptions of both/and thinking broaden our perspective, helping us better respond to adaptive, complex problems. As Heifetz, Grashow, and Linsky argue, such thinking is particularly vital for leaders. Given their roles, leaders increasingly move from solving technical problems to facing adaptive challenges—challenges that have no road map and that bring paradoxical demands to light. Leadership means being able to move from the dance floor to the balcony, where leaders can better embrace and learn from the dynamic complexity.

The dancing metaphor can help us all learn to navigate paradoxes. Moving to the balcony is similar to shifting our focus from the elephant's trunk or tail to the whole elephant. We can step back from our own individual perspective, the one that keeps us stuck in a rabbit hole or engaged in trench warfare, and instead appreciate the multiple sides of competing demands and how they inform one another. We can move from seeing competing demands locked in a static relationship to seeing how they shift over time. That is, we can let go. We can embrace the need to cope, allowing situations to unfold over time as we learn, adapt, and grow through our responses.

To be clear, Heifetz, Grashow, and Linsky recognize that although the balcony offers perspective, leaders can only act while on the dance floor. Addressing complex situations, therefore, requires leaders to be both on the balcony and on the dance floor. As they note, "the challenge is to move back and forth between the dance floor and the balcony, making interventions, observing their impact, and then returning to the action. The goal is to come as close as you can to being in both places simultaneously, as if you had one eye looking from the dance floor and one eye looking down from the balcony, watching all the action, including your own."[26]

This metaphor brings to mind a recent meeting I (Wendy) attended. Amid increased awareness about systemic racial injustice, the other leaders and I debated the efforts toward becoming a more equitable organization. Everyone in the room agreed that work needed to be done. But what work? Some people proposed an intervention that would start by working with a small group on their own perspectives and biases and use this as a pilot to inform broader efforts. Other people resisted, suggesting that these efforts were too small, too expensive, and too hasty. They proposed studying the issue for a longer period in search of more efficient, systemic-level changes. Small steps or large system change? Responding or planning? Everyone believed in the overall goal but felt the struggle of how to get there.

This was not the group's first meeting. I was joining it late in its process. The "let's just get going" camp had already done significant groundwork toward an experimental project that would facilitate difficult conversations about bias among a small selection of leaders. This camp had reached out to several consultants and had received a proposal to start the work. The get-going people were ready and raring to go. But the "let's slow down to have a bigger impact" folks still had reservations. Everyone turned to me, looking for an unbiased and novel perspective.

As I listened to everyone's arguments, my own biases kicked in. I'm prone to act first and think later; I'm driven by impatience. Siding with the get-going group, I opened my mouth to add my support. But then I closed it. Many years ago, I learned that when meetings surface debates like this, I would do better to sit back, listen, and take in the full argument before I speak. This approach took some training. I was so disposed to jumping into the debate (acting first, being impatient) that I had to work hard to hold off and be more thoughtful at first. To this end, I used to draw a black X on the back of my hand before joining a meeting to remind myself to spend more time listening than talking. The big black X was my reminder to get onto the balcony. To listen. To hear both sides. To see the broader picture. To do all of that before jumping to a conclusion.

So that's what I did. I stepped up to the balcony. I saw myself on the dance floor and recognized my own preference for early action over longer reflection. Then I listened to the people who came from the other side. What were their goals? What were their concerns? And finally, I asked myself whether there were options to go both slow and fast, to focus on both pilot experiments and system-level change. Then I started to talk. But instead of offering a solution, I presented an alternative question— what would it look like to honor these different perspectives? The question shifted the conversation from defensive conflict to synergistic thinking and offered a chance for new ideas. It took me out of my own sense of control, a leaning to fight for what I initially believed, and into a sense of coping, of being open to change and inviting others into broader thinking.

• • •

Table 4-1 summarizes the differences between the dichotomous and paradox mindsets. As we have described thus far in this chapter, how people with these different mindsets approach knowledge, resources, and problem solving has an enormous impact on their ability to creatively face persistent challenges.

Paradox Mindsets in Cambodia

Faced with the dilemma of joining a for-profit or a nonprofit in 2000, Jeremy Hockenstein, the new MBA whom we introduced at the beginning of the chapter, felt stuck. He was grateful to be in Hong Kong. He needed time away from his home in Cambridge, Massachusetts. While there, he decided to take some extra time to explore the region while also examining his own career decisions. The opportunity opened him up to new ideas and allowed him to change the question. Rather than asking himself whether to join a for-profit or a nonprofit—an either/or question—he started asking how he could build a career that allowed him to have an impact on

TABLE 4-1

Assumptions of dichotomous and paradox mindsets

Assumptions about . . .	Dichotomous mindsets (either/or)	Paradox mindsets (both/and)
Knowledge	Contradictory One truth One right answer Win/lose	Consistent Multiple truths Multiple competing ideas Win/win
Resources	Scarcity Zero-sum approach Implies competition	Abundance Positive-sum approach Implies cooperation
Problem solving	Control Resolving Minimize uncertainty and risk	Coping Adapting Accept uncertainty and risk

people while using the skills and talents he learned in business and in business school.

He found a novel answer to that question in Cambodia. While Hockenstein was still in Hong Kong, someone recommended that he travel to Siem Reap, Cambodia, to visit Angkor Wat, the twelfth-century temples and one of the wonders of the ancient world. Hockenstein took the advice. Yet it was not the temples that amazed him, but the people.

Many visitors to Angkor Wat experience the local people, who often beg tourists for money, as a distraction from the temples. Hockenstein felt the opposite. He was intrigued by the people. Looking beyond the begging, he noticed the motivation and creativity of the local community. Cambodia is one of the poorest countries in the world, held back economically by the rule of Pol Pot and the Khmer Rouge party from 1975 to 1979. The regime's policies led to the death of nearly two million citizens, particularly the intellectual and middle class, through execution, starvation, disease, overwork, and other atrocities. More than twenty years later, this genocide left the next generation impoverished. Yet amid this current poverty, Hockenstein saw a spirit of hope. He climbed into a tuk-tuk, a bicycle taxi, with a driver who would not stop talking because he wanted to practice his limited English with Hockenstein. When Hockenstein visited internet cafés to email home, he would have to wait in long lines because of all the local youth hanging out there, trying to gain access to the broader world.

Like these Cambodians, Hockenstein was raised by a generation devastated by genocide. Yet unlike them, his family members had escaped Europe and rebuilt their lives in Canada. Was there something that he could do to pass forward his stroke of good luck to this next generation of Cambodians?

He ended his travels but kept wondering how he could help. Six months later, he returned to Cambodia with four friends—two friends who worked with him in consulting and two friends with a background in nonprofits and social work. Together, they set out to determine the most pressing needs of the country, to identify what already existed to address these needs, and to explore what they could add. They rented an apartment in Cambodia's capital and only major city, Phnom Penh, and knocked on doors of organizations, looking to meet local people. They learned that most Cambodians worked either as rice farmers with an unpredictable income from this commodity product or as garment workers manufacturing clothing exported to mostly Western countries. Family poverty often resulted in sending young kids from their rural homes to the big city to find jobs. Unfortunately, these kids from the rural areas faced significant discrimination in the big city. So too did the huge population of orphans raised by monks after their parents were killed in Pol Pot's genocide or the tremendous number of citizens with a physical disability from contracting polio as children or from being hit by one of the many still-live Khmer Rouge land mines scattered in the rural fields. Too often, faced with significant poverty, families sold their daughters into the sex trade. Numerous nongovernmental organizations sought to help by offering Cambodians classes to learn English and computer and other job-readiness skills. Many people lacked the time or money to take advantage of these programs. For those who did attend classes, there were few jobs available to use their new skills.

Hockenstein and his friends realized that they could make the biggest impact by creating good jobs for some of the most disadvantaged people in Cambodia. They focused on those left behind in the job market—orphans, rural migrants, physically disabled people, and women rescued from the slave trade. Hockenstein set up what would become Digital Divide Data (DDD)—an entry-level IT business that hired the most disadvantaged and unemployable citizens of Cambodia for data entry jobs. He encouraged employees to learn new skills and eventually apply for higher-level jobs. Now in its twentieth year, DDD has had more than twenty-five hundred employees in four countries. More than ten thousand people have "graduated" from the organization and moved to jobs where they earn more than ten times their national wage average. DDD won the prestigious million-dollar Skoll Award for Social Entrepreneurship and a million-dollar Rockefeller Award. Pulitzer Prize winner Thomas Friedman called Hockenstein "one of my favorite entrepreneurs" in his book *The World Is Flat*.[27]

Soon after Hockenstein founded DDD, I (Wendy) discussed his business model with a colleague who asked, "So, are they a nonprofit or a for-profit company?" The legal restrictions on nonprofits and for-profits affect how business can be carried out and the kinds of decisions that management make. I remember finally asking Hockenstein which one his company was. "Neither," he said. "Both. Does it really matter?" The truth is that he incorporated as a for-profit organization in Cambodia because of deep cultural resistance to nongovernmental organizations (NGOs). Cambodians experienced NGOs as dominating and highly exploitative. But in the United States, Hockenstein created a nonprofit venture that supported DDD. This venture could more easily accept the grants and donations that helped the organization launch and train many of its employees. It wasn't that Hockenstein shunned the legal implications; rather he found ways to allow the legal structures to support, rather than restrict or define, the social mission of his revenue-generating organization. At a time when social enterprises were becoming more common, Hockenstein was an early adopter.

Building DDD required that Hockenstein adopt a paradox mindset. He sought a world where he could make a strong impact with the social mission of a nonprofit and the focus and efficiency of a for-profit. Rather than choose between the two structures, he found a third option, a social enterprise that could accomplish both aims.

• • •

Both/and thinking begins with an awareness of paradoxes that underlie our daily tensions and most vexing dilemmas. If we reframe key assumptions from either/or to both/and, we rethink how we see knowledge, resources, and management; we start the journey toward a more complex, creative, and paradoxical approach. As philosopher Søren Kierkegaard encouraged, the results can open new and powerful possibilities:

> One must not think slightly of the paradoxical . . . for the paradox is the source of the thinker's passion, and the thinker without a paradox is like a lover without feeling: a paltry mediocrity.[28]

 **CHAPTER TAKEAWAYS**

- **Assumptions form the mindsets and cognition that inform our action.** A paradox mindset involves both experiencing tensions and reframing those tensions from an either/or (dichotomous) to a both/ and (paradox).

- **Both/and thinking begins with shifting our underlying assumptions in three areas:**

  - *Knowledge:* from thinking about truth as a singular issue of right versus wrong to recognizing that multiple truths can coexist;

  - *Resources:* from thinking about scarcity to abundance, from how to slice the pie to designing creative approaches to increase the pie's value and impact;

  - *Problem solving:* from desiring control to coping, recognizing that vital capabilities for navigating the uncertainty of paradox involve adaptability and learning.

5

Creating Boundaries to Contain Tensions

Structures to Stabilize Uncertainty

Life is as complex as we are. Sometimes our vulnerability is our
strength, our fear develops our courage, and our woundedness
is the road to our integrity. It is not an either/or world.

—Rachel Naomi Remen

Janet Perna felt immense pressure. In 1996, as the general manager of the
Data Management Division of IBM, she was tasked with completely revamp-
ing her business unit without losing billions of dollars' worth of existing
revenue. The task was daunting. She could easily fail. She knew how the
threat of failure felt: only several years earlier, she, and the rest of IBM,
had faced the near death of the organization. IBM laid off more than a hundred thousand people within three years. Perna was one of the lucky ones
to remain. Or was she so lucky? The heat was on to prove to senior management that the company had kept the right person.

IBM's massive decline in the early 1990s was legendary. Although many
companies fail when new technology enters the market, IBM was then

perhaps the biggest to have ever experienced such a fate. For decades earlier, the multinational firm was the market leader in mainframe computers. This expertise positioned IBM to introduce the next generation of personal computing—and also to be jeopardized by it. In the 1980s, smarter, faster, and cheaper semiconductor chips opened up a new world in which large mainframes were replaced by smaller and faster microcomputers. Several companies moved in to develop these computers. Seeing the potential of microcomputers, IBM's R&D team built out its version—what would ultimately become the IBM personal computer. To enter this market quickly, the firm licensed components from other companies. The microprocessors came from Intel, and the operating system came from Microsoft.

IBM started to sell these smaller computers to its marquee corporate clients. These clients could then connect the smaller computers to larger servers, whose value would be extended. The result was a client-server environment that helped companies grow their access to computing power while reducing the price. The increase in computing power legitimized and expanded the market for these smaller machines far beyond their current use by just a small group of computer enthusiasts and hobbyists. IBM's sales grew considerably, but their approach to computing also opened up opportunities for new companies to move in. IBM both created the market and then allowed that market to destroy the company.

At first, IBM leaders were not worried about the new competition. Their bread and butter was the mainframe computer, for which IBM remained at the top of the market. But this strength created blinders. The leaders had gone too far down a rabbit hole with the mainframe computer and remained committed to what they considered their core product. Meanwhile, growth of the microcomputer market was accelerating. As corporate budgets tightened during the declining economy in the late 1980s, the client-server approach was a cheaper option for computing. As increased demand opened up a broader market for home computing, IBM continued to reinforce the value of the mainframe and was, as a result, starting to lose ground in hardware computing. It was trench warfare in the IBM C-suite as the traditionalists dug in, defending their current strategy, rationalizing bad news, and avoiding major changes. They were caught in a swirling vicious cycle.

As the history of disruption has proven again and again, haughty complacency is no match for hardworking passion and feisty innovation. The marketplace was being taken over by what was then scrappy entrepreneurial firms—Dell, Microsoft, Oracle, Compaq, Digital Equipment Corporation, Sun Microsystems, Hewlett-Packard, and, eventually, Apple. IBM faced dire consequences. The mainframe business lost billions of dollars in 1992. By 1993, IBM had laid off more than a hundred thousand employees—a particularly painful blow given that many had joined IBM with expectations of lifetime employment. Newspapers and analysts were drafting IBM's obituary. The *Economist* wrote a series of articles, stressing the damaging ripple effects and saying that "IBM's fall from grace is difficult to exaggerate."[1]

Amazingly, executives were able to resurrect the firm. In 1993, IBM hired Lou Gerstner. With experience in taking bold strategic action, he began to dig the company from out of the rubble. He shifted IBM's focus from a predominantly hardware organization and invested significantly in software and computer services.[2] Yet he barely had time to let the dust settle on this new strategic focus when the next technological wave started to swell. The World Wide Web was becoming popular in the early 1990s, quickly enabling tremendous new possibilities for what has now become cloud computing, extensive apps, and constant connectivity. IBM leaders were not going to make the same mistake they did last time. This time they would be ready for this new technology.

Learning from IBM's previous disaster, Gerstner wanted to build innovations to meet the emerging internet and e-commerce opportunities, while at the same time managing the company's existing business. To do so, the leaders of IBM focused on building products in three horizons. Horizon 1 products were already in the market. Horizon 2 innovations could enter the market within six months. Horizon 3 innovations focused on a more distant future.[3] To embed this kind of innovating across the company, Gerstner wanted every business unit to be investing in Horizons 1, 2, and 3 products. Doing so meant that each business unit needed to be managing existing products for short-term revenue, while looking out to the long term by building innovations—innovations likely to cannibalize the existing products.

Janet Perna felt the tug between ensuring market leadership for today while innovating for tomorrow. Her business unit built, sold, and connected traditional databases that stored office data for large companies. Yet she recognized several significant changes in the future for databases. First, they would no longer be centralized in only one computer but would have to be distributed across many platforms from different vendors. This change would require IBM engineers to start writing code in a new programming language that would allow the software to function across different platforms. Second, the databases would need to store not just numbers and characters as they had until then, but to store all kinds of content, including audio and visual data such as photos, videos, and sound clips. This new content was more complex and required new ways of thinking about data storage. Finally, the engineers also realized that they would need to develop new products able to handle exponential growth of data of all types, and to store and retrieve information on the internet. In an ideal world, IBM's current position as a leader in the database management space would translate and support its work to develop, market, and sell these new products. Perna's business unit was developing Horizon 2 and 3 products that allowed it to store different types of data in new ways. This capability would not only be applicable to back-office functions but would also be a driver of computing.

While the engineers worked to build new databases, trying to focus on both the existing product and innovations for the future proved challenging. The R&D leaders wanted to allocate engineers to experimentation but also felt pressured to respond to customer requests to update the current database. These leaders felt the tug of war in how to allocate their engineers' time. The business unit also needed to build out a whole new sales team and new channels to reach customers, beyond the traditional IBM accounts. The sales team, however, was still rewarded by meeting their quotas which was easier to do when calling on existing customers rather than taking the time to build new ones. Many of the Data Management

Division employees felt threatened that their skills would no longer be valued and that they would be out of a job. Perna felt pulled in multiple directions.

Underlying Perna's dilemmas are classic *learning paradoxes*—competing demands in how we grow from the past to the future. Learning paradoxes include interdependent opposites such as between the short term and the long term, risk aversion and risk taking, stability and change, tradition and modernization. In 1991, Stanford University professor James March described this paradox as a tension between *exploring* new opportunities and *exploiting* old certainties. He noted how these paradoxes emerge whenever organizations need to adapt over time to survive:

> Exploration includes things captured by terms such as search, variation, risk taking, experimentation, play, flexibility, discovery, innovation. Exploitation includes such things as refinement, choice, production, efficiency, selection, implementation, and execution. Adaptive systems that engage in exploration to the exclusion of exploitation are likely to find that they suffer the costs of experimentation without gaining many of its benefits. They exhibit too many undeveloped new ideas and too little distinctive competence. Conversely, systems that engage in exploitation to the exclusion of exploration are likely to find themselves trapped in suboptimal stable equilibria. As a result, maintaining an appropriate balance between exploration and exploitation is a primary factor in system survival and prosperity.[4]

Organizations can be outdated, but so can people. Learning paradoxes arise for us on a personal scale as well, such as when we grapple with updating, retooling, and reskilling ourselves. These paradoxes arise when we try to make the time for learning something new amid so many current responsibilities. We know that we should prepare for the future, but we barely have enough time to live in the present. Herminia Ibarra, professor at London Business School, recognizes these tensions in what she describes as the *authenticity paradox*. We seek to be authentic to who we are. But to grow and learn over time, we need to step outside our comfort zone and act in ways that feel inauthentic. Sometimes, we need to fake it until we make it, feeling inauthentic to stretch toward a new and expanded sense of authenticity.[5]

Building Boundaries

As part of my (Wendy's) doctoral dissertation, I studied IBM leaders while they worked to reinvent the company in the early 2000s. IBM wanted to better understand how to navigate the past and the present, how to juggle its multiple time horizons. For help, company senior leaders turned to Michael Tushman, professor at Harvard Business School, and Charles O'Reilly, professor at Stanford Graduate School of Business.

Tushman and O'Reilly argue that to navigate these kinds of challenges, organizations need to be ambidextrous. One way to overcome the tragedies of success is to explore and exploit simultaneously. Leaders have to achieve operational excellence on the one hand while taking risks to generate novelty on the other.[6]

IBM hired Tushman and O'Reilly to help all the business unit leaders understand how to be ambidextrous. As a doctoral student, I joined the two of them, seeking to understand what it took for the business unit senior leadership team to navigate this exploration and exploitation paradox. I observed how Janet Perna and some of her peers grappled with these tensions. Some leaders, like Perna, adopted approaches that allowed them to effectively navigate learning paradoxes. Some did not. They went down rabbit holes and got stuck in a rut of the past. Some leaders saw the potential of the future, but their entrepreneurial spirit became a wrecking ball. They went all in on innovating, ignoring, and, in some cases, destroying millions of dollars of revenue from their existing businesses.

One key factor impacting the outcome of these business units was how they created boundaries to cope with paradoxes. As described earlier, boundaries are the structures that sustain our mindsets, emotions, and behaviors (figure 5-1). These structures include a broad array of features,

FIGURE 5-1

The paradox system: boundaries

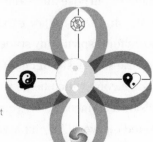

Creating boundaries to contain tensions
- Linking to a higher purpose
- Separating and connecting
- Building guardrails to avoid going too far

Shifting to both/and assumptions
- Accepting knowledge as containing multiple truths
- Framing resources as abundant
- Problem solving as coping

Finding comfort in the discomfort
- Building in a pause
- Accepting the discomfort
- Broadening our perspective

Enabling dynamics that unleash tensions
- Experimenting using measured steps
- Preparing for serendipity
- Learning to unlearn

including goals, routines, formal organizational structures, and roles. They can also include the allocation of time and arrangements of the physical environment. In this chapter, we explore the tools that allow these boundaries to contain tensions. The more clearly we can put such boundaries into place in our lives and in our organizations, the more dynamic, experimental, and bold we can be in navigating paradoxes.

Linking to a Higher Purpose

Building the scaffolding around paradox starts with identifying a higher purpose—the overarching reason, meaning, and direction that captures why we do something. Psychotherapist Viktor Frankl argued that purpose, above all else, defines and motivates our lives. As a Jew in Vienna in the middle of the twentieth century, Frankl was arrested by the Nazis and sent to a concentration camp. Frankl noticed that even while people in the concentration camps were surrounded by so much seemingly senseless suffering and death, they grasped for an existential meaning of life. Finding meaning, it turned out, offered the will to live.[7]

A higher purpose invites us to define that meaning in our own lives. It can structure our actions and enable our success. Many high performers write a personal statement of purpose and values. Oprah Winfrey, media mogul and talk show host, told *Fast Company* that her mission was "to be a teacher. And to be known for inspiring my students to be more than they thought they could be." In the same issue of *Fast Company*, Amanda Steinberg, founder of DailyWorth.com, which helps women build their wealth, said her own personal vision statement was "to cultivate the self-worth and net-worth of women around the world." Steinberg stressed the importance of empowering both financial wealth and emotional strength.[8] Likewise, organizational success depends on purpose—more than strategy or structure. Consider LEGO's mantra "to inspire and develop the builders of tomorrow" or Nike's mission "to do everything possible to advance human potential." These statements of purpose inspire and energize.

Statements of purpose also provide a critical tool for navigating paradoxes. Specifically, in the face of conflicts and uncertainty, a higher purpose can (1) energize us to continue pushing through in the face of competing demands, (2) help unite opposing forces, and (3) provide a long-term focus to help align our short-term decisions.

Persistence amid challenges

Navigating paradoxes can be taxing. The uncertainty and ongoing conflict can wear us down. Purpose helps energize us. It reminds us why we do the work we are doing and can help us push through day-to-day challenges and find more commitment to the work. American preacher Harry Emerson Fosdick captured this idea when he argued, "People will work hard for money. They will work harder for other people. But people will work hardest of all when they are working for a cause."[9] As an illustration, you may be familiar with the classic parable of the three bricklayers.

Three bricklayers were working side by side. The architect approached the first and slowest of the three. "What are you doing?" asked the architect. The bricklayer replied, "I'm a bricklayer. I'm laying bricks so that I can feed my family." The architect asked the second-fastest bricklayer, who replied, "I'm a builder. I'm building a wall." Finally, the architect asked the third and fastest bricklayer. This bricklayer noted, "I'm a cathedral builder. I'm building a cathedral allowing people to connect with each other and with God."

Antoine de Saint-Exupéry, author of the beloved book *The Little Prince*, captures a similar idea in his *Wisdom of the Sands (Citadelle)*: "Building a boat isn't about weaving canvas, forging nails, or reading the sky. It's about giving a shared taste for the sea, by the light of which you will see nothing contradictory but rather a community of love."[10] We articulate purpose not only to motivate ourselves but also to motivate others. Simon Sinek preached the value of a higher purpose to a small TEDx audience in Puget Sound. He told people to start with explaining *why* to do something: "People don't buy what you do; people buy why you do it." Sinek uses the example of Apple. The multinational tech company doesn't say that it makes great computers; rather it says that it wants to challenge the status quo and think differently. Making great computers is just one means to accomplish this vision.[11] Focusing on the aspirational value and impact of our actions can help people be excited to complete the tactical work. Sinek argued that great leaders inspire action by describing why something matters—its purpose—before describing how to implement it or even what it is. This simple message resonated and quickly went viral.

Clayton Christensen highlighted the value of higher purpose in an address to the 2010 graduating class from the Harvard Business School. As an accomplished Harvard professor, consultant, and management guru, Christensen could have offered deep advice about using purpose to motivate strategy and business results. Instead, he noted more poignantly how the tug of careers, professional success, and wealth often competes with personal happiness, familial ties, and communal commitments. When we navigate the paradoxes between work and life, the pursuit of money, status, and fame often pull harder and can lead us toward a vicious cycle.

Without mincing words, he reminded the class that Jeffrey Skilling, convicted felon of Enron infamy, was a fellow alum of Harvard Business School. Two of the thirty-two people who were Rhodes scholars with Christensen also served time in jail. Christensen implored the students to take the time to find a deeper personal purpose and to use that purpose to motivate themselves to continually value both work and life; to achieve professional success alongside, and not despite, personal happiness.

Purpose particularly bolsters us when we experience challenging tensions that can strain our time, energy, and patience. Both/and thinking requires emotional engagement and cognitive effort. Purpose can offer both the cognitive reasons and motivational boost to help us engage paradoxes.

Uniting opposing forces

Paradoxes can also be divisive, as competing demands pull in opposite directions. In the face of those divisions, a higher purpose statement can serve to unify. Negotiation experts often stress the value of a higher purpose to serve as a touchpoint that reminds opposing parties of their shared commitment. The nonprofit Seeds of Peace offers a good example. The organization brings together youth from conflict-ridden zones to learn and connect with one another in service of enabling courageous leadership in these areas. The nonprofit provides the young people with a shared purpose that they all agree with: "the pursuit of peaceful change in communities divided by conflict." Achieving peace is something that youth from all sides of conflict can agree upon. The pursuit of peace transcends their differences, helping to connect the youth when they are facing particularly divisive issues.[12]

Research in the 1950s by social psychologist Muzafer Sherif demonstrated the power of a higher purpose to unite sparring factions. He started by fostering warring factions. He and his research team brought twenty-two twelve-year-old boys to the Robbers Cave Camp in Oklahoma, split them into two teams, and created competitive activities across teams. At the end of five days, the competition drove the boys toward prejudice and anger against one another. Could the researchers then turn around this divisiveness? To do so, they set up situations that involved what they described as a "superordinate goal," a goal that appealed to both teams but that required their collaboration for success. Motivated by these overarching goals, the warring groups started to minimize their conflicts and work together.[13]

A long-term focus for short-term decisions

Finally, a higher purpose allows us to raise our sights toward a far-off horizon which can help us work through short-term tensions. The ongoing struggle between opposing forces can be dizzying and destabilizing in the moment. When we are caught in such throes, the oscillations can feel like being on a boat in a storm, as the boat thrashes from one direction to the next. But looking out toward the distant horizon offers an inner calm amid the chaos. No matter what kind of local movement we experience, the horizon remains stationary, giving us a sense of stability in the moment. Similarly, looking out to a higher purpose can reduce the chaos of paradox. Focusing on an overarching vision can minimize the anxiety and uncertainty we feel when confronting competing demands.

This long view also helps us avoid either/or traps. Short-term decision making tends to be more myopic; we focus on what is more tangible, quantifiable, and certain over what is more abstract, qualitative, and uncertain. This focus can lead us to overemphasize one side of paradox over the other. The pressure to achieve short-term profit frequently overwhelms the desire to have long-term impact. The demand to accomplish our short-term to-do list edges out any interest in learning and changing for the future. If we allow our short-term thinking to always drive our decision making, we will end up reinforcing either/or choices and leading ourselves down rabbit holes. For Janet Perna, short-term pressures reinforced efforts to advance the existing product. She and other leaders needed to keep focused on the long term in order to continually remind themselves of the value of investing in riskier innovations.

Professors Natalie Slawinski at University of Victoria in British Columbia and Pratima Bansal at Western University in London, Ontario, confirmed the value of a long-term focus when they were studying companies in the Alberta oil sands. The Canadian province of Alberta is home to the third-largest oil reserves in the world, after Saudi Arabia and Venezuela. In the early 2000s, the Alberta oil sands faced tremendous pressure from environmental groups. Activists and celebrities portrayed the industry as producing "dirty oil," noting that compared with conventional crude oil, extracting energy from Alberta's oil sands produced significantly more greenhouse gas emissions, used more water, introduced more noxious pollutants into the air, and required more deforestation. In addition, thousands of ducks had landed on and died in the retention ponds built to hold the oil sands' extraction waste.

The extraction of the Alberta oil sands is a cutthroat commodity business where any costs, particularly those that introduce environmental practices, could diminish short-term competitive advantages. Slawinski and Bansal's deep entrenchment in the industry, however, revealed an important insight. Despite the competitive nature of the industry, some companies did engage in a greater number of environmental practices. These companies were the ones that adopted a longer-term vision for their own organization. In the short term, leaders viewed environmental practices as costly and diminishing their company's profits. But shifting the focus to the longer term, company leaders saw a different picture. Taking a long-term view, they recognized environmental practices as opportunities that pushed them to innovate, improve stakeholder relationships, and reduce costly accusations from environmental activist groups while fostering greater passion and commitment from employees with aligned personal values.[14]

At IBM, I (Wendy) and the company leaders watched as tensions between the short term and long term surfaced again and again. Big dilemmas, such as whether to restructure the organization to enable greater efficiency or more experimentation, would arise in their business meetings. Likewise, ongoing decisions emerged almost daily about whether to allocate an engineer's time to satisfying an existing client need or to developing products for a new market. Effective senior teams could frequently oscillate between supporting the existing product and the innovation, being consistently inconsistent. They were the tightrope walkers.

But this tightrope walking was supported by the team's higher purpose. For Perna, the vision was simple—be the number one player in database management. There was nothing magical about the vision. More important was how she used this vision. Perna would start every senior leadership meeting by restating the vision. She would then remind the other leaders how they each contributed to achieving the vision. Like the boys in Sherif's experiments at Robbers Cave, achieving success for the Data Management Division vision required contribution from all parts of their team. The business unit had to remain critical to current database customers while figuring out how to compete with internet startups that were creating new database options. By starting each meeting with the business unit's higher purpose, Perna reinforced the importance of her team's cooperation to embrace the tensions and find options that were more creative. As a senior leader on Perna's team once told us, "There's no grandstanding on this team." You couldn't just praise your successes; you had to contribute to the overall solutions for the entire business.

Separating and Connecting Competing Demands

We are frequently asked how to effectively structure tasks to navigate paradoxes. Should people split opposing poles to ensure that the focus means that each side will achieve what it needs, or should they bring the opposing poles together, fostering increased potential for synergy? Differentiate or integrate? Separate or connect? Perhaps unsurprisingly, the answer is both. Effectively navigating paradoxes requires finding ways to both separate and connect opposing poles. As we've said, navigating paradoxes is paradoxical.

Separating and connecting involves how we structure the boundaries around paradox—both in our personal lives and in our organizations. To help pull apart or bring together the poles of a paradox, organizations can rely on different features to create these boundaries, including formal structures, specified leadership roles, goals, metrics and rewards, time, stakeholder relationships, and more. Separating might involve pulling apart the poles into distinct subunits or allocating responsibilities to different leaders. It might also involve identifying alternative times to talk about each pole or articulating distinct goals and different reward structures. Likewise, connecting might involve identifying senior leaders responsible for building links across the subunits, creating time to bring together the opposing forces, or fostering a culture that stresses exploring synergies and integration.

We can also build boundaries in our personal lives to help separate and connect paradoxical poles. Similar to an organizational context, boundaries in our personal lives might include goals, personal roles, times, network connections, and physical location. For example, some people create boundaries that clearly demarcate work from life. We might use physical space or time, focusing on work and life in different places or during different hours of the day. We might even use different technology—the work computer and phone are put away as soon as we come home. Others prefer less demarcation. For some, work doesn't stop at home and home doesn't stop at work—time is more fluid. The laptop might come out in the evenings so that we can finish work at home. Or we answer emails at all times of the day. Sometimes these boundaries work, while at other times they pose challenges. Enter the global pandemic. People who once had clear work-life boundaries felt them blur or disappear. As we write this book, organizational leaders and employees are learning to navigate new ways of thinking about work and life boundaries as they explore possibilities of working from home or enabling hybrid options.

Features to separate and connect might even include things like the clothing we wear. Remember *Mister Rogers' Neighborhood*? Fred Rogers famously started each show by entering his house and trading his business jacket and loafers for a comfortable cardigan and sneakers. By doing so, he signaled the transition from a more formal business role into the friendly neighbor character. Michael Smets, Paula Jarzabkowski, Gary Burke, and Paul Spee, professors of organizational theory, recently studied reinsurance underwriters working with Lloyd's of London, and noted that they often adopt the *Mister Rogers* strategy at work. Reinsurance underwriting involves deals that help protect insurance firms from large claims that could wipe out their resources because of such catastrophic events as floods and hurricanes. Underwriters from various firms compete to bid on deals, but once the deal is accepted, the firms cooperate to parcel out parts of the risk. The underwriter interactions are both transactional as well as communal, competitive as well as cooperative. Smets and colleagues found that dress was one way they navigated this boundary. They put on a professional jacket and shoes to signal their more formal and competitive stance on the trading floor. When they return to their offices, however, they remove the jacket, change their shoes, and roll up their sleeves to show that they are ready for more informal, cooperative connections.

The insurance underwriters also found strategies to build connections and synergies between these two worlds. For example, knowledge and information can foster connection. The give-and-take of information in a more relaxed, communal interaction can impact the transactional business deals, while the value that the companies gain in their deals has spillover effects on how they build community.[15]

Separating and connecting at IBM

When managing innovation, Tushman and O'Reilly suggest business unit structures that emphasize separating and connecting. Specifically, they recommend creating a separate subunit that differentiates the new products from the rest of the organization. They focus on the senior leadership to foster points of connection, as well as pointing to integration through tactical synergies created by leveraging technology, sales, and other resources.

Given the potential for the new product to threaten the existing world, a distinct subunit incubates experimentation in a more protected and focused environment. Consider the creation of the microcomputer at Data General in the late 1970s. The company was one of the early computing firms that challenged IBM's hardware hegemony. Data General executives believed that they could lead in the microcomputer market, but they too were losing the race in this new space to other companies, most notably Digital Equipment Corporation. Despite the excitement to develop a new machine, Data General leaders found that they fell prey to a familiar challenge; the existing business took precedence for their time and resources. Finally, buoyed by vision and purpose, as well as some frustration, the company's innovative leader Tom West created a sort of Skunk Works team. He moved a small team of engineers to a totally different location from the main headquarters and gave them a year to produce the new machine. Author Tracy Kidder captures the focus and frenzy of this innovation team in his Pulitzer Prize–winning book *Soul of a New Machine.*

Importantly for Tushman and O'Reilly, these innovation incubator teams need strong ties back to the organization. For a business unit to value its innovations and for the innovations to benefit from the existing products, the senior leaders need to foster ongoing connections across the organization that enable integration and synergies.

Perna implicitly understood this need to separate and connect when her business unit was developing a new database for distributed computing. IBM had a proprietary database that operated on its own mainframe computers. In the new client-server computing world, IBM needed a database that would work on a broad array of platforms. The company could start with the insights from its existing database but would need to build this new software in Java, a completely different programming language. The expert team of engineers in California working on the existing mainframe database included some of the best people in the industry. However, they resisted creating the new program. As Perna told us, "These engineers were so busy taking care of the existing customers and maintaining competitiveness on the mainframe that they just couldn't come up for air to build the new database."[16]

Trying to shift the focus of these engineers would be counterproductive. Perna realized, however, that she could tap into the skills of a team of Toronto engineers who had already started to work on new database software for the Unix operating system. Perna moved from California to Toronto to lead this team. With the California research team separated from the Canadian team, each could focus on its distinct mandates. Yet this separation also gave both groups more flexibility for connection. Rather than see the new database as a threat, the California engineers saw the work of the Toronto team as extending the Californians' own mainframe database and were happy to serve as consultants through the process. Separating the R&D for the new database enabled the teams to find new ways to foster connections.[17]

When a separate unit is not possible

When an organization's critical tasks are intertwined, separating strategic goals into distinct subunits may not always be possible. Senior teams might have individuals who identify with more than one agenda, requiring leaders to work together closely. In these cases, leaders can find other ways to foster separation, beyond creating a distinct unit. They could highlight separate practices, identify unique times to explore each goal, use different decision-making processes, or develop discourse and communication to pull strategies apart.

In chapter 4, we introduced Digital Divide Data (DDD), an award-winning social enterprise. DDD's social mission to alleviate poverty depends on its hiring practices and is intricately linked with the financial demands of running a sustainable business. Yet the social mission and financial demands frequently conflict for critical strategic questions, such as whom to hire and how to grow. A number of advisers suggested that DDD's leadership consider building different units—one unit that hires college graduates and makes greater margins on their work and another unit that hires a greater number of disadvantaged people and serves the social mission. The first unit could provide the needed financial support for the second.

The DDD leaders, however, realized that this bifurcated structure would fuel too much discord. They also gained significant value in leveraging the business to best support their employees. Creating separate units would diminish these advantages. Instead, DDD leaders found ways to separate its social mission from its financial demands and ensure that they focused on both. DDD leaders developed two sets of independent practices. For example, they created two sets of financial statements—one for the social mission activities and one for the primary business activities—identifying different metrics so that they could better understand the drivers of success for each goal. They further allocated different times in business meetings to address each goal.

CEO Jeremy Hockenstein would also emphasize the distinctions in his communications. He would pose questions such as "How does this decision impact our social mission?" and then, "How does this decision impact our business?" in board meetings, inviting leaders to consider the different needs of each strategy.

Both Perna and Hockenstein built boundaries in their organizations for separating and connecting, yet they did so in different ways. Tushman and O'Reilly describe Perna's approach as *structural ambidexterity*—creating a separate innovation subunit to incubate new ideas, while a senior leadership team manages strategic integration and enables synergies with the core products. In comparison, Julian Birkinshaw and Christina Gibson describe the DDD model as *contextual ambidexterity*, as efforts of separation and connection are built into the informal context, practices, and culture of an organization, not into the formal structure.[18]

Avoiding false dichotomies and false synergies

These examples offer varied approaches to building boundaries that can separate and connect. No approach is particularly right or wrong; it depends on an organization's circumstances. However, all these approaches must balance both separation and connection. Relying only on separating or only on connecting is problematic. We need both approaches to navigate paradoxes.

Some IBM teams tried to separate without connecting; they created subunits to keep their innovation distinct from the rest of the organization. Doing so allowed them to avoid tensions in the short term. Yet these units failed to benefit from one another. The innovation had little access to the existing knowledge, skills, markets, and other resources related to the current product. And the existing product gained no benefit from the new insights and energy created by the innovation. Over time, the lack of shared value and purpose fueled competition between the subgroups. Their polarized agendas resulted in vicious cycles. As the IBM situation shows, when political conflicts intensify, leaders are locked in permanent battle and become emotionally weary and deflated. Ultimately, the result is organizational decline. This approach emphasizes a *false dichotomy*—the pulling apart of opposite poles without valuing their integration.

Just as problematic, however, is connecting without separating. We call this practice a *false synergy*—a veiled attempt at unity that does not address the underlying needs of both poles. In these situations, the pole with more power eventually takes over. One of the IBM software business units became enthusiastic about the idea of being an ambidextrous organization. It created an emotionally engaging statement of higher purpose. The unit leaders posted this mission statement all around their office— they made posters, wallet cards, and so forth to highlight this integrative, aspirational statement of purpose. They also built connections into their structures. Responsibility for the innovation was embedded in their existing functional structures. The vice president of R&D managed development for the existing product and exploration of the innovation. The vice president of sales had to figure out how to continue to sell to the current markets while scoping out new markets. The senior leadership meeting agenda focused on reports from each functional leader. Nothing about the structure of this business unit spotlighted the innovation. Not surprisingly, the existing world, with all its inertia, took over. Innovating became something that busy executives did "off the side of their desk." Given the tremendous demands of the existing products, the more uncertain, short-term, and risky innovations were often swept aside completely. To effectively navigate paradoxes, leaders must create strategies to both separate and connect.[19]

Building Guardrails to Avoid Going Too Far

When separating the poles of a paradox, we often pull too far. Our either/ or thinking takes over. We focus on one pole to the exclusion of the other. We start heading down a rabbit hole, focused heavily on one side, and our cognitive, emotional, and behavioral traps keep us stuck there. We fail to see the other side, obscuring potential synergies and connections.

We can, however, build structures to keep us from going too far. As I (Wendy) and my colleague Marya Besharov at University of Oxford saw in our research, Hockenstein drew on people, practices, and formal structures to reinforce the value of each pole and to reinforce connections. We called these boundaries *guardrails*—the features that act as guardians of each pole. These guardrails serve two functions. First, like the guardrails on a road, these barriers ensure that we do not veer too far to one pole. They help us avoid vicious cycles and instead aid in tightrope walking, encouraging us to move fluidly and frequently between opposing demands without fearing that we focus too heavily on one direction or another. Second, guardrails also create constraints. They scope out the field within which we are navigating paradoxes. These constraints inspire novel ideas. Bringing together the opposing poles to foster creative integration, we can find new mules.

Staying on track

Social enterprises like DDD that seek to engage both a social mission and business purpose face a significant risk of moving too far toward one pole of paradoxes. These organizations often emphasize their social mission at the expense of the business purpose, or vice versa. Some social entrepreneurs may launch a venture with such passionate idealism that they eschew the business end of the project. Taken to the extreme, idealism can bankrupt the entrepreneurship, ultimately killing its chances of achieving the mission. Other social entrepreneurs may set out with mission-driven goals but then quickly see the profit potential and start to cut corners on the mission. Diminishing the commitment to the mission means that they could lose the unique features that might have offered them a competitive advantage in the marketplace.

When DDD was founded, Hockenstein's determination to stop the cycle of poverty in Cambodia was passionate, inspiring, and infectious . . . and it almost sank the business. The organization hired the most disadvantaged citizens in Cambodia and provided them on-the-job training that enabled them to enter the labor market and move on to even better jobs.

DDD hired people who were orphaned during the Pol Pot genocide. It also hired people who had physical disabilities from a polio outbreak or left-over land mines from the wars and who couldn't find jobs elsewhere. At one point, DDD leaders launched a program to hire women rescued from sex trafficking, knowing that these women would return to the trade if they did not have alternative work.

The problem was that many of the people the organization hired had limited skills to do the work at DDD. These employees needed to do data entry, but many had no typing skills. Early hires averaged eight words per minute. Much of the work was in English, but many people were barely literate in Khmer, let alone English. Trying to train these employees while also meeting client needs was a challenge. Every once in a while, one of the company leaders would raise the question of whether they wanted to hire people with more skills—like some of the college graduates of Cambodia—who could do a better job meeting client needs. The idea was always rejected; it did not fit DDD's mission.

Several years into the work, Hockenstein created a board of advisers. At one of its first meetings, a board member who had previously run a multibillion-dollar business unit explicitly laid out the situation for the DDD leaders: "You know you guys have a great idea here, but if you keep on the way you are going, you will be bankrupt in three months." Hockenstein and the management team knew they were struggling with revenues, but the board member's frank exclamation served as a wakeup call. The leaders needed to pay more attention to the bottom line.

The DDD management team took this feedback seriously. They developed more efficient processes, built in additional financial controls, and became tighter with their human resource practices and benefits. But soon they started to go too far. What once felt like a mission-driven business seemed more bureaucratic. Increased goals, targets, and rewards left employees feeling frustrated. Despite DDD's mission to be a work-integration social enterprise to support its employees, the workers said they felt exploited by the organization. DDD had apparently moved too far toward managing its bottom line, and its leaders needed to rethink their approach.

Board advisers served as a guardrail for DDD. So did the organization's employees. These groups of people prevented the organization from getting stuck too far down rabbit holes by overemphasizing either the social mission or the business purpose. Hockenstein began building more guardrails to keep the organization from falling prey to the fate of so many other social enterprises. The guardrails explicitly ensured that the management team included some people with a business background and some people with experience in international development. DDD did the same with its board of advisers. The enterprise also created relationships with other stakeholders to guard each mission. For example, in its early years, DDD had strong ties to other data entry firms in India. These firms could help ensure DDD's sound business practices. Likewise, DDD's ties to a network of nonprofits and NGOs helped keep its leaders attuned to its social mission. Honoring these varied roles and relationships allowed DDD to move more fluidly between decisions that supported its social mission and those that advanced its business; the organizational leaders could more comfortably walk the tightrope when they knew that guardrails were in place to keep them from falling too far in either direction. Over time, the senior leaders started to ask one another, "What are my guardrails?" to ensure that they maintained a commitment to their strategic goals.

Janet Perna also built guardrails for her team to make sure that people remained committed to both the existing product and the innovation. The guardrails guided both the team members' roles and the team's goals. At one business meeting, Perna's vice president of finance blurted out a concern that she had been struggling with for some time. The team members were talking about next steps for the innovation—hiring. They needed to extend offers to new engineers to help build the innovation—engineers who had specialized skills and who would expect high salaries. The vice president told the group that the innovation's return on investment deeply concerned her. They were taking a huge risk, she said, and she struggled to justify the costs, given the uncertainty about when they would recoup the investment.

As in most cases, it is the job of finance experts to manage an organization's financial risk. And Perna's vice president of finance had her performance review linked to her ability to manage that risk. Yet the executive was not alone in her concerns. Other team members also felt frustrated. They worried that they were spending too much time on the innovation while current customers waited for them to fix bugs in the software or build out important extensions. The existing issues seemed much more urgent.

These current concerns were important, but Perna knew that there would always be immediate needs that would keep the company from planning for the longer term. She knew that she had to honor these challenges but additionally needed to protect the innovation from being taken over by people experiencing short-term pressures. The value of having different people responsible for the innovation or the existing product spurred Perna to build guardrails that prevented IBM from going too far in either direction. She worked with these senior leaders to create new metrics for the innovation that differed from those of the existing product and highlight a different process for making decisions about how to advance the innovation through the development process.

Guardrails as the mother of invention

Guardrails create constraints that can actually foster increased innovation and creativity. As the adage says, necessity is the mother of invention. The same is true for navigating paradoxes. By scoping out the playing field, we bring competing demands together. This juxtaposition forces us to find more mules—more creative integrations.

In his book *Stretch*, Scott Sonenshein argues that people who stretch seek out constraints that enable their creativity. He offers the example of Theodor Geisel, better known as Dr. Seuss. Geisel wrote one of his most famous books in response to a challenge and clear set of constrains from his editor: could Geisel write a blockbuster that used only fifty unique words? The result was *Green Eggs and Ham*. With only fifty different words, Geisel produced a book with catchy phrases that left kids not wanting to put the book down and with repetition that stayed with them long after they did. The book sold more than eight million copies, earning its place as one of the bestselling children's books.[20]

Guardrails also force us to generate creative possibilities in response to competing demands. Consider the challenge set forth by Lou Gerstner to all of IBM's business unit leaders to excel in multiple-horizon businesses. Doing so forced them to be more creative in how they managed their businesses. Similarly, by juxtaposing a social mission and business purpose, social enterprises discover new organizational norms. They have to move beyond more standard nonprofit or for-profit norms, rethink their legal status, and reconsider their strategy.

Or consider the pressure placed on dual-career couples. With two adults working outside the home, these couples face more dilemmas around how to address family and domestic needs. Underlying these dilemmas are so many of the paradoxes we have raised in this book such as self and other, work and life, planning and spontaneity. In her work on dual-career couples, INSEAD professor Jennifer Petriglieri finds that one of the most important things that keep these couples thriving is their creation of constraints which inspire them to be more creative in the face of conflict. Petriglieri describes these constraints as a *couple contract*—the shared values they build together while clarifying the boundaries that neither person wants to cross. These boundaries can look different for different couples. For some, they might involve clarifying geographic locations or the amount of work travel and time away from family, the couple's financial needs, their commitment to their careers, or their decision on whether to have children. These guardrails create the boundaries within which couples can then negotiate and innovate. Like all boundaries, the solutions are not one-size-fits-all. For example, guardrails around work travel might lead the partners to search for new jobs that accommodate these demands. Or a commitment to their careers might lead the partners to identify what parts of domestic responsibilities they can outsource. While the solutions are different across different partners, the process is similar. Set out boundaries, and use them to uncover new ways of grappling with competing demands.[21]

Boundaries at the Personal Level

The examples that we shared in this chapter have, until now, predominantly focused on senior leaders navigating paradoxes in their organizations. However, as the preceding paragraph suggests, boundaries also help us navigate paradoxes in our personal lives.

We explored these kinds of structures with one of our friends whose challenging dilemmas and underlying paradoxes left her practically in tears. Our friend, we'll call her Maya, had just started a prestigious residency after finishing her medical degree. Maya was a great student and excelled in medical school. She felt honored to be accepted into this particular residency; however, she was also nervous about whether she was up for the challenge. Soon after she began the residency, she quickly lost her confidence.

Residency programs help physicians translate the information they learned in medical school into actual patient treatment. In Maya's program, everyone reminded residents to use this time as an opportunity to learn. The chief resident and attending doctors encouraged the residents to ask questions. The residents frequently checked in with the chief resident to talk through the diagnosis and treatment of all the patients they saw. The residents also participated in grand rounds, when doctors present and discuss with their colleagues the specific medical problems of the patients.

Despite these efforts to encourage the students to participate freely, Maya found the social norms sent a different message. The highly prestigious residency program was also highly competitive. Residents knew that their performance in the program dictated their potential for their next jobs. Maya's fellow residents seldom asked true questions. Instead, they all tried to express their knowledge and talents, rarely showing any vulnerability. Furthermore, the chief resident did not encourage uncertainty. While he told residents that they should ask questions, he never seemed to have patience to answer them. Instead, he appeared to expect the residents to have their own answers.

Maya felt uncomfortable. She stopped asking questions. She did not share her uncertainties or discomforts with anyone at work. She second-guessed herself before making any comments. Looking for external validation for her diagnoses, she often shared her insights about a patient with a nurse in the hope that the nurse would offer confirmation. The stress grew over time until Maya finally cracked.

Sitting together with us, Maya broke down, saying she wondered if she should be a doctor after all. Had she just wasted the last four years of medical school, not to mention her four years as a pre-med in college? Was she really able to do this job? When she was four years old, all she had wanted to do was to be a hairdresser. Maybe she should go back to that profession. Although she feared messing up someone's hair color, it could be fixed far easier than could a botched medical diagnosis.

The underlying paradoxes of Maya's dilemma are actually quite similar to Janet Perna's. At the heart of the issue are paradoxes of learning and performing, growing and achieving, planning for tomorrow and living for today. Residency programs are structured to help a new doctor learn the art of their craft. However, new doctors are expected to act with confidence, to avoid a sense of uncertainty, and to perform well. The more they learn, the better they can perform. The better they perform, the more comfortable they feel expressing uncertainty and pushing to learn.

Many of us have experienced this learning-versus-performing paradox. When we step into a new position and have a lot to learn, we may experience this tension the way Maya did. We may also experience it when we find that the world does not value our skills and experience as it once did or when we encounter a new challenge that we cannot resolve. Ultimately, we have to balance performing well with learning new things.

After listening to Maya and letting her vent her emotions, we started talking through the problem. The challenge was not that she had new things to learn. The challenge was how to maintain her confidence while learning those new things. Performing well breeds confidence. How could she regain and retain her confidence when she was still learning?

First, we talked about her higher purpose. Why was she studying to be a doctor? Why did she go into the profession in the first place? Maya had always wanted to help people. When she was young, she had been in a car crash with her family. In the end, everyone was fine, but both her mom and her brother had needed surgery. Maya saw the importance of health professionals in such serious situations and felt inspired and grateful. She remembers how, after the accident, her family had waited anxiously for an ambulance. She felt so helpless waiting and so grateful when it finally

arrived. Maya wanted to have those skills to help others. She had identified her higher purpose—to provide comfort and care in times of crisis.
Reinforcing this statement reminded her why she needed to always learn
more about medicine, her patients, and herself.

We then talked about what experiences made her feel confident and those
that made her feel vulnerable. Could she think about separating her performance from her learning? Were there periods, such as when she felt that
she was performing well, that bolstered her confidence? Could she separate those moments from those when she needed to learn? In medical
school, Maya had volunteered in a clinic for several hours a week, offering
patients advice on wellness and preventive measures. She loved doing that
and felt really good about it but had stopped volunteering, knowing that
she would have little time to do so when she started her residency. Would
it make sense to go back to volunteering for a little while? Even though it
took away some of her free time to rest and relax, she would again have
moments of reclaimed self-confidence. Doing so would help in the moments
during the residency when she felt so uncertain.

We also talked about how she could connect her experience of confidence in her performance with her experience of learning. Research from
Brené Brown emphasizes the value of vulnerability. Vulnerability is not a
weakness. Showing vulnerability conveys our strength and allows us to
learn.[22] Were there ways that Maya could convey her vulnerability with
more power and strength, inviting her to learn more?

Finally, what guardrails did Maya need in her life? Some people spiral
out of control because they become too self-assured about their successes
and need guardrails that remind them to return to learning new things.
In this case, Maya faced the opposite situation. She was spiraling out of
control because the need to learn new things was taking over, diminishing her sense of performing well and sapping her confidence. Ultimately,
focusing on learning without performing limited her potential to learn.
What guardrails could she put in place to avoid her spiraling downhill again?
We talked about a number of options. She could reach out to her medical
school friends to compare experiences, commiserate together, and remind
one another of their talents. She could reconnect with a mentor from her

undergraduate education who encouraged her to apply to medical school. She could also generously give more compliments to her fellow residents. If she was feeling insecure, chances were that so too were the other residents in the program. Reaching out to authentically value their skills would boost their confidence while also helping her to value her own at the same time.

Building these boundaries and structures into her life allowed Maya to navigate the paradoxes of learning and performing, to reclaim her confidence in her medical skills, and to address the dilemmas she experienced. Three years later, she was seen as one of the top residents in the program. The hospital invited her to remain as a full-time employee.

 **CHAPTER TAKEAWAYS**

- **Boundaries are the structures, practices, and people that we put in place to support our ability to navigate paradox.** We identify three core boundaries to help us engage more both/and thinking:

  - *Higher purpose:* An overarching statement of vision can motivate us to embrace tensions, unite opposite poles, and focus on the longer term to minimize the short-term chaos;

  - *Separating and connecting:* Structures, roles, and goals help us pull apart opposing demands, appreciate each demand independently, and bring them together to value their interdependence and synergies;

  - *Guardrails:* Structures can prevent us from going so far in the direction of one tension that we end up moving down a vicious cycle.

6

Finding Comfort in the Discomfort

Emotions That Accommodate Tensions

What I know for sure is that your breath is your anchor, the
gift you've been given—that we've all been given, to
center ourselves in this very moment. Whenever I have
an encounter that involves even the slightest tension,
I stop, draw in a deep breath, and release.

—Oprah Winfrey

I (Wendy) remember my first night at college. I slumped back on my new bed against the dark red brick of Lawrence Hall feeling a swirl of relief and anxiety. The road to college is always a long one. Mine was a bit longer, having deferred my enrollment at Yale to spend a year working in the leadership of an international youth group. I had finally arrived.

My parents stood by me through every step of the process. They neither hovered nor smothered. They listened to pitches on college tours, printed out application materials, and helped me stock my new college dorm. In our final goodbye, I felt relieved to finally arrive at the starting block.

However, I also felt anxious about what lay ahead. My most pressing challenge crystalized before me: How was I going to belong in this new place that felt so wildly different from the one that I came from? Alone in my dorm room for the first time, I sat in the liminal space betwixt and between and felt the tug between my past and my present.

In my mind, Yale belonged to smart, rich people who wore uniforms at prep schools, vacationed in Tahoe, and had the same last name as one of the buildings on campus. I believed that people attended Yale to become future national leaders or Nobel Prize winners. I was the kid who got good grades from working really hard at a public high school near Fort Lauderdale, Florida. Our school "uniform" involved T-shirts and flip-flops. I spent many vacations hanging out with my cousins, having watermelon seed spitting contests in our backyard. Any campus building that might bear the name Smith was a happy coincidence. I had no idea how to negotiate this new world defined by residential colleges, a cappella groups, secret societies, and political unions. I felt as if I had landed in a foreign country.

In 1848, Horace Mann, US politician and activist, wrote, "Education then, beyond all other devices of human origin, is a great equalizer of the conditions of men—the balance wheel of the social machinery."[1] Mann became an inspiration for public education in the United States and for expanding university access. For me, like so many, college was a beacon of opportunity.

Yet, as with anything, there's a catch. That equalizing experience, the ability to move up in social and economic status, comes with considerable challenges. Research by our colleagues Paul Tracey and Kamal Munir from Cambridge University, along with Tina Dacin at Queen's University in Kingston, Ontario, points to these overlooked costs. They studied the social dynamics at Cambridge University, an institution known to play an outsized role in reinforcing the upper class in the United Kingdom. They found that the university's rituals and norms, such as formal dinners, school socials, and interactions with the college porters, teach the unwritten rules of the elite in British society. The rituals and norms are so strong that they quickly taught these rules to students who didn't come from that background. Yet many of these students reported that although they could play the part, they never felt that they truly belonged. More importantly, their newfound experiences of talking about wine over dinner or attending punting regattas meant that they now also felt like outsiders when they returned home. They felt caught in between. Seeking to belong, they asked themselves, "Who am I?"[2]

The question "who am I?" presents a dilemma at various points in our lives. This fundamental human question has been debated and discussed by philosophers, poets, therapists, and the like for millennia. Underlying this dilemma are what we describe as *belonging paradoxes*—contradictory but interdependent elements in our roles, goals, memberships, values, personalities, and other aspects of our lives. Belonging paradoxes include tensions between our varied roles, such as those of parent and child, employee and family member, or subordinate and superior. They also include tensions between our past selves and our future selves—the tension I felt so acutely on my first night of college.

Putting Our Emotions to Work

In this chapter, we turn to another set of tools that help us navigate paradoxes—our emotions. Paradoxes trigger complex and conflicting emotional reactions. To open ourselves to tensions, we must move beyond focusing on our mindsets and thinking to be able to engage our heart. We need to use our emotions as an enabling resource, rather than crippling obstacle.

Einstein's diaries offer insight into such complex emotions.[3] Grappling with foundational principles of physics, he confronted the paradox of how an object could be in motion and at rest at the same time. The problem was both vexing and energizing. He felt uneasy knowing that his thinking would challenge core assumptions about how people understood the world, but also felt invigorated to discover new insights. In his diaries, Einstein described feeling as if the foundation beneath him was shaking, as if he was no longer standing on stable ground.

Professors Russ Vince and Michael Broussine examined conflicting and intense emotional reactions to a major change initiative in the UK's National Health Service. Conducting workshops with doctors, nurses, and administrators, study participants explored the tensions they felt, surfacing underlying paradoxes of past and future, stability and change, and idealism and pragmatism. The researchers asked the participants to draw pictures to tap further into their feelings. Three participants drew images that conveyed excitement for new possibilities, such as an image of an ugly duckling turning into a swan. The other eighty-three participants drew pictures that suggested the uncertainty of change sparked deeper negative reactions—dark clouds, gravestones, a sick patient in bed, the sinking of the organizational ship. Vince and Broussine turned to psychoanalysis to categorize five defensive reactions expressed: repression, regression, projection, reaction formation, and denial.[4]

Uncertainty alone does not trigger a defensive reaction. Uncertainty can be beneficial or detrimental. It can spark curiosity and open-mindedness, but it can also lead to more defensive closed-mindedness. Ingrid Haas, professor at University of Nebraska–Lincoln, and William Cunningham, professor at University of Toronto, found that the different reactions to uncertainty depend on our level of threat.[5] Greater threat drives us to respond to uncertainty with a more closed, narrow focus. We avoid the information or ideas that raised the uncertainty in the first place. That is, we turn to either/or thinking seeking to minimize the uncertainty, and thereby the threat.

The bigger problem is that once triggered, our defensive reaction can spiral into a vicious cycle. Uncertainty and threat together intensify anxiety, frustration, or even anger. Our brains then tell us that we shouldn't feel this way. As we judge our own emotions, we start to pile on additional emotional responses. We might feel guilt or even shame. Brené Brown offers an important distinction between the two ideas. Guilt suggests that we did something bad. Shame is more personal and pervasive; it suggests that we ourselves are bad. Feelings of guilt and shame lead us to disconnect and hide from others, lest they discover all the reasons that we are bad, at the very moments when connection is most important.[6] The negative emotions continue to spiral downward.

The Buddha, writing in the fifth century BCE, described this downward emotional spiral as shooting the second arrow. Some experiences in our lives can be uncomfortable or even painful. These are inevitable. As the Buddha describes, such experiences are like being shot with an arrow. Often we respond to this first arrow with a variety of negative emotions—horror, shock, anger, grief, blame, shame—that cause us additional suffering. These responses are like shooting *ourselves* with a second arrow. We have no control over that first arrow; however, we do have control over our reactions, the second arrow. This Buddhist wisdom is often summarized as "Pain is inevitable. Suffering is optional."[7]

Restated in our context, the uncertainty created by paradox is inevitable. The detrimental outcomes from that uncertainty are optional. Our underlying paradoxical dilemmas can surface deep fear, anxiety, and defensiveness. All those are real and important emotions to accept. However, it is these emotions that can also lead us to narrow our focus and resort to either/or thinking. If we ruminate on fear for too long, we end up pushing ourselves farther and farther down our rabbit holes. We need to honor our fear but then find a different approach to respond to competing demands. That is, by recognizing our emotional discomfort we then can use tools to find comfort with the discomfort. We identify three practices to do so (figure 6-1).

Building In a Pause

To address the discomfort of navigating paradoxes, we can start by building in a pause—a space between the initial stimulus and the ultimate response. A pause could be a mental or physical break and can include practices like taking a deep breath or stepping away from the emotional intensity for a moment. The goal of taking a pause is to enable a more considered, rather than kneejerk, reaction.

A pause allows us to draw on different parts of our brain. When we experience something fearful and anxiety-producing, our limbic system, or what has been called our old mammalian brain, is triggered. The limbic

FIGURE 6-1

The paradox system: comfort

Creating **boundaries** to
contain tensions
- Linking to a higher purpose
- Separating and connecting
- Building guardrails to avoid going too far

Shifting to both/and
assumptions
- Accepting knowledge as
  containing multiple truths
- Framing resources as abundant
- Problem solving as coping

Finding **comfort** in
the discomfort
- Building in a pause
- Accepting the discomfort
- Broadening our perspective

Enabling **dynamics** that
unleash tensions
- Experimenting using measured steps
- Preparing for serendipity
- Learning to unlearn

system helped our prehistoric ancestors react quickly to threats in the wild. If our ancestors saw a bear, their limbic system yelled "Danger!" and triggered an immediate response to freeze and then to quickly react with fight or flight. Our survival as a species no longer depends on constant vigilance for bears . . . and lions and tigers. Yet our limbic brain remains in gear, always on the lookout for threats.

Paradoxes feel like bears to many of us. Paradoxes are uncertain, absurd, irrational, and complex. We don't know what will happen when we encounter them. Will they upend all that we know to be true and right in the world? Will they tap into our deeper fears? Paradoxes trigger our limbic brain, and our brain yells "Bear!" We could then either flee—retreating from the discomfort of paradox to our dichotomous thinking, which diminishes the immediate discomfort but leads us down into our ruts—or we could fight, defending our favored pole and thereby fueling trench warfare. Either reaction sparks a vicious cycle.

Building in a pause gives us the chance to find a different reaction. Rather than a quick fight-or-flight response, we can consider other options. We can feel the discomfort from the initial trigger but then tap into our more developed brain to adopt a more open and flexible response.

Keep calm and carry on

The idea of building in a pause in the face of discomfort is not new. Yet somehow the practice requires continual reminding. Consider the vast popularity of memes that remind us to include a pause by keeping calm in the face of threat. This advice is so universal that the phrase "keep calm and carry on" has been adopted, adapted, and reproduced millions of times over the last twenty years. The original use of the phrase, however, had much less impact.

The British government created a poster with this phrase on the eve of World War II. Brits felt anxious, anticipating massive air attacks on major cities in the United Kingdom. The government knew that an outcry of pandemonium would only make matters worse. To quell the anxiety, the government created a set of posters to try to manage everyone's emotions. It expected to distribute millions of these posters around the country. In the end, the attacks came too soon and the distribution was minimal. The posters had little impact.

But in 2000, Stuart Manley, co-owner of Barter Books in Alnwick, Northumberland, was flipping through some secondhand books about the war and found an image of the Keep Calm poster. "It had a really nice feeling about it," he said. He showed it to his wife, Mary. They decided to reprint it and sell it in the store. Customers loved it, and the bookshop quickly sold out of the reprinted poster.[8]

The reminder to keep calm was so well received that people started to replicate and adapt the phrase in tens of thousands of ways. We have signs telling us to keep calm and stay focused, be yourself, study hard, bake bread, eat cupcakes, love unicorns, and more. As we write the first draft of this chapter, one of our universities just sent out an invitation to join a training course for online teaching. The course is titled Keep Calm and Carry ONline.

The sentiment of the saying resonates in part because it taps into a deeper sense of wisdom: the power and value of keeping calm when the uncertainty and confusion in the world around us triggers our anxiety and chaos. We don't always have control over our surroundings. But we do control our inner world. Rather than allow experiences to automatically spark defensive reactions, the British war propaganda is instead encouraging a different path—keeping calm. But how do we do that?

Let the heart do the talking

One of the easiest and most effective strategies to keep calm and create a pause between stimulus and response is breathing. When you look up techniques for anger management, this is the first and most popular technique. In fact, among the techniques recommended for most kinds of emotional regulation—managing physical pain, triggering happiness, diminishing anxiety—breathing is a critical one. A long inhale and exhale require us to pause, to shift our focus momentarily, and to slow down our heart rate. Together, these physiological tweaks allow us just enough space and time to move from an automatic response to instead consider a more thoughtful alternative reaction. When we are navigating paradoxes, a pause can help us shift from the automatic defensive emotions that keep us trapped in narrower either/or thinking to a mindset more open to broader options.

This is the approach Raouf (Ron) Gharbo developed for his clinical patients. Gharbo, a physician, is board certified in physical medicine and rehabilitation and neuromuscular electrophysiology and is director of the Cardiac and Wellness Integration Center at Virginia Commonwealth University. He works with patients with chronic illness and disabilities. In doing this work, he noticed the paradoxes embedded in the experiences of pain and healing. Long-term adaptive health requires attention to both physical pain and emotional pain—the head and the heart. Healing depends on recognizing our deeper fears that keep us trapped in narrow spaces while unleashing our potential for trust that opens up to new possibilities.

Gharbo connects these responses to the physiological system. As he notes in his work, we not only need to address the fight-or-flight response to pain trigged by our sympathetic nervous system but must also simultaneously enable the parasympathetic nervous system, which controls recovery responses. These poles are not just distinct levers that pull in opposition to one another but are highly interdependent, enabling solutions to accommodate both emotional and physical responses. Physical pain and emotional suffering reinforce one another to trigger a vicious cycle that diminishes our flexible thinking. This vicious cycle releases a cascade of hormones, including cortisol, the persistent production of which has countless detrimental health consequences.

We need to minimize the hormonal cascade so that we can return to flexible thinking and produce healthier responses. Doing so involves the parasympathetic nervous system, which, Gharbo argues, is fueled instead by the emotion of trust. Managing our health depends on living in the ongoing navigation between both trust and fear, sympathetic and parasympathetic, care for the pain and avoidance of the pain. Gharbo finds that pain management requires a balancing act—tightrope walking between the multiple opposing levers of the body. Drawing on these paradoxical physiological approaches gives us strategies for more effectively engaging the paradoxes in our lives.

The first step, however, is taking a pause and becoming aware of the potential overload of hormones that trigger a fear-based sympathetic response. That pause then allows us to move toward a more purpose-driven, trust-based trigger of the parasympathetic system. As Gharbo notes, a fluctuating heart rate is an early warning indicator of the need to rebalance our response. If we can monitor our heart rate variability, we gain more information about when we need to pause, check in, and seek an alternative course of action. Gharbo describes this process as *autonomic rehabilitation*. His patients, for example, might have chronic back pain that causes ongoing anguish in walking, sleeping, or even sitting. One response is pain medication—a strategy that in the extreme has led to the opioid crisis that we now face globally. Gharbo offers alternatives, emphasizing the role of becoming aware of the underlying emotional pain, recognizing how it triggers greater physical pain, and learning to manage it. In the moment, this starts with breathing.

Gharbo then advocates for continued strategies to use the breath to trigger the parasympathetic nervous system. By focusing on our breathing, we can zoom in on our immediate physiological responses. With these skills in hand, we can then zoom out and further improve their parasympathetic responses by moving to conversations around purpose, building relationships that value trust, and minimizing the energy spent on conflicts that advance fear.[9]

Accepting the Discomfort

We can pause to encourage us to consider a different response, but what will ensure that our response after our pause will be any different from what we would have done otherwise? How do we shift to a more productive response after the pause? To make sure the pause works for us, we need to first accept the underlying emotions, particularly the difficult emotions, that trigger us in the first place. Often our response to negative emotions is to reject and deny them, in hopes that they would go away; however, doing so only encourages them to come back even stronger. Instead, accepting and honoring these emotions allow them to fade.[10]

Radical acceptance

Tara Brach holds a PhD in clinical psychology and was trained in Buddhism at the Spirit Rock Insight Meditation Center in Woodacre, California. She offers dharma talks and guided meditations online for a wide audience. Her offerings draw heavily on both the Buddhist and the dharma traditions and are peppered with a significant dose of good humor. Core to these talks is acceptance, or what Brach calls *radical acceptance*. She argues that we can only minimize the suffering from our difficult emotions if we first surrender to them. In her book *Radical Acceptance*, she illustrates this key idea with the powerful allegory of the Tibetan yogi Milarepa, who continually faced demons while living in a cave:

> The great Tibetan yogi Milarepa spent many years living in isolation in a mountain cave. As part of his spiritual practice, he began

to see the contents of his mind as visible projections. His inner demons of lust, passion, and aversion would appear before him as gorgeous seductive women and terrifying wrathful monsters. In the face of these temptations and horrors, rather than being over-whelmed, Milarepa would sing out, "It is wonderful you came today, you should come again tomorrow . . . from time to time we should converse."

Through his years of intensive training, Milarepa learns that suffering only comes from being seduced by the demons or from trying to fight them. To discover freedom in their presence, he has to experience them directly and wakefully, as they are.

In one story, Milarepa's cave becomes filled with demons. Facing the most persistent, domineering demon in the crowd, Milarepa makes a brilliant move—he puts his head into the demon's mouth. In that moment of full surrender, all the demons vanish. All that remains is the brilliant light of pure awareness. As Pema Chodron puts it: "When the resistance is gone, the demons are gone."[11]

Acceptance, Brach argues, is the first step toward healing. In the language of the Buddha, acceptance is recognizing the pain without adding more suffering, noticing the first arrow without shooting the second arrow.

The rebound effect

Radical acceptance works to diffuse difficult emotions, partly because our brains are wired to engage with the things that we try to push away. If we try to reject or deny negative emotions, we will only start to experience them stronger. Daniel Wegner, who was a Harvard psychologist, describes this rebound effect as the *ironic processing theory*. He famously demonstrates the effect through his white bear experiments.

Wegner's research was inspired by Russian novelist Fyodor Dostoevsky. In his book *Winter Notes on Summer Impressions*, Dostoevsky poses a question to the reader: "Try to pose for yourself this task: not to think of a polar bear, and you will see that the cursed thing will come to mind every minute."[12] Intrigued, Wegner asked participants in his studies to not think about a white bear. If you haven't tried it before, you might want to consider trying it now. If so, put this book aside, set a timer for one minute, close your eyes, and tell yourself not to think about a white bear for one minute. See what happens.

As Wegner's research found, and as we would guess, most of you thought about white bears (some people tell us that they decided that they would not think about white bears by thinking about brown bears instead). Ironically, however, they often ended up comparing the brown bear to the white bear.[13]

Similarly, trying to reject or negate our emotions creates a rebound effect. It is rarely useful for someone to tell you to cheer up when you feel sad, depressed, or worried. As we try to bury the underlying emotions, our defense mechanisms kick in. We reject the attempts to avoid the emotions and start to engage with them. Eventually the emotions will rebound, often creating more damage. Instead, as Brach argues, the more we can accept our negative emotions, the more we can diffuse their impact on our thoughts and behaviors.

When paradoxes perplex, overwhelm, or frustrate us—the first thing to do is to honor the moment. Brach tells her listeners to say yes to each emotion that emerges. For example, while lying in my college dorm, I might have told myself, "Yes, I feel overwhelmed by how I will fit into this new environment. Yes, I feel scared that the old me won't really fit with the new me. Yes, I feel anxious about where this all leads to. Yes, I worry about what it will feel like when I return home." As Brach notes, this first step of acceptance provides us some comfort with the discomfort and gives us some space to find new ways to address our dilemmas.

Admitting our struggles

Sometimes it is hard to accept our own emotions but easier to do so with others. The other day, the two of us were in conversation with one another.

I (Wendy) was struggling with a strategic question. I had long been teaching an in-person executive education program. We canceled the program during the pandemic. Now I was debating whether or not to reopen the program in person, knowing that we still faced uncertainty in the pandemic.

Deeper issues surfaced around how to make the program feel physically safe but flexible amid the long tail of the pandemic; how to address racial equity, an important and challenging issue that had been brought forward in the program; and other concerns. Instead of grappling with the opportunities and possibilities of the program, I went straight for an either/or approach: Should we go forward with the in-person program or cancel it altogether?

Marianne gave me that look—the one that we reserve for when we catch ourselves going into either/or thinking. She then asked directly, "Wendy, what are you afraid of?" She knew that fear lay beneath my concerns. The opportunity to articulate my deeper emotions gave me some space to accept them rather than allow them to reflexively dictate my responses.

Broadening Our Perspective

Once we have paused and accepted the difficult emotions, how do we then shift to find comfort in, and to proactively engage with, emotions to allow us to move forward in navigating paradoxes? Positive psychology offers insights into how we can broaden our perspective when navigating paradoxes and tap into positive emotions, moving from narrow, either/or approaches to more open and expansive both/and thinking.

Broadening and building

Barbara Fredrickson, professor at the University of North Carolina at Chapel Hill, argues that tapping into positive emotions helps expand our mind, opening us to new ideas and alternatives. As we generate new possibilities, we then create emotions that are more positive. That is, over time, our positive emotions fuel a virtuous cycle. She called this positive feedback loop the *broaden and build theory*.[14]

Positive emotions such as joy, pride, contentment, and gratitude lead us to broaden our perspectives. The better we feel, the more we take in varying information and can explore integrative ideas. Doing so leads us to be more creative in our thinking and more generous in our behaviors. Importantly, Fredrickson shows that changing our thinking and behaviors has lasting impacts. When we become more generative and creative, we build new knowledge, expand our social circles and networks, develop resilience, and grow in other ways. We develop a tool kit of resources that we can draw on over time. These resources allow us to be healthier and more fulfilled, a state that ultimately sparks more positive emotions, and the virtuous cycle continues.

Extensive scientific research underlies Fredrickson's argument that positive emotions can actually undo the harm of negative emotions. These outcomes manifest themselves in our own physiology. Whereas negative emotions may lead to a flood of cortisol and a rush of blood flow, positive emotions can quickly return us to a more neutral state. Negative emotions raise our blood pressure, but positivity lowers it.

Shifting from negative to positive emotions

People have pointed to many actions we can take to trigger positive emotions when we are stuck in a negative emotional rut. A list of such actions would require volumes. For the purposes of this book, the recommended actions can be summarized as twofold: (1) become aware of when our negative emotions are taking control, and (2) know how to tap into our underlying positive emotions. Together, such purposeful practices work to flip our primary emotional drivers from the negative to the positive.

First, we must beware of letting our negative emotions take the wheel; we cannot change what we do not know needs changing. Gharbo teaches patients to stay attuned by considering their actions during the day. Ask yourself if you were involved in conflicts that triggered a negative emotional cycle. Did you spend too much energy on something that provided limited return? Did you move from worry to fear and down a rabbit hole of unproductive what-if scenarios? Gharbo then encourages patients to compare those efforts to their broader meaning and purpose. Zooming out to explore purpose allows us to shift to healthier responses. From a more physical viewpoint, he reminds us to consider our own heart rate. Heart rate fluctuations—particularly sharp changes—signal that our negative emotions are leading us toward counterproductive thoughts and actions.[15]

Second, find practices that help you flip the switch from detrimental emotions to healthy ones. Martin Seligman, a founding thought leader in positive psychology at the University of Pennsylvania, offers an extensive review of such efforts in his book *Flourish*.[16] For example, you might consider practices of gratitude, social connection, and physical exercise or some combination of these practices.

Gratitude journals have become quite popular, and science supports their value. Philosophers have long considered gratitude as a core moral expression. The Roman statesman Cicero considered it the mother of all virtues. More recently, psychologists find that gratitude leads to a broader perspective and more generative and integrative thinking. Seligman dives further into various exercises, such as identifying and building gratitude for our signature strengths or enjoying a "gratitude visit" by writing a letter of thanks or popping by someone's office or a friend's place to share your appreciation.

Efforts like the latter overlap with practices of social connection. Connecting with others reduces stress and expands our thinking. Yet in the Covid-19 era and in personal times of negativity, we can counterproductively isolate ourselves. Need an excuse to connect? Try a practice such as Seligman's kindness exercises: "Find one wholly unexpected kind thing to do tomorrow and just do it."

Likewise, consider the value of physical exercise, which releases endorphins in the brain and thereby reduces our experience of pain. Pick your favorite way to exercise, be it a brisk walk or a triathlon. Exercise triggers positive emotions and increases blood flow to our brain; the increased flow enhances brain function.

Benefits of emotional ambivalence

It may seem that the way to respond to our emotionally defensive reactions to paradox is to take a dose of positivity. Yet, as astute readers, you likely realized that just focusing on the positive is too simplistic a response. The full antidote is more complex—and more paradoxical. Healthy responses spring from engaging both negative and positive emotions. As we have often said in this book, navigating paradoxes is paradoxical. Two of the previously described practices already indicate that navigating paradoxes involves contradictory emotions. *Accepting discomfort* requires you to tap into and own your negative emotions, while *a broader perspective* invites you to explore and expand your positive ones.

Naomi Rothman, professor at Lehigh University, embraces a paradoxical approach to emotions. Through her research, she finds that connecting with positive and negative emotions simultaneously can be tremendously beneficial. She describes this experience as *emotional ambivalence*. Ambivalence does not indicate uncertainty about our emotions but rather an acceptance of our multiple, conflicting emotions. Like being ambidextrous—equally skilled with both hands— being emotionally ambivalent means we feel both a sense of negativity and a sense of positivity at once. We might not realize it, but we often feel this way.

For example, attending a family wedding can evoke both a deep sense of joy for the new couple and a deep sense of loss for what the couple might be leaving behind from their single days, or an awareness of the people who are not with us on that day. Similarly, we might feel overwhelming grief at a funeral for losing a person we loved while also feeling sparks of joy for our beautiful, happy memories of the deceased. We have a word that we use for these moments of emotional ambivalence—*bittersweet*.

Rothman notes that we don't like to think of ourselves—or our leaders—as ambivalent. We prefer that they convey clarity, specificity, and consistency not only in their thinking, but also in their emotions. Yet her research shows that emotional ambivalence might actually be a key to better interactions and more productive leadership. Engaging the negative along with the positive may be healthier and more realistic. In one study, Rothman and Gregory Northcraft, professor at University of Illinois at Urbana-Champaign, explored how emotional ambivalence affects the outcomes of a negotiation. Negotiations require us to take competing demands and try to work out a cooperative deal. In a negotiation, each of us wants to get as much as we can from the situation—a competitive stance—yet we also want to reach an agreement, which requires a cooperative stance.

Scholars point to the importance of adopting an integrative approach that allows for both parties to learn more about what the other needs and to expand the potential solution set before taking a more distributive approach that divides the resources among the parties. Intuition might suggest that we would be more willing to engage in integrative thinking with people showing positive emotions. If people are pleasant, engaging, and happy, we might feel more welcoming and willing to cooperate. Instead, as Rothman and Northcraft find, expressing emotional ambivalence triggers negotiations that are more integrative. It turns out that if one party demonstrates emotional ambivalence, the other party feels as if they can have more influence in the negotiation and will be more involved in problem solving that promotes more discovery and development of integrative possibilities. The study suggests that engaging our complex emotions simultaneously may be more powerful than we think.[17]

Back to School

Ambivalent. That's how I (Wendy) felt my first night at college. As I sat in my dorm, my fears started to get the better of me. I was exhausted and alone. How would I navigate this place? When would someone figure out that I didn't belong? The uncertainty of how to manage my past with my future, to both honor who I was and explore who I could be, all flooded in. I was brooding and becoming more fearful by the minute.

Then I heard a knock on my door. My five other suite mates were planning to head out for dinner at Yorkside Pizza, the family-run, classic Greek restaurant feeding hungry Yale students since 1969. Nervous and excited, I jumped up and joined them. As we got to know each other, I started to see myself and my suite mates more fully. The six of us had such different backgrounds. One of us was a Korean American who grew up in Chicago, another was Chicana and grew up in Los Angeles, another was an Irish American raised in Boston, another an Indian American from New Jersey, and the final one was a Jew straight from Texas. No one reflected my image of the typical Yale student hailing from a super-wealthy New England prep school. I was not alone. In fact, we all were working through questions of how to fit in at the university.

Sitting and eating pizza with my suite mates was just what I needed. It offered me an external pause to stop my negative thinking. It provided me a sense of connection to others. It gave me a chance to laugh and bond with people and to trigger my positive emotions.

I can't say that all my Yale experiences reflected such smooth emotional shifts that allowed me to feel comfortable with my discomfort, but I can say that we ate a lot of pizza my freshman year.

 **CHAPTER TAKEAWAYS**

- **Underlying paradoxes trigger discomfort—fear, anxiety, and defensiveness.** Acting on those emotions can lead to narrow, more limiting either/or thinking. To enable both/and thinking, we need to address these negative emotions, while also sparking their positive counterparts by using three tools:

  - *Building in pauses:* By creating a space (taking a breath or a break to step briefly out of the situation) between our negative emotions and our reactions, we can honor the emotions without triggering a more immediate and often counterproductive reaction to paradox.

  - *Accepting the discomfort:* Trying to deny negative emotions can cause a rebound effect, a strengthening of the negative emotions. We can minimize the impact of our negative emotions by accepting them and submitting to them rather than trying to deny or bury them.

- *Broadening our perspectives:* Reaching for positive emotions, such as the energy, wonder, and excitement of uncertainty, leads to expanded thinking, which spurs us to reach for further positive emotions. This feedback loop invites us to adopt a more open, both/and approach to paradoxical tensions.

- **Navigating paradoxes is paradoxical—we need to engage with both negative and positive emotions (emotional ambivalence) to effectively respond to competing demands.**

7

Enabling Dynamics That Unleash Tensions

Changes That Avoid the Ruts

Today's successful business leaders will be those who are most
flexible of mind. An ability to embrace new ideas, routinely
challenge old ones, and live with paradox will be the effective
leader's premier trait. Further, the challenge is for a lifetime.
New truths will not emerge easily. Leaders have to guide the
ship while simultaneously putting everything up for grabs,
which is itself a fundamental paradox.

—Tom Peters

Terri Kelly faced competing demands when she became the fourth CEO of
W. L. Gore & Associates (Gore) in 2005. A Gore family member had led the
company for forty-two of its forty-seven years. The leaders of the organization built up an impressive legacy based on treasured cultural values
of innovation and independence, fueling significant growth and expansion.
Yet as Kelly took over as CEO, the company's success challenged the very

culture that had created it. Could Kelly maintain this cultural heritage while still shepherding the company into a more global enterprise?

Bill Gore founded the chemical product development company in 1958 to build the kind of place where he wanted to work. An inspired innovator, he believed in the power of self-reliance, experimentation, and personal connections. Family folklore tells of his backwoods camping trips. Before a trip, he spent weeks methodically packing only the necessary supplies to ensure his survival once on the tundra alone for weeks. Another metaphor for his values was the iconic swimming pool on the Gore family ranch in Wilmington, Delaware. Gore designed the pool himself. He built it with a small crew of family and friends, rebuilt it when the first attempt leaked, and then used the beautiful result as a beacon for community gatherings. The pool reflected his own engineering prowess and his love of bringing people together. This self-reliant and entrepreneurial personality clashed with the hierarchical and bureaucratic culture in his first position. Gore left that job and, along with his wife Vieve, founded his own company.

An avid reader of social science, Bill Gore relied on two scholars to help develop a more engaging company culture in his own organization. Abraham Maslow's book *Toward a Psychology of Being* inspired Gore to create a culture where humans could reach toward self-actualization, and Douglas McGregor's *Human Side of Enterprise* helped him identify managerial practices that would allow his employees to do so.[1] As Gore once said, "I dreamed of an enterprise with great opportunity for all who would join in it, of a virile organization that would foster self-fulfillment and which would multiply the capabilities of the individuals comprising it beyond their mere sum."[2]

To implement this dream, Gore encouraged employees to identify projects on their own, to make a case for how these projects could advance the company strategy, and then to enroll other employees to join the project. He minimized bureaucracy, removing formal roles and titles, instead calling all employees "associates" and ensuring that employees had "sponsors" to help them grow, rather than bosses to control them. He structured the organization on the "power of small teams," encouraging people to innovate in groups of five people or fewer. He capped the size of each physical facility at two hundred to make it possible for every employee at a location to know one another. These structural innovations paid off when, in 1963, Gore's son, Robert, finished a PhD in chemical engineering, joined the company, and eventually found and patented the firm's main compound, Gore-Tex. Small teams went into action, identifying all kinds of new applications and markets for this material, including rugged outdoor jackets, dental floss, aortic grafts, military apparel, and even guitar strings.

By the time Kelly took the lead in 2005, the company had grown to more than $3 billion in revenues, with ten thousand employees in forty-five sites around the globe. The firm had spent years on the World's Great Places to Work lists.[3]

Having been in the company for twenty-two years, Kelly deeply valued the Gore culture and understood the power of small teams. Yet she also started to see cracks in this cultural armor. Small teams sparked engagement and generated new ideas, but they also created problems as the company tried to build an industrywide strategy to compete in a global marketplace. Gore employees often engaged the same market from varied approaches and developed innovations that pulled the company in a wide range of directions, creating confusion in the marketplace. Each local team also often established its own systems for communication, IT, and HR, causing tremendous redundancy and ineffective integration.

By 2008, the organization needed even more discipline and efficiency at the enterprise level to weather the global economic downturn. As Kelly told us, "It used to just happen organically as groups would just gather and something innovative would come out, and they would take it and drive it through, and voilà . . . But when you try to manage multibillion-dollar businesses, there is a lot more discipline and decision-making around investment and global coordination."[4]

Kelly felt torn. The company's growth created new challenges that needed a strong, integrated, enterprise-wide strategy to allow Gore to play in the global market. Yet the idea of introducing central controls felt like an assault to the empowered and flexible identity that served as the company's cornerstone. As only the second CEO from outside the Gore family, she grappled with how to honor Bill Gore's legacy while growing a global company.

Kelly saw the paradoxes underlying her dilemmas. She identified opposing yet interwoven forces between centralization and decentralization, control and flexibility, small teams and large organizations. These tensions fall into the category of *organizing paradoxes*, which reveal conflicts in how we structure our lives and organizations. We see other examples of organizing paradoxes in firms we have worked with—pulls between autonomy and independence, emergence and planning, control and flexibility. As we move into an era of greater artificial intelligence and machine learning, companies are now increasingly navigating paradoxes of human and machine, or technology-centric cultures and people-centered ones. And in our personal lives, we see organizing paradoxes between being deliberate and being spontaneous, or between more structure or more adaptation.

Recognizing these paradoxes is a good start. Kelly told us, "What I've learned over time is that I don't hide these from the organization—all these tensions—because we all constantly need to manage them."[5] Still, she felt the conflict among these paradoxes, with advocates holding strong and opposing positions.

Building In Dynamism

Kelly knew that W. L. Gore & Associates could be sliding down a rabbit hole. Its entrepreneurial culture led to tremendous success, yet this success motivated the company to double down on this culture that, as times changed, became more of a noose than an enabler. It was headed toward a vicious cycle.

To avoid falling into rabbit holes in the first place or to help us emerge quickly, we need tools that enable dynamism (figure 7-1). Dynamism involves actions that spur learning, enable adaptation, and encourage ongoing shifts between competing demands. Not only can such dynamic actions prevent us from getting stuck in ruts, they also help us take advantage of creative tensions. By constantly reconsidering the nature of alternative sides and the relationship between them, we can unleash the creativity in paradoxes—finding new mules or more effectively walking our tightropes.

FIGURE 7-1

The paradox system: dynamics

Creating **boundaries** to
contain tensions

- Linking to a higher purpose
- Separating and connecting
- Building guardrails to avoid going too far

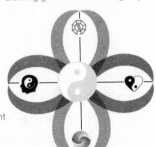

Shifting to both/and
assumptions

- Accepting knowledge as
  containing multiple truths
- Framing resources as abundant
- Problem solving as coping

Finding **comfort** in
the discomfort

- Building in a pause
- Accepting the discomfort
- Broadening our perspective

Enabling **dynamics** that
unleash tensions

- Experimenting using measured steps
- Preparing for serendipity
- Learning to unlearn

Being dynamic does not mean being indecisive. People can make clear decisions when navigating paradoxes; however, being dynamic ensures that they are open to new information, can tolerate ambiguity, and are willing to rethink decisions with new information. In particular, we identify three core tools for enabling dynamism: experimenting using measured steps, preparing for serendipity, and learning to unlearn.

To illustrate dynamism in practice, consider the organizational example of Toyota.[6] Emi Osono, Norihiko Shimizu, and Hirotaka Takeuchi find that engaging paradoxes is the key to fostering the company's ongoing creativity and success. In their book, *Extreme Toyota*, they identify six paradoxes that inform the company's strategy and drive its success:

- Move gradually while taking big leaps

- Cultivate frugality while spending huge sums of money

- Operate both efficiently and redundantly

- Cultivate both stability and a paranoid mindset

- Respect bureaucratic hierarchy while also encouraging dissent

- Maintain both simplified and complex communication[7]

These paradoxes are embedded in the company. Toyota's guiding principles help them to stay dynamic as the employees navigate competing demands. For example, consider two of the firm's guiding principles. First is *jidoka*, meaning automation with a human touch. The company website explains that "craftsmanship is achieved by learning the basic principles of manufacturing through manual work, then applying them on the factory floor to steadily make improvements. This cycle of improvement in both human skills and technologies . . . helps to reinforce both our manufacturing competitiveness and human resource development."[8] A second principle is just-in-time (JIT) manufacturing. To reduce waste, each manufacturing plant is challenged to have all the inventory ready for what it needs to build cars, and all cars produced to meet customer demand—but no extra inventory or production. Together, jidoka and JIT allow the employees to engage in experimentation and change that enable everyone at Toyota to address their most pressing paradoxes. These guiding principles are reinforced by a system of continuous learning and improvement called the Toyota Production System. People work in small self-managed teams to minimize overall leadership, to empower more local decision making, and to encourage everyone to experiment and improve processes and outcomes. Together these principles and their production system allow them to navigate paradoxes in dynamic ways that fuel the company's virtuous cycles.

Experimenting Using Measured Steps

The more that we invest in something, the more we become committed to it. As we introduced in chapter 2, psychologists call this almost pathological behavior *escalating commitment.*[9]

Even when a behavior, habit, or culture no longer serves our purposes, and even if we know we need to change, we still hold on, afraid to let go of the known and to move into new and uncertain possibilities. Measured experimentation allows us to dislodge ourselves from these commitments.

When confronting our dilemmas, experimentation allows us to conduct purposeful tests, putting new ideas into action and then evaluating what happens. We do not just think about options in our minds, but actually implement them in small ways, collect data to see the impact of these actions, and then consider whether to continue down a particular path or shift to a new one. Doing so keeps us on our toes.

Rapid prototyping

To allow you to shift tactics often, experiments should be low-cost, frequent, and rapid. David Kelley, CEO of the award-winning Palo Alto, California, design firm IDEO, built a process to encourage this kind of experimentation. Designers create prototypes, sample models of their designs, to learn what works and what doesn't work and then improve the design. Kelley realized, however, that most designers did not use prototypes in this way. Most designers would spend lots of time analyzing the problem and thinking through a solution up front. By the time they created the prototype, they invested so much effort in the process that they would be hesitant to change the design. The prototype no longer served as a tool for dynamic learning and change.

To counteract this common situation, Kelley encouraged IDEO designers to engage in "rapid prototyping." He expected them to build frequent, small models. The goal was not to get the design perfect with each model but to try out ideas, learn from and improve on them, and then experiment again. Importantly, these low-cost experiments ensured that the designers did not get stuck committing to ideas too early.[10]

As writers, we know the value of rapid prototyping. In writing this book, we reflected on our early years as solo researchers. We would spend hours agonizing over every word put on a page. It would take so long to finish a first draft that we hated to return to edit it. Ironically, our anxieties to produce a high-quality first draft would leave us unable even to get started, delaying the process even more. The more we spoke to other writers, the more we saw this pattern of anxiety and paralysis as the norm; however, what we came to appreciate was that it was in the editing that great writing happens. While writing helps us think, editing polishes these thoughts.

Great writers are not necessarily those people who write a good first draft, but rather those people who can write a bad first draft quickly and then edit it to develop their ideas. Authors with writer's block are encouraged to use free association just to get the words down on paper so that they can start editing and improving. As coauthors, we learned to work together toward rapid prototyping, sending drafts back and forth to one another, helping to clarify each other's thoughts along the way. One of us would write the messy first draft. The other would edit it. We would then volley the paper back and forth multiple times—constantly improving it along the way.

Toyota is built on a culture that encourages rapid prototyping. When the company leaders started to explore possibilities for shipping cars to the United States in 1957, they knew that the only way to learn about the US market was to try something out and learn from it. As a past Toyota president stressed, "Even if our cars don't quite measure up at the moment, we don't have time to just stand around and watch. We need a bridgehead. Initially we may experience some setbacks in entering the market, but all the time we'll be gaining precious experience and gradually improving our business performance."[11] Developing the Prius to enter the hybrid market offers an example of ongoing experimentation. Toyota leaders set an audacious goal: a car that makes the air cleaner. Engineers started to work on achieving this goal. Their first experiment produced an engine that wouldn't start. The next engine moved the car only a few hundred yards. Ongoing small experiments continually moved Toyota toward achieving its seemingly impossible goal.

Uncovering synergies

Experimentation helps us navigate paradoxes, in part, by exposing hidden synergies. When we first examine a presenting dilemma, we more easily see the contradictions between the opposing options. We can see how different decisions serve each side. Less obvious to us are the synergies: how one option can prove valuable for the opposing side. Experimentation helps make those synergies more salient.

Kerry Ann Rockquemore grew up valuing paradox and understanding how experimentation could enable synergies. The child of one white parent and one Black parent, she grew up straddling multiple cultures and realities. She knew that her ability to easily flow from one culture to the other was a source of strength.

This kind of easy movement between identities helped Rockquemore build a successful career. Rockquemore started her career as an academic exploring how biracial people navigated their differing backgrounds. As an academic, she realized how few formal opportunities exist to mentor and support faculty. Successful faculty often benefit from informal mentorship. The most nuanced and personal—and often the most important—advising happens with drinks at the end of the day, on a golf course or squash court, or over dinner at someone's home. The problem is that this kind of informal mentoring often introduced biases into the system. People often connect more easily with others who are similar to them. With fewer underrepresented minorities among senior faculty, there were fewer opportunities for informal mentorship for junior faculty. Junior faculty needed more mentoring and support, particularly the underrepresented minorities.

Comfortable with crossing boundaries and trying new things, Rockquemore engaged in her own experimentation. She launched an entrepreneurial business as a side hustle. She created an online community providing mentoring, advising, and support to faculty. Filling an important need in the marketplace, this side hustle soon grew to a full-scale company—the National Center for Faculty Development and Diversity (NCFDD).

Rockquemore built paradoxes into the core strategy of NCFDD. Most ed-tech companies like NCFDD focused more on the "tech" than the "ed"—hiring more engineers and entrepreneurs than academics. As Rockquemore told us, "Most other companies see faculty as an obstacle to move around . . . rather than as essential partners in advancing the business."[12] Rockquemore knew if she was building a product for faculty members, they needed to inform the process from the beginning. She recognized that the success of her venture would depend on the input and ideas of both educators and entrepreneurs.

Trying to integrate the approaches of these different groups, however, created challenges. As Rockquemore noted, "Academics take a year to study a problem and experiment in order to be thoughtful and intentional about making a decision. Entrepreneurs fail as fast as possible to shift and pivot."[13] Academics and entrepreneurs also had different priorities. The academics wanted a useful and accessible product, creating the greatest content that could be available to the broadest range of faculty. The entrepreneurs came from a more commercial background and took a more pragmatic and market perspective. They asked, what could they sell at the highest revenue for the lowest cost? These differences created ongoing conflicts.

One dilemma was particularly acute—grad students. If NCFDD's goals were to support faculty and to address inequities in academia, the company would be more effective if it started early by working with graduate students. Doing so would have a high "return on mission." But the entrepreneurs saw this option as killing their return on investment. Grad students have notoriously limited resources, and universities don't invest in them the same way they would their faculty.

Rockquemore and her team decided to conduct an experiment, creating their key program—a twelve-week intensive boot camp where people learn new skills to manage time and to improve their productivity—for grad students. The participants attend these programs in small groups of four, facilitated by a coach to help them. Typically, universities pay for their faculty to join. As predicted, few universities sent their grad students. As the cost was too high for these students to pay for themselves, NCFDD decided to significantly lower the cost to accommodate the grad students. But doing so meant that the company would have to reduce its own costs. One of the biggest costs was paying the dedicated coaches to facilitate each group. The coaches added tremendous value, but in light of its current budget, NCFDD experimented with forgoing the coaches and allowing the groups to self-organize.

The experiment proved tremendously successful. The participants valued the significant content and support, even without the facilitators. Importantly, this experiment helped expand the rest of the company's business. The leaders recognized that they could continue to offer this lower-cost option to other faculty who could not afford the full program. Their experiment allowed the company not only to advance its mission but also to ultimately develop a new opportunity to increase profits.

Leaving the nest

As I (Wendy) was writing this section, a longtime friend called and shared a dilemma. The insights about experimentation to navigate paradoxes proved valuable in her personal life. My friend and her husband lived as expats in China for years, raising their three children there. In 2020, at the start of the pandemic, they moved back to the United States to be closer to the grandparents. Their oldest daughter was in eighth grade and about to enter high school. As they looked around their community, they struggled to find a high school where their "third-culture" kid, who had roots and familiarity with both US and Chinese cultures, fit in and felt challenged. On a whim, they applied to several boarding schools. When we spoke, they had just heard the good news. Several boarding schools accepted their daughter. Now they had to decide whether to send her.

The dilemma raised tensions and emotions. The parents and the daughter all felt excited about the boarding schools' opportunities. On the other hand, they feared the pain of living apart from one another, breaking up their tight-knit family unit before they were ready. Their daughter was a real leader in the family. How would the other two kids react when she was gone? No one in either of their extended families had ever gone to boarding school; it was just not what their families did, and the decision left them feeling ill at ease. Listening to their dilemma, I could spot the underlying paradoxes between holding tight and letting go, between doing what they thought was best for one family member and doing what they thought was best for the whole family system.

I was in the middle of writing this chapter when we spoke. "What if," I asked, "you thought of the boarding school decision as an experiment?" The truth is, while they could assume what impact the boarding school decision might have on their daughter, on them, and on the rest of their family, they did not really know until they tried it. What if they tried out boarding school for six months, with the understanding that, in six months, they would reevaluate? Perhaps the loss would be too much for everyone and they would decide that she needed to come home. Or perhaps the move, while a loss, might create new possibilities for everyone in the family—opportunities that they might not even have anticipated. This reframing—thinking of the decision as an experiment—helped my friends move away from being stuck in an either/or tradeoff and live in a more dynamic approach to both advancing their daughter's education while still ensuring the closeness of their family.

Preparing for Serendipity

New possibilities sometimes come to us when we least expect them. The challenge is to notice these ideas and be open to engaging with them—that is, to be open to serendipity. We define serendipity as planned luck—finding something valuable when we are not looking for it. While we may not be actively looking, we can, however, put ourselves in a position to surface new possibilities and be aware of them when they do arrive. As individuals and as leaders, we can create the conditions for serendipity; this approach allows us to engage in novelty and will prevent us from getting stuck in a rut.

Classic examples of serendipity are Post-it notes from 3M, Velcro, penicillin, and even Columbus's journey to the Americas. In each case, an inventor, a scientist, or an explorer focused on solving one problem, when an accident introduced a solution to something else. Columbus was on a mission to find a new trade route to China. Instead, he reached the Americas. Sir Alexander Fleming was conducting research on influenza when he discovered penicillin to treat infections.

It was also serendipity that led Robert Gore to identify the polymer that became Gore-Tex. He had been experimenting with the chemical compound for months, looking for ways to make it more durable. Yet everything he did—from heating it to cooling it—only made it more brittle. One day, out of frustration, he yanked hard on the material, ultimately noticing that it stretched by more than 800 percent but did not break. That moment led him to ultimately develop Gore-Tex, the material that would serve as a foundation of so many products developed by the company. The question for Kelly as she took over as CEO was whether the company could create the opportunities for serendipity to help them similarly innovate on their culture.

I (Marianne) have experienced the power of serendipity many times in my life, possibly most clearly while on a Fulbright scholarship in London. I pushed myself out of my Cincinnati comfort zone to explore, to step away from my then associate dean responsibilities, and to extend my research and its impact. To make the most of that experience, I presented my work at numerous business schools in and around London and enjoyed incredibly positive experiences, such as my day at then Cass Business School (now Bayes Business School).

Yet some days were not so positive. My most intense trial was at the London Business School, where I faced a ninety-minute grilling of my work, its underlying assumptions, my methods, and so forth. I fought my emotions, particularly my defensiveness, to stay calm so that I could listen and learn from the faculty members' critique. In fact, rather than take the Tube home, I walked for an hour to metaphorically lick my wounds and process the insights.

It was only a year later, when I was at Cass Business School as the new dean, that I understood my planned luck. A senior faculty member who had been on the search committee for the dean's role joined me for tea (we were in London, after all). I told him how grateful I was for my Fulbright scholarship, which had enabled my day at Cass and the surprising turn of events that led me to later become dean. He smiled, telling me that it wasn't my visit to Cass that had helped me get the dean interview. Rather, he had been in the audience at London Business School, and afterward, he told his university president that anyone who could take such an interrogation with poise and a collaborative, learning approach could certainly handle being dean.

I share that story often with my students. You never know where your opportunities will come from. But you can put yourself purposefully in places that might make them happen, and you can adopt a mindset to be aware enough to recognize them. Plan so that you can explore purposefully and with an explorer's mindset.

Effectively navigating paradoxes depends on creating the conditions that can enable serendipity. That is, we prepare for luck to occur. Louis Pasteur captured the idea of serendipity in the often-paraphrased quote "Luck favors the prepared mind."

Importantly, preparing for serendipity itself is paradoxical. How do we prepare for luck to emerge? Colleagues Miguel Pina e Cunha, professor of management at Nova School of Business and Economics in Lisbon, Portugal, and Marco Berti, professor of management at University of Technology Sydney in Australia, warn against the dangers of becoming too mechanistic in preparing for luck. If we mandate serendipity in organizations or try to seek it out in our lives, we lose the essence and delight of novel discovery. Instead, they suggest a more organic approach, one that involves embracing uncertainty, encouraging doubt, and enabling improvisation.[14] Christian Busch, director of the Global Economy program at New York University's Center for Global Affairs, adds to this kind of preparation. Serendipity, he argues, depends on our mindsets. We can foster them to be open to luck as it presents itself to us.[15]

Teach our children well

Children's book author Stephen Cosgrove relied on serendipity to navigate paradoxes that brought him to new opportunities in his life. As he told us, "My whole life is a story of serendipity."[16] This comment is particularly apropos, as the first book he wrote was titled *Serendipity*. The process that led him to writing it was indeed one of planned luck. I (Wendy) had a particular fondness for Cosgrove's books, having had the word *serendipity* rattle around in my six-year-old head when I initially read his books in first grade. After I reached out to Cosgrove to learn his story, my fondness grew to admiration.

In 1974, Cosgrove, an executive at a midsize company, wandered into a bookstore looking for something to read to his three-year-old daughter. He wanted short stories yet ones that included good characters and offered positive messages with good values. He wanted high-quality ideas but inexpensive books so that he could buy a number of them. What he found was mostly pricey hardcover books with either a long story or a collection of oversimplified short stories with no morals. Facing a crossroads, he decided not to accept the options before him. Rather, he opted to experiment with writing his own children's books.

He had grown up reading great stories and had spent time in college as an actor and a storyteller. Yet he never imagined that these interests would lead him to a career. Instead, he assumed roles in business, first working for his father and then as the vice president of a leasing company. Standing in the bookstore, he saw the opportunity to try writing again. While still working in leasing, he would lug out his typewriter at 4 a.m. and write. He wrote four books, among them *Serendipity*. The books were lyrical and fun while also offering admirable characters and positive values. He had Robin James create the colorful illustrations.

As Cosgrove tried to publish the books, he faced a new dilemma. He wanted to publish them as softcover books and make them available to mass markets. But he struggled to find a publisher. After a year of trying to sell the stories, he finally received an offer from a publisher that would pay Cosgrove well for his books, as long as he stripped out the overly colorful illustrations, removed the value-laden lessons, and published the books in hardcover. That was not what Cosgrove wanted at all. Frustrated, he again looked internally. Turning now to his business background, he decided to self-publish. He became a one-man publishing company—Serendipity Press. The Serendipity series became a huge hit. Within three or four years, Cosgrove sold more than three million copies of the first twelve books. The series now includes more than seventy titles, even inspiring the creation of a Japanese anime series and another cartoon series. Now nearing the fiftieth anniversary of first launching the Serendipity books, Cosgrove is working on an English television series and is launching translations of the books in Chinese.[17]

Cosgrove was prepared to embrace new opportunities as they presented themselves. He sought out books, and when he couldn't find them, he drew on his own creative past to create them. He sought out a publisher, and when he couldn't find one, he drew on his own business acumen to become one. His own background created the preparation that allowed him to experiment with new opportunities that came his way; in doing so, he could navigate the ongoing paradoxes underlying his core dilemmas.

Motorcycles for the masses

A well-cited example of serendipity in business occurred with an automobile manufacturer—Honda. In fact, a tremendous debate has raged about the extent to which Honda relied on luck or on thoughtful preparation in its tremendously successful entry into the US motorcycle market in the 1960s.

In 1975, the Boston Consulting Group was commissioned by the British automotive industry to write a report about how the UK share of the US motorcycle market had declined from 49 percent to 9 percent.[18] The report tells of how in the 1950s, motorcycle use declined in the United States, with the primary demographic riding the bikes being a segment of leather-jacketed Hell's Angels and other rowdy groups. In 1960, Honda brilliantly entered the United States and created a new market by introducing its smaller, lighter-weight motorcycles that had successfully sold in Japan for urban dwellers who wanted to get around town more easily and run errands. At the same time, Honda was running a marketing campaign declaring, "You Meet the Nicest People on a Honda." The report suggests that it was Honda's brilliant low-cost differentiated strategy and creative marketing that drove company revenues from $500,000 in 1960 to $77 million in 1965, capturing 63 percent of the US market. Honda's success became a paragon of market analysis and strategic brilliance taught in business schools around the world.

Richard Pascale, professor at Stanford Business School, wondered if this account really told the full story. The narrative seemed too sanitized and too rationalized. Motivated by what he called "a quest for amusement," he invited six of the Honda executives who had led the 1960s US motorcycle launch to reconvene in 1982. Their post hoc recollection reflected a very different tale from the one described by Boston Consulting Group. In the executives' view, the success relied more on dumb luck, an overconfident leader, and a willingness—albeit after an initial reluctance—to follow unforeseen opportunities. That is, the executives planned for serendipity, and took advantage when it struck them.

Soichiro Honda, the company founder, was a bit of an inventive genius and a maverick. His ethos pervaded the organization, helping inform the decision by his partner Takeo Fujisawa to authorize $1 million to send three executives to the United States to figure out how to build a market for their motorcycles. With only minimal understanding of the US market, the executives knew nothing about selling to the main demographic of leather-jacket users. And on top of it, they barely spoke English. They rented a one-bedroom apartment in Los Angeles for all three of them and tried to sell bikes.

With their limited understanding of the US market, their initial strategy focused on selling their heavier motorcycles (350 cc—cubic centimeter—bikes). Unfortunately, these engines could not accommodate the kind of long trips and heavy usage needed for the current US market. The machines repeatedly leaked oil, and the clutch failed.

Within the first month, it looked as if Honda's US efforts were doomed. The executives used up their cash reserves shipping the motorcycles back to Japan so that their R&D teams could fix the problems. Strapped for cash, waiting for the retrofitted bikes, and unsure of their next move, they caught a lucky break. While in a holding pattern, the team drove the lighter-weight motorcycles (50 cc bikes) they had brought along with them from Japan to help them run errands around Los Angeles. An executive at Sears noticed the lightweight machines and saw the possibilities of selling these bikes to urban dwellers. The three Honda executives initially resisted the offer by Sears to sell these bikes; they didn't want to tarnish their reputation as a contender in the heavyweight market by selling their lightweight motorcycles. Not only did this new idea seem risky, but they also worried that selling through places like Sears or other sporting goods stores could diminish Honda's position with motorcycle dealers. Nevertheless, facing a precarious position as they awaited the remodeling of their heavier motorcycles, the executives finally relented—the first of many fortuitous shifts along their way to eventual success in the US motorcycle market.

Pascale framed his recounting as the "Honda effect," explaining that some observers overemphasized preparation and foresight when they tried to define Honda's success and neglected to take into account luck. Replacing the Boston Consulting Group's rationalized story of brilliant strategic planning, the Honda effect became a lightning rod for dynamic balancing. "Little did I realize," Pascale notes, "that this small foundation of an anecdote would find itself at the epicenter of tectonic debates between the 'design' and 'emergent' schools of strategy." Yet the debates raged, including those among management scholars who offered strong arguments for the alternative approaches.[19]

Pascale has gone on to elaborate on some of the tools that allow for sustained serendipity. These tools include valuing different options, honoring and creating opportunity for debate, and diminishing the power dynamics in a company to allow for input from across the ranks. Pascale and his colleagues describe these practices as *cultivating agility*. We agree that this dynamism is necessary for long-term success—the planning that allows for luck.

Our colleagues Miguel Pina e Cunha, Arménio Rego, Stewart Clegg, and Greg Lindsay studied the Honda story. They highlight the paradoxical nature of Pascale's approach. Serendipity not only helps manage paradoxes. Serendipity, these scholars argue, is itself paradoxical, integrating thoughtful preparation with lucky breaks, planning and emergence, stability of strategy and the willingness to make changes. The Honda executives cultivated what Cunha and colleagues refer to as the *potential for generative doubt*—they drew on their willingness to know that there might be opportunity amid the uncertainty. Their analysis of the Honda story reinforces a core message of this book—navigating paradoxes is paradoxical.

Learning to Unlearn

Earlier in the chapter, we mentioned the design firm IDEO. Its design practices, including its commitment to rapid prototyping, allow the company to be exceptionally dynamic, constantly learning and always open to change. Yet one thing that challenged the firm along the way was whether IDEO could change its fundamental processes when needed. We describe this effort as *learning to unlearn*—finding ways to let go of our old mental models to make space for new ones, allowing us more flexibility in navigating paradoxes.

In 1998, IDEO designer Dennis Boyle faced a new opportunity that stumped him. Boyle had successfully worked on a team with IDEO to help 3Com design their PalmPilot V project. The version of the early handheld computer was designed to be more durable, lightweight, and sleek than the previous PalmPilots. The design project took more than two years. It involved extensive research to study how people used their PalmPilots and to identify opportunities for improvement. The team had to work with manufacturers to create new lithium ion batteries and needed to develop new methods to replace the traditional plastic case with anodized aluminum. The product was now in production and expected to ship in February 1999.

In 1998, however, several leaders running the Palm V project left 3Com on amicable terms in search of greater autonomy and more direct financial gain. They launched a new company called Handspring and looked to make a product that would be half the price of the Palm V, with novel features and with an agreement to license the operating system from 3Com. They wanted to design this new product in half the time it took to launch the Palm V in order to be ready to sell the product during the 1999 December holiday season market. To achieve this goal, they would need a rapid design completed by April 1999. The Handspring team, having worked so successfully with Boyle on the Palm V, asked him if he would take on the project at IDEO.

The project created a dilemma for Boyle. Taking on the project required him to compromise IDEO's well-developed design. First, the design process involved extensive conversations as employees brainstormed across projects and used informal hallway connections to spark serendipity and deepen learning. For example, much of the learning for the Palm V project occurred when Boyle purchased PalmPilots for more than two hundred IDEO employees in Palo Alto, inviting them to provide informal feedback about how to improve the product. Given IDEO's ongoing relationship supporting the launch of the Palm V, the Handspring project would need to be conducted in secrecy, diminishing the possibility of learning from colleagues at IDEO that were not directly on the team. Second, the short time frame required the IDEO team to significantly condense the experimentation phase of its design process, minimizing the opportunities to rapidly prototype, get feedback, and improve.

Should Boyle take on the Handspring project knowing that it would challenge their core process? Doing so would require that they not only generate new ideas for a new product, but that they generate new ideas about their core process for product development. Ultimately Boyle accepted the project. He knew that if IDEO truly was a design firm committed to learning and design, then it had to commit to redesigning its own processes as well.

Double-loop learning

Harvard professor Chris Argyris, considered one of the founding thinkers of organizational development, describes the challenge that Boyle faced as one of *double-loop learning*. We practice single-loop learning regularly and nearly automatically. We make a decision, try it out, get feedback, and use the new knowledge to improve our future decisions. Double-loop learning challenges our embedded assumptions, mental models, and decision rules that led us to our decision in the first place. Argyris uses a thermostat as a metaphor. Imagine that a thermostat is set to sixty-seven degrees Fahrenheit. The thermostat monitors the temperature in the room, collects data, and then responds accordingly, adding colder air (or reducing heat) when the temperature is too high and adding warmer air (or reducing cold) when the temperature is too low. That process reflects single-loop learning. Double-loop learning involves questioning the assumption about why the thermostat is set to sixty-seven degrees.[20]

Our assumptions constantly inform our thinking and decision making, particularly our reactions when we are facing paradoxes. Consider some of the paradoxical tensions that we have introduced throughout this book and how we have challenged some of the assumptions that informed these tensions. In chapter 4, we introduced the tension that organizations face between focusing on mission or on the market. We described the work of Jeremy Hockenstein, who launched the social enterprise DDD. As Hockenstein started to develop ideas for DDD, he faced a profound assumption that organizations either focus on profit-oriented work or mission-oriented work and cannot address both. Throughout the book, we've raised work-life tensions. Our own assumptions about our identities and responsibilities as career-driven and/or as family-oriented people strongly inform how we navigate this tension.

In his recent book *Think Again*, author and scholar Adam Grant invites us to learn how to unlearn, to rethink that core assumptions that inform our thinking.[21] His research encourages us to build into our lives an acute awareness of our assumptions and the humility and practices to continually challenge them. Rather than think as politician, preacher, or prosecutor—defending our stance, ideology, or case, respectively— Grant calls for us to think as scientists, questioning our questions as well as our evidence, and seeking competing data and views. A dynamic approach to navigating competing demands means being willing to learn how to unlearn; it allows us more flexibility to oscillate on the tightrope. It might even mean being willing to ask ourselves if we are on the right tightrope.

At Gore, Terri Kelly needed to do what IDEO did. She needed to introduce new practices that would allow the organization to innovate its core processes. Dynamic and innovative when it came to product development, the company was stuck and rigid when it came to its culture and structure. Ironically, the organizational leaders had been applying McGregor's management theory with a dogma that McGregor himself discouraged— thinking like preachers, not scientists.

The challenge for Kelly was how she could help the firm live more on the tightrope. Kelly realized that she needed a more dynamic approach to having a small team culture within an integrated global structure. She started to slowly introduce enterprise-wide thinking. She created a company harmonization process, collecting data about what was working in each of the subunits and what was being suboptimized.

This effort required great transparency and communication to help the organization see how a global strategy for the whole enterprise would not diminish local power and creativity but rather could advance it. Kelly held a number of town halls. She listened closely to feedback. Through these sessions, her team adopted a guiding metaphor—breathing. To stay alive, we have to both breathe in and breathe out. Like breathing, Gore's survival depended on both thinking globally and acting locally—living in the dynamic ongoing dance between the two demands.

 CHAPTER TAKEAWAYS

- **Either/or thinking can lead us to get stuck in ruts.** In response, we need both/and thinking that enables us to learn, develop and change. This set of tools seeks to help us enable vital and ongoing dynamics:

  - *Experimenting with measured steps:* Taking small, frequent, and low-cost steps to test new ideas, learn from feedback, and move forward allows us to push ahead even while still experiencing uncertainty.

  - *Enabling serendipity:* Through planned luck, we can better open possibilities for innovation and change. Through purposeful exploration, we can put ourselves in positions to experience or create opportunities, and in the mindset to engage them.

  - *Learning to unlearn:* Paradoxes are dynamic, asking us to constantly rethink and change what we know. To do so, we must be prepared to let go of our existing certainties.

PART THREE

APPLICATIONS: BOTH/AND THINKING IN PRACTICE

How do you respond to dilemmas in your personal life? How do you address intractable conflicts that split groups of people into sharply defined factions? How can you lead an organization to integrate, value, and achieve competing demands? These are the kinds of situations ripe for both/and thinking. The paradox system offers a framework for such messy problems. But how do you put these tools into practice when deeply mired in a challenge?

This part explores the how—the processes of adopting both/and thinking. Each chapter focuses on these processes at a different level—individual, interpersonal, and institutional. We describe specific examples that bring the paradox system to life.

8

Individual Decisions

Should I Stay or Should I Go?

How wonderful that we have met with a paradox. Now we
have some hope of making progress.

—Niels Bohr

Imagine an issue that you are facing in your life. It could be something that
you are grappling with at work. It might be a problem you are struggling
with at home. Write it down.

When we lead workshops about both/and thinking, we often start with
this question. We first invite people to describe a challenge they are facing more generally. We then encourage them to frame a more particular
dilemma and, finally, more vitally, to recognize the underlying paradoxes.
It is at this point that, in the words of quantum physicist Niels Bohr, "we
have some hope of making progress."

In this chapter, we describe a process to identify and make progress on
underlying paradoxes in order to address some of the most challenging
problems that people face. To illustrate this process, we introduce a career
dilemma facing Ella Franke. Franke is a pseudonym. The details of her story
are an amalgamation of experiences from several people we have worked

with over the years. Given that we have seen a version of this career problem many times, we think it offers a good example for demonstrating how the paradox system can apply to personal decision making.

Define the Dilemma

Ella Franke finally felt confident and energized in her career, but getting to this point had been a bumpy road. She had worked in a variety of departments in a hospital system, including finance, strategy, and operations. Each role had its upsides but mostly lots of downsides because of stifling bureaucracy, stressful coworkers, and a toxic boss.

After ten years, she now worked in development in a role that she really loved and with people that energized her. She valued the opportunity to raise funds for the hospital's new initiatives. She enjoyed connecting with donors and helping them feel excited about the impact of their philanthropy. She also had great colleagues and supervisors. In this position, she truly felt like she could bring her whole self to work and was valued for who she was and how she contributed to the team. Successful in the work, Franke was recently promoted to lead a significant capital campaign for the hospital. Having developed strong relationships with her colleagues, she was able to handpick a dream team to work on the campaign. Together they identified aggressive goals for the next six months.

Good work rarely goes unnoticed. Two months into the campaign, as her dream team hit targets impressively ahead of schedule, she received a call from a headhunter. Would she consider a job as the head of development in another hospital—the largest system in the area?

Franke was honored but unsure. She had finally hit her stride. She loved her job. She thought she would never move. Yet she also knew that the best time to take a new job is when she was at the height of her current role. She recognized the downsides of staying on one S curve for too long, as we described in more depth in chapter 2. A mentor further reminded her that it was always worth exploring new opportunities, because you never

TABLE 8-1

Both/and thinking for Franke's dilemma: define the dilemma

FRANKE'S DILEMMA AND BOTH/AND THINKING

1. Define the dilemma	After years of struggling to find the right place in my career, I now really love my job, my role, and the people I work with. Yet I have the opportunity to move to a new and potentially better job and have to decide what to do.

know what you might learn in the process, so Franke applied for the new job. There was no harm, especially as she convinced herself that the larger hospital would never offer the position to someone with her limited experience. But the unthinkable happened: she received an offer. She now had a challenging decision to make.

Table 8-1 illustrates the first step in Franke's use of both/and thinking to address her challenges—defining the dilemma. She recognized the problem she was facing and noted the tug-of-war she felt between choosing alternative options. If you are following along with this process, you may want to take a moment to consider an issue you are facing in your own life and write down the dilemma on table 8-6 at the end of the chapter.

Surface the Underlying Paradox

Franke's dilemma is a good one to have—a problem of too many valuable options. Yet it is still a dilemma that requires a decision. Her challenge boils down to a set of alternative options, "Should I stay or should I go?" We have all faced this kind of question, whether focusing on a career decision, a physical move, or a relationship. The punk rock band, The Clash, captured this universal dilemma in their 1981 song.

As you thought about a dilemma you are currently experiencing, you too may have identified a question about a career move. Alternatively, you might have considered a work-life tension or perhaps something about conflicting priorities. You might instead be grappling with how to hire diverse talent at work, how to allocate a budget, or how to give feedback to subordinates.

Embedded in our dilemmas are underlying paradoxes framed as competing demands. Many of these dilemmas involve a scarcity of resources such as time, space, and money. The paradoxes emerge as we experience the tug-of-war between the options for allocating these resources. Work-life dilemmas, for example, involve competing demands for how to spend our time. Dilemmas about hiring often boil down to alternative options of how to spend our finances. Some of our dilemmas include tensions between opposing aspects of our identity, values, goals, and actions. The question about how to give feedback to a subordinate raises opposing identities. We may value our identity as being kind, friendly, caring (i.e., likable), but giving difficult feedback means that some people might not like us. Work-life dilemmas often involve issues of consistency of our identities, as we grapple with trying to be known as a good professional but also wanting to uphold other identities such as being a good parent, child, or community member. These competing demands start to surface the underlying paradoxes. As we move from either/or thinking to both/and thinking, we first need to identify these alternative options. Once we frame the alternatives, we can start to shift our assumptions and mindsets and value their paradoxical nature. We can recognize how these options are both in conflict with one another, but also can reinforce and define one another.

Table 8-2 identifies deeper paradoxes within Franke's dilemma. Underlying the decision about whether to stay with her current job or move to the new job are interdependent tensions between stability and change, loyalty to an existing team and opportunity to try something different, performing well and learning new things. If you are following along with your own dilemma and wrote down your challenge in table 8-6, now go back and consider the contradictory, yet interdependent tensions that inform this dilemma. Usually, paradoxes involve two alternatives such as those between self and other, today and tomorrow, stability and change. Your dilemma may involve multiple options, and if so, feel free to add a column and write down the additional options as well.

TABLE 8-2

Both/and thinking for Franke's dilemma: surface the underlying paradox

FRANKE'S DILEMMA AND BOTH/AND THINKING

2. Surface the underlying paradox	Option A: Remain in my current job	Option B: Move to the new job
	Stay	Go
	Stability	Change
	Loyalty	Opportunity
	Performing well	Learning new things

Reframe to a Both/And Question

After people define the dilemma and identify the competing demands, our common reaction is to treat these alternatives as mutually exclusive. We tend to think that we can choose only one of them. If our dilemmas involve tensions of resource allocation, we might be thinking of those resources as limited and zero-sum. If we spend the resources on one thing, we no longer have them to spend on something else. We may also be thinking about our identity, goals, and values as needing to be consistent. If we want to achieve a consistent identity, then we need our actions to align with that identity. This kind of reasoning leads us to either/or thinking.

How can we shift our assumptions to adopt more complex both/and thinking? To do so, we need to start thinking about our competing demands as paradoxes that are not only contradictory, but also interdependent. We need to start surfacing how these opposing forces define and inform one another. As we have argued throughout the book, the most basic and powerful tool to start shifting our assumptions and engaging paradoxes is to change the question we are asking. Reframing the question helps us rethink the nature of alternative options and start seeing their interdependence as well as their differences.

This power of changing the question cannot be understated as a means of shifting our assumptions and enabling both/and thinking. In fact, whenever we facilitate workshops, we usually pause at this point to make sure that the people participating heard this key idea. If their mind briefly wandered off to think about their to-do list or if they started to check texts or emails on their phone or computer, we invite them to bring their mind back to the workshop and we repeat this idea. *The most basic and powerful tool to start navigating paradoxes is to change the question.* In the quest for nirvana and meditative bliss, you can start by focusing on just one breath. Similarly, in the quest for both/and thinking, you can start by just changing one question.

When we face competing demands, instead of asking, "Should I choose A or B?" we can ask "How can I engage both A and B?"

Changing the question has become for us a bit of a professional reflex—or a professional hazard. Our colleagues all know by now that when we hear people debating alternative options, we will interject and pose a both/and question. Our kids know it, too. When my (Wendy's) twins were young, they knew that if I got involved in one of their conflicts, I would inevitably invite them to come up with a both/and alternative where everyone got what they needed. It was fairly rare that they would find an integrative solution to their conflict, but at the very least, their shared annoyance with my question would offer a moment of twin bonding.

Returning to Franke, she can change the question in her dilemma, shifting from asking "Do I stay with my current job or move to the new job" to instead ask "How could I both stay and move?" Table 8-3 shows this step. Of course, that new question feels like an impossible situation. We can't be in two places at once or take on two full-time jobs at once. Or can we?

Such questioning invites us to do a deeper dive into our dilemma to consider the underlying paradoxes further. For Franke, this might mean explor-

TABLE 8-3

Both/and thinking for Franke's dilemma: reframe to a both/and question

FRANKE'S DILEMMA AND BOTH/AND THINKING

3. Reframe to a both/ and question *How can I engage both competing demands?*	How can I both stay with my current job and accept the new job?

ing how aspects of her current job inform and expand her potential for the new job or how engaging with the new job could be valuable to her current job. As you will see below, delving deeper into the different elements of each competing demand will result in a more nuanced question. But for now, just asking a both/and question invites us into new thinking.

If you are following along, add your both/and question to your own worksheet (table 8-6). Even if the question feels impossible, it can open up new avenues of thinking for you.

Analyze the Data: Separating and Connecting

If we were adopting a traditional either/or approach, we would process the situation by separating and analyzing—pulling apart the alternative options and analyzing the pros and cons of each one. In contrast, in the paradox system, we highlight the value of creating structures to instead enable separating and connecting. This step in the process provides such structure by guiding purposeful analyses that help you to both separate and connect the opposing options.

People take different approaches to analyze their options. Some people might adopt a more rational approach by collecting detailed data about each alternative and making extensive pro-and-con lists. Others take a more relational approach, reaching out to mentors, advisers, and friends (or the internet!) to ask for advice and input. Still others go with more of an intuitive approach, trusting their gut to inform their decision. Usually, whether consciously or not, we all tend to adopt some mixture of these approaches. For example, we might have a gut instinct and then look for the data that confirm our instinct (also known as confirmatory bias).

Franke could easily separate and analyze each option. The new job excited her. The larger hospital system was about to expand significantly, and the leadership of this hospital wanted her to develop a fundraising strategy that would reach out to many new donors with great projects. The new position would pay her significantly more than what she earned at her current job, and it offered additional resources for her to succeed.

Yet she also had some significant reservations. First, she wasn't sure about the people. While they all seemed nice enough throughout the interview process, the larger hospital had a much more competitive culture. She had heard rumors from colleagues who worked there about some challenging dynamics among senior leaders. Having been in a previous toxic environment, she was concerned about this information.

She was also uncertain about the timing of a move. Franke had a lot of loyalty. It pained her to think about abandoning her current team members and their ambitious goals. The leaders at the new job, however, would want her to start as soon as possible to get the hospital moving quickly on its major campaign. For several days after being offered the job, Franke walked around in a fog of uncertainty. One minute she convinced herself to go; the next she convinced herself to stay. Her either/or thinking kept her feeling stuck between the two options.

Both/and thinking involves slightly shifting the evaluation process. Rather than separate options and analyze them, both/and thinking involves separating options and connecting them. We still pull apart the options and consider each one. Separating allows us to fully examine the upsides and downsides of our alternatives. But then, unlike a traditional approach, the data collecting continues when we search for points of connection.

One way to start looking for connections is what Harvard psychologist Ellen Langer described as "moving up a level" and "moving down a level."[1] Moving up a level means connecting the options to a larger, overarching vision. For Franke's "should I stay or should I go?" dilemma, moving up a level would involve defining her more universal values and higher purpose. What are her overarching goals in life, and how could this decision help progress those goals? Long-term aspirations widen our lens and can prove vital in helping us explore links between competing options. For instance, if Franke's vision was to have an impactful career and to make a positive and meaningful difference, she could find ways to see how both her current role and the new opportunity would inform that goal.

Moving down a level involves finding what is really at stake for each option. For example, Franke might ask, "How could completing my current campaign impact the new campaign?" Working with prospective donors is tricky. The same donors might contribute to more than one place. But out of loyalty, integrity, and professionalism, she could not go back to a donor whom she had approached for the current campaign while they were still in conversations with that hospital. Once they had solidified a gift, however, she might be able to approach them either for an additional gift to the new hospital or to put her in touch with others who might be potential donors. So finishing out the current campaign might be a benefit to the new organization.

She could also ask, "How could allowing myself to move into a new job create opportunities for my current team?" She worries about abandoning her team, given her sense of loyalty and commitment. Yet when a leader leaves a team, they open opportunities for others to assert leadership. In fact, great leaders cultivate leadership in others on their team so that they do not always have to be there. By moving on, Franke might see new leaders emerging within her team. Alternatively, she might ask, "How can the existing team inform my work on the new team?" She loves her current team. One option is that she brings some of the team members with her, creating more opportunities for them to grow and expand their careers. Table 8-4 captures how Franke could separate and connect the options in her dilemma.

TABLE 8-4

Both/and thinking for Franke's dilemma: analyze the data

FRANKE'S DILEMMA AND BOTH/AND THINKING

4. Analyze the data	**Option A: Stay pro/con**	**Option B: Go pro/con**
Separating: *How are the competing demands different from one another in terms of their goals, costs, and benefits?*	• Loyalty: finishing the project	• Opportunity: engaging new possibilities
	• Focus on people: sticking with the dream team	• Focus on role: moving to the dream job
	• Prioritize others	• Prioritize myself
Connecting: *What is an overarching vision that accommodates both? How are the competing demands reinforcing and synergistic?*	Overarching vision: having an impactful career Reinforcing synergies: • How could completing my current campaign impact the new campaign? • How could allowing myself to move forward create new opportunities for my existing team and its members? • How could my existing team inform the work on my new team?	

If you've ever studied negotiations, you might recognize these tactics as strategies that help us get to a win/win or an integrative decision. In their classic negotiation book, *Getting to Yes*, Roger Fisher and William Ury suggest that direct conflict often comes when we assert our specific positions.[2] As we confront our own dilemmas, we often create this kind of direct conflict when we first list our options, specifying and pitting them against each other. From this starting point, if each party in the negotiation (or each option in our own dilemmas) can dive deeper, sharing what they are actually interested in, we might find common ground. That is, separating the options to learn more about each one can enable more possibilities for connection.

Imagine you are trying to buy a house. Let's say the house is listed at $250,000. You think it is worth no more than $200,000. Perhaps you and the seller cannot close that $50,000 gap. You might think that you need to give up this possibility and look for another house. Or maybe you and the seller can compromise and agree to a price of $225,000. Fisher and Ury suggest that there is still another option that starts with discovering what you are really interested in. Imagine that the seller is interested in selling the house but does not want to have to manage any of the repairs that need to happen. What if you know a contractor (or you are a contractor!) who can easily make repairs? The seller might be willing to come down in price significantly if you agree to take on the repairs, and you've determined that the repairs won't cost you that much. Or imagine that you are eager to move into a house quickly. You might be willing to spend extra to have a closing date sooner than what the seller initially suggested.

As you go back to your own dilemma, consider what is unique about each alternative and how you can find connections between the opposing demands by moving up a level and identifying your overarching vision. Then move down a level and find reinforcing synergies. You can add this to table 8-6.

Consider the Outcome: Choosing

When we adopt traditional either/or thinking, our goal is to make a choice between alternative options. In contrast, for both/and thinking, we describe the goal as choosing. The difference involves how we understand the choice within a broader context. Making a choice feels final. Choosing feels like identifying a workable solution that moves us forward even as we might reevaluate and reconsider the options in the future. Choosing leaves us open to recognize that we are never solving the underlying paradoxes, but always ready to reengage with them. Choosing invites us to recognize the dynamic nature of paradoxes and draw on approaches that value this dynamism.

We defined two patterns of choosing in this book—mules and tightrope walkers. The easier solution for people to get their heads around is the mule. The mule, a hybrid between a horse and a donkey, illustrates a creative integration, offering an elegant (and practical) solution that accommodates competing demands simultaneously. Franke has some mule options. She can take the new job and bring some of her current team along with her—therefore having the chance to value the new challenges without worrying about the new people. She could also use the new job offer to negotiate with the current job, seeking to move into a more senior role and therefore enabling new challenges without leaving her current work environment.

She might also have some options that exemplify tightrope walking, small shifts between alternatives that lead to a consistently inconsistent pattern over time. Tightrope walkers move forward with an overall balance by constantly shifting their weight left to right. Rather than find a static balance, they are continuously balancing. We see the same thing when we are navigating a paradox—a constant shift between alternative options over time. Franke has some tightrope-walking options. For example, she could negotiate with the new job to delay her start date—an option enabling her to spend more time shoring up a transition plan for her current role and finishing the current campaign. She might also explore how she could work as a consultant to the old job until the hospital has trained a new leader. Table 8-5 captures these various options.

In the end, Franke decided to take the new job at the larger hospital, but she negotiated with the senior leaders in the new hospital to allow her to serve as an adviser to the old team for a transition period. Overall, this

TABLE 8-5

Both/and thinking for Franke's dilemma: consider the outcome

FRANKE'S DILEMMA AND BOTH/AND THINKING

5. Consider the outcome *Mules:* creative integration. What options might build synergy between both demands?	Mule options: • Take the new job and bring some of my current team along • Use the new job offer to negotiate with my current organization to move into a more senior role
Tightrope walkers: consistent inconsistency. What options might allow for micro-oscillations between options over time?	Tightrope-walking options: • Negotiate with the new job to delay my start date in order to spend more time to ensure succession planning for my current role • Figure out how I could work as a consultant with the new job for a period of time until they have trained a new leader

arrangement turned out well. Her new boss valued her loyalty to the old company and commitment to the existing capital campaign, seeing these attributes as assets to the large hospital as well. He also recognized that she would be more engaged with the new work if she could first tie up loose ends in the old job. He offered her the option of taking one day a week for the first four weeks to work with her current team. In doing so, Franke identified and trained her replacement, a rising star from the old team. But Franke also knew of another rising star on the same team, someone with outstanding capabilities but not ready for such a leadership role. Knowing this second rising star's skills, and recognizing that this person might resent having a former peer as a new boss, Franke hired her into the new team, ensuring some consistency of colleagues.

Going back to your own dilemma, consider potential mules and tightrope walkers—your own creative integrations and consistent inconsistencies. You can continue to fill out table 8-6 to lay out your ideas. As you do so, we offer a caution: most of us usually see other people's both/and opportunities more clearly than we see our own. When it comes to personal paradoxes, the defensive emotions described earlier kick in, and we can become paralyzed by the tensions. We have far less emotional investment when it comes to someone else's dilemma. One way that people can find some com-

TABLE 8-6

Both/and thinking for your own dilemma

YOUR OWN DILEMMA AND BOTH/AND THINKING

1. **Define the dilemma**	My core dilemma is . . .	
2. **Surface the underlying paradox**	**Option A:**	**Option B:**
3. **Reframe to a both/and question** *How can I engage both competing demands?*		
4. **Analyze the data** Separating: *How are the competing demands different from one another in terms of their goals, costs, and benefits?*	**Option A: Pro/con**	**Option B: Pro/con**
Connecting: *What is an overarching vision that accommodates both? How are the competing demands reinforcing and synergistic?*	Overarching vision: Reinforcing synergies:	
5. **Consider the outcome** • *Mules:* creative integration. What options might build synergy between both demands?	Mule options:	
• *Tightrope walkers:* consistent inconsistency. What options might allow for micro-oscillations between options over time?	Tightrope walker options:	

fort in their discomfort and move beyond their emotional defenses is by reaching out to others and asking for help to brainstorm their own dilemmas.

We invite you to try this out: If you get stuck in your own either/or thinking, invite a friend to consider your dilemma and offer some both/and possibilities. Now note your reactions. There is a good chance that your defensive brain will creep in and tell you all the reasons that your friend's ideas won't work. We encourage you to ask your defensive brain to take a little vacation and just listen to what your friend has to say. You might be surprised.

9

Interpersonal Relationships

Mending a Widening Divide

Difference must be not merely tolerated, but seen as a fund of
necessary polarities between which our creativity can spark like
a dialectic. Only then does the necessity for interdependency
become unthreatening. Only within that interdependency
of different strengths, acknowledged and equal, can the
power to seek new ways of being in the world generate . . .
Difference is that raw and powerful connection from
which our personal power is forged.

—Audre Lorde

Paradoxes can foster persistent interpersonal tensions—conflicts between
individuals or between groups of people. One person or group adopts one
perspective, and another person or group opposes it. I (Wendy) remember
once striking up a conversation with the person sitting next to me on a
long plane ride, as is typical for me. When she asked about my research,
I described the idea of exploring competing demands among leaders of

organizations. Senior teams often create fault lines, where differences of opinion can become etched into their ongoing dynamics. My flight neighbor gave a nod suggesting that she understood from personal experience. She had been the general manager of a circus. For the rest of our flight she shared harrowing tales of ongoing conflicts she and the rest of the managers had with the performers—the egotistical elephant trainer, the demanding acrobats, and others. The types of conflict she recounted in these stories are not new ones; organizations have long experienced tensions between administrators and creatives or between managers and employees. Yet even amid these persistent tensions, our world has experienced an uptick in interpersonal conflicts as people increasingly line up on opposite sides of issues. Political polarization has intensified, halting governmental action while also tearing apart families, friends, and even workplaces.[1]

Other scholars have written extensively about strategies to manage interpersonal conflicts.[2] We believe that paradox adds an important lens to deepen our understanding of these rifts and new approaches to mend them. Interpersonal conflicts often involve tensions where the poles are split across different parties. Individual experiences and group dynamics can easily turn up the volume on defensive emotions, exacerbating our fears, amplifying our anxieties, and catapulting us even faster into vicious cycles. The challenge is to surface and then navigate the underlying paradoxes, working together amid opposing views and heightened emotions.

In this chapter, we demonstrate how you can use the paradox system to address interpersonal conflict. To do so, we draw on a framework and process developed by our colleague Barry Johnson and his team at Polarity Partnerships. Johnson and his team have successfully brought together warring factions across varied settings, inviting them to recognize the paradoxes embedded in their tensions and to find points of synergy and connection. The work they do breaks down the challenges, recognizes deep emotions, and identifies novel solutions. We share this approach using a story of their success around a particularly poignant, timely, and challenging divide between law enforcement and citizens while also suggesting its applications to other, widely varying interpersonal conflicts.[3]

Ensuring Community Safety in Charleston

On Wednesday, June 17, 2015, a young white man entered the Mother Emanuel AME Church in Charleston, South Carolina, during a weekly Bible study. He sat down next to the pastor, Clementa Pinckney, and participated in the discussion. As the Bible study concluded around 9 p.m., the small group started to pray. It was then that Dylann Roof, age twenty-one, pulled a gun from his fanny pack, shouted racial epithets, and started shooting at the Bible study members. He loaded his gun five times and killed nine of the twelve people in the room. One woman and her granddaughter survived by playing dead under a table. Roof told one other woman that he spared her life so that she could be the bearer of the tale to others. He then turned the gun to his own head to kill himself but was out of ammunition. He fled.

That night, the Charleston chief of police, Greg Mullen, told the press that the tragic hate crime was "the worst night of my career."[4] This was not the first racially motivated crime in Charleston. In fact, the Mother Emanuel AME Church lay its foundations on racial crime and on mistrust between Black and white people in the community. In 1822, white community leaders suspected Denmark Vesey, a freed slave and one of the Black church cofounders, of planning a slave rebellion. To thwart the rebellion, white community leaders burned down the church and then hanged thirty-five church members and banished thirty-five other members from the state or country. More recently, only months before the shooting at Mother Emanuel, another racial incident stirred the community. A Black man was killed by a Charleston police office. Police officer Michael Slager stopped Walter Scott because of a broken brake light on his car. When Scott got out of the car, he fled from the police, and an altercation ensued. Slager shot his Taser at Scott. But as Scott continued to run away, Slager took out a gun, shooting eight bullets and fatally hitting Scott five times. Slager reported that Scott had tried to take possession of the Taser, prompting Slager to go for his gun. A bystander's video of the incident contradicted the report. In response to this event, Mother Emanuel's Pastor Pinckney actively advocated for the increase of body cameras on police officers to more accurately capture what happens in such incidents.

Ever since Chief Mullen joined the Charleston Police Force in 2006, he had been working hard to address the deep mistrust and divide between Black community members and the police. The tragedy in the Mother Emanuel Church intensified the importance of the work.

Law Enforcement and Citizens:
At Odds for a Similar Goal

The tension between law enforcement and citizens over community safety, with its underlying context of racial justice, is particularly timely and challenging. Indeed, we would invite you to pause here for a minute before you keep reading to consider your own perspective on this issue. Our guess is that, at least for our US-based readers, your own knowledge or background experiences probably mean that you have already taken a side on this issue.

If so, you would be in good company. This issue of policing in Black communities has become a lightning rod of political polarization in the United States. In the summer of 2020, police killings of Black men and women such as George Floyd and Breonna Taylor expanded the rift. Protests erupted, violence ensued, and the debate became a central feature of the 2020 US presidential election. One side called to defund the police, while its opposition called for increased law enforcement. One side rallied around the Black Lives Matter movement, while another declared that Blue Lives Matter. This persistent conflict raises deep emotions on all sides.

We chose this example because enabling community safety and ensuring underlying justice are critical to the fabric of our society, yet the issue poses a polarized and polarizing dilemma. Group conflicts start in local communities, yet they have been reverberating and reinforced by national and international movements. Chief Mullen certainly felt this conflict in South Carolina. Both/and thinking suggests that we can come to more creative, effective, and lasting solutions if we engage the opposing sides rather than choose between them. Chief Mullen worked with Polarity Partnerships consultants. Together they sought to address the underlying paradoxes they were experiencing in the Charleston community. Their approach was a process that Polarity Partnerships has applied to bring people together over questions of homelessness, racial and gender inequity, access to health care, and beyond.

Before you go further in the chapter, we invite you to pause and think about a group conflict that you are experiencing. The conflict could involve opposing perspectives around national politics. It could also be a more local tension that you experience within your organization, within a community group, or even within your own family. We invite you to try using this process for your own interpersonal conflicts.

Polarity Partnerships' Model for Analyzing Complex Paradoxes

Barry Johnson defines a polarity as an interdependent pair that (1) consists of two poles that (2) are interdependent and have ongoing challenges.[5] As he notes, polarities are similar to paradoxes. Used in the way that Johnson describes, we agree that we are addressing the same ideas—persistent contradictory, yet interdependent elements that lurk beneath our presenting dilemmas. We use the terms *paradox* and *polarity* interchangeably in this chapter to emphasize the link between the ideas that we introduce in this book and the work of Polarity Partnerships.

Johnson and his colleagues at Polarity Partnerships developed what they abbreviate as the SMALL model to analyze paradoxes in complex situations:

- Seeing the polarities

- Mapping the polarities

- Assessing the polarities

- Learning from the assessment

- Leveraging the polarities

TABLE 9-1

Polarity Partnerships' SMALL model

POLARITY PARTNERSHIPS' FIVE-STEP **SMALL** MODEL OF TRANSFORMATION

1. Seeing the polarities	• Identify opposing poles in neutral or positive language.
2. Mapping the polarities	• Define the greater purpose statement (overarching vision) and the values associated with each pole.
	• Identify the deeper fear and the specific fears associated with each pole.
	• Unpack the upsides and downsides of each pole.
3. Assessing the polarities	• Evaluate how the upsides and downsides of each pole emerge in the current system.
4. Learning from the assessment	• Reflect on the data to help reveal the paradoxical nature of tensions.

5. Leveraging the polarities	• Develop an action plan that includes consideration of these questions:
	  ○ What can we do to ensure the upsides of each pole?
	  ○ What can we do to reduce the downsides of each pole?

This process offers an exceptional approach to applying a paradox system, one that works particularly well for intergroup conflicts because it explicitly invites both sides to reflect on the upsides as well as the downsides of their position. The SMALL model involves taking small steps to unpack the polarities that both honor differences across groups and invite integration. Table 9-1 unpacks the details of each of these five steps of the SMALL process. In the following sections, we examine each step in detail, linking it to the tools in the paradox system.

The SMALL model applied

Margaret Seidler, an organizational development consultant trained in Polarity Partnerships' processes and a Charleston resident, helped guide Chief Mullen through the process. In 2010—five years before the shooting at the Mother Emmanuel Church—Seidler was working with neighborhood committees in Charleston to address increased crime. She was finding the initial process derailed by either/or thinking. The community members included people living in neighborhoods with single-family homes. These people blamed crime on the residents of the nearby multifamily apartment units and called on the police to more effectively patrol the area. Seidler recognized how the residents adopted an us/them split; the single-family residents blamed the problem on "them"—the multi-family apartment residents—and called for others—in this case, the police—to fix the problem rather than take accountability for their own role in the challenges. She even started to see herself falling into this either/or thinking trap.

Seidler realized that adopting a paradox lens could help shift gears for everyone involved. She thought about how to bring people with conflicting points of view into a conversation to explore underlying paradoxes. She invited leaders of both the single-family home community and the multifamily apartment community into conversation with one another. Holding a dinner, they collaboratively explored the tensions they all experienced and their shared desires to enable greater community safety.

Mullen attended that dinner. He recognized that the tensions Seidler addressed paralleled what he was seeing in his own work. At the end of the dinner, he asked Seidler if they could meet the next morning. Together they set out on a path to address tensions between the Charleston police force and the community.

Seeing the polarities

People need to first recognize paradoxes to effectively navigate them. As we've noted, paradoxes often lurk beneath the surface of our presenting challenges. The SMALL process starts with shifting assumptions to help people dive deeper.

Polarity Partnerships draws on the polarity map to help reveal the underlying paradoxes. As described in chapter 2, a polarity map depicts the upsides and downsides of opposing views, or poles. The first step involves examining the conflict to identify and label each pole. This step helps people to start shifting their assumptions and move away from either/or thinking that pits sides against one another to adopt both/and thinking that values both their opposition and integration.

Importantly, individuals filling out the polarity map can come up with the labels that work best for their situation. However, these labels should define the poles in neutral or positive terms. Language is important. If we are in favor of one approach, we often adopt a positive label for our side and a negative label for the other side. Consider, for example, the debate over abortion in the United States. Depending on your beliefs, you might use very different language to label opposing views. Using even subtly loaded language, particularly with someone from a conflicting stance, quickly raises defenses and limits discussion.

If the paradoxes underlying the dilemma are not obvious, Johnson often helps people discover them by first thinking about change. He invites people to describe their imagined future. Ideally, what would their community (work, organization, family, life, etc.) be like if the challenge were resolved? Then he asks people to describe their current reality. As he notes, we are often moving toward an imagined future that is the opposite of our current reality. Paradoxes are embedded in the differences between where we are coming from and where we are going to. For example, an organization may be moving away from excessive bureaucracy that seems to slow down processes and toward a more agile approach. Underlying this change are ongoing tensions between flexibility and control. This tactic of considering the current reality and imagined future is one way to surface paradoxes lurking beneath the presenting dilemma.

Seidler sat down with Mullen the morning after the community leaders' dinner. Mullen had been living through the tensions in Charleston for quite some time and knew all too well the underlying paradoxes erupting in the quest for community safety. Together with Seidler, Mullen labeled the main poles of the conflict "enforcement" and "community support" (figure 9-1).

If you are working through conflicts within your own group or organization, take a moment to consider the whole system. You'll want to identify the opposing poles of the paradoxes that underlie the challenges and to find neutral or positive labels for each pole. You can use the blank polarity map toward the end of the chapter (figure 9-4) or find one at the Polarity Partnerships website.

FIGURE 9-1

Polarity map for Charleston community safety: seeing the polarities

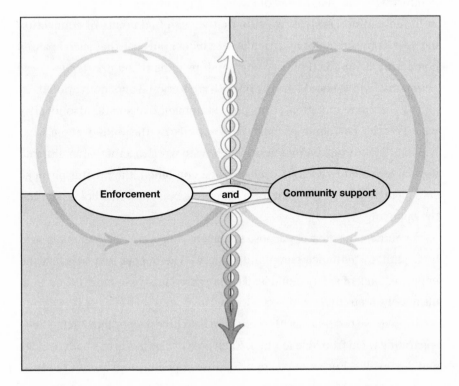

Mapping the polarities

In the paradox system, we stress the need to create structures (boundaries) that separate and connect—separating the poles to show the value of each while also seeking points of connection and synergies between the poles. When using the SMALL process, the step of mapping the polarities encourages us to separate and connect poles. In interpersonal or intergroup conflicts, this may be one of the hardest steps for people, because doing so requires us to really listen to and appreciate a truth potentially opposite from our own. To listen carefully, we need to manage our emotions. We need to recognize and work through the inherent defensiveness when we face conflicting perspectives. As we've noted in this book, we need to feel comfort with the discomfort of navigating paradoxes.

In the paradox system, we note that we can find points of connection between opposing poles by articulating a higher purpose that encompasses competing demands. Polarity Partnerships calls this a *greater purpose statement*, which should ideally be both aspirational and motivational. To clarify the value of a greater purpose statement, we should also identify what Polarity Partnerships calls the *deeper fear*—the anxiety about what happens if the group cannot figure out how to work together—the ultimate downside fueled by vicious cycles. When combined, the greater purpose statement and the deeper fear form a unifying boundary that holds together the opposing sides.

For Mullen, the greater purpose statement sharpened the goal of his strategic plan, to "enhance community safety." The deeper fear was just the opposite. Lack of safety could lead to increased mistrust, more crime, and, ultimately, anarchy.

Given these boundaries, the next step is to dive deeper into each pole—separating them from one another. Each pole of a paradox has both upsides and downsides. For example, consider the opposing approaches to creating an organizational strategy—a planned approach and an emergent approach. The upside of a planned approach is that it enables more certainty and encourages people to get on board to implement the strategy together. But on the downside, it is inflexible and unresponsive to change. In contrast, the upside of an emergent approach is its flexibility and responsiveness, but on the downside, strategic implementation is harder to coordinate. Getting a full picture of each pole involves probing both the upsides and the downsides.

When facing an interpersonal conflict, an important aspect of unpacking the opposing poles is engaging with a broad group of stakeholders. When people supporting each pole honestly share with, and listen to, one another, we can all obtain a more detailed understanding of the conflict. Open dialogue is a powerful tool to bring people together across contrasting perspectives. Yet such openness is another potentially challenging part of the process, particularly in an era of deep divides. Across the world today, people with different opinions and perspectives have taken to shouting their ideas from the safety of a social media soapbox rather than engaging in respectful listening. Effectively navigating paradoxes across opposing groups depends on our ability to be in conversation with one another.

To examine each pole, Mullen and Seidler invited thirty-five employees of the police force into a discussion. These employees included both officers and civilians of different ages. To be successful, Mullen and Seidler knew they needed to introduce the idea of polarity thinking to the police employees before they reached out to members of the broader community.

Seidler led the thirty-five employees through their first session. These participants quickly filled out the polarity map. They noted the upsides and downsides associated with enforcement and with community support (figure 9-2). However, as we have emphasized several times in this book, paradoxes are knotted. Rarely do we experience one single paradox; rather, we experience multiple paradoxes informing one another. While Mullen and Seidler initially identified poles of enforcement and community support, by diving more deeply into the challenges of community safety, the police employees in the workshop quickly uncovered other knotted paradoxes. For example, they identified the paradox of change, noting the conflict between wanting to honor traditional practices of the police force while recognizing the need for new directions. With Seidler's encouragement, the group expanded their focus by surfacing five different paradoxes of community safety. They filled out five polarity maps within a couple of hours. By drawing out the complexity and nuances beyond the focus of each opposing pole, the group also helped loosen the boundaries—and grip—of those poles.

If you are following along with the paradoxes from your own interpersonal conflict, take a moment to fill out the greater purpose statement, or your overarching vision, as well as your deeper fear in figure 9-4. Now consider all four boxes in detail. What are the upsides of each pole, and what are the downsides of focusing too singularly on that pole? As you ask

FIGURE 9-2

Polarity map for Charleston community safety: greater purpose, deeper fears, upsides, and downsides

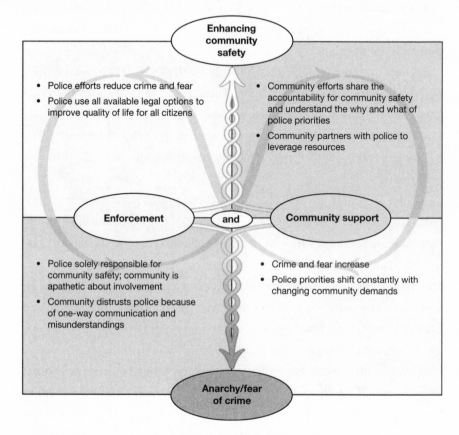

yourself these questions, you may want to notice any additional tensions about this issue that start to arise.

Assessing the polarities

After identifying the possible upsides and downsides of each pole, the next step in the SMALL process is to assess the polarities in the specific light of your current situation. To what extent does the current reality value the upsides of each pole, and to what extent does the current reality display the downsides of each pole?

Groups and teams can adopt various approaches to assess their current reality. They could use a more informal approach—asking people to come together and offer their perspectives. They could adopt a more formal survey, asking different people to rank the situation. In the first meeting with the police department employees, Seidler sought to surface initial reactions about the current reality. She divided the employees into subgroups, asking each participant to write down their own ratings for the upsides and the downsides of each pole. The participants then shared the ratings with one another in the subgroups and discussed them to come up with a consensus.

Polarity Partnerships consultants indicate this assessment on the polarity map by where they position the cyclical loop. The polarity map in figure 9-3 shows the ideal loop in which the loop moves high through both upsides while avoiding both downsides. However, if the reality is that the current situation emphasizes the upside of one pole and the downside of the other, your loop could reflect that reality instead. The Polarity Partnerships website includes examples of polarity maps with the loop reflecting different realities of the situation.

In your own polarity map, how well does your organization display the upsides and downsides of each pole? If you are working in a group, you could collect some data from the group and then discuss the results to reach a consensus about your organization. Figure 9-4 shows the polarity loop emphasizing the upside of both poles, however, you can draw in a different loop to more accurately reflect the reality of your situation.

Learning from the assessment

To effectively navigate a paradox, the goal is to value the upsides of each pole while minimizing the downsides. In reality, however, most organizations or teams advance the upsides of one pole while focusing on the downsides of the other pole—an either/or approach. This kind of approach

FIGURE 9-3

Polarity map for Charleston community safety: action steps and early warnings

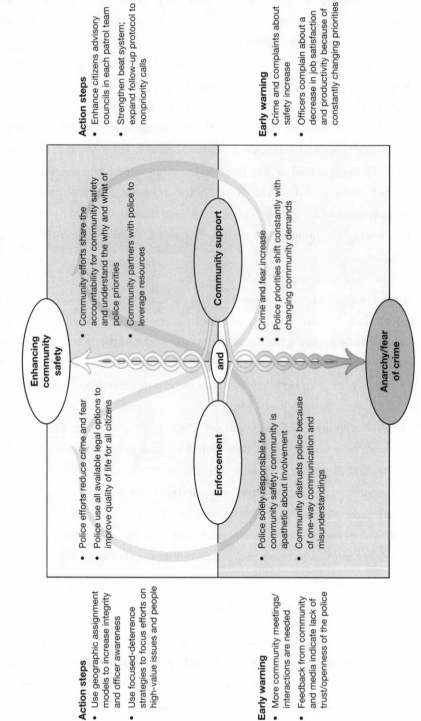

Action steps
- Enhance citizens advisory councils in each patrol team
- Strengthen beat system; expand follow-up protocol to nonpriority calls

Action steps
- Use geographic assignment models to increase integrity and officer awareness
- Use focused-deterrence strategies to focus efforts on high-value issues and people

Early warning
- Crime and complaints about safety increase
- Officers complain about a decrease in job satisfaction and productivity because of constantly changing priorities

Early warning
- More community meetings/ interactions are needed
- Feedback from community and media indicate lack of trust/openness of the police

Enhancing community safety
- Police efforts reduce crime and fear
- Police use all available legal options to improve quality of life for all citizens
- Community efforts share the accountability for community safety and understand the why and what of police priorities
- Community partners with police to leverage resources

Community support
- Crime and fear increase
- Police priorities shift constantly with changing community demands

Enforcement
- Police solely responsible for community safety; community is apathetic about involvement
- Community distrusts police because of one-way communication and misunderstandings

and

Anarchy/fear of crime

FIGURE 9-4

Polarity map from Polarity Partnerships

Greater purpose statement:
Why leverage this polarity?

Positive results: What are the positive results from focusing on pole A?
- _____
- _____
- _____

Action steps: How can we gain or maintain the positive results from focusing on pole A?
- _____
- _____
- _____

Positive results: What are the positive results from focusing on pole B ?
- _____
- _____
- _____

Action steps: How can we gain or maintain the positive results from focusing on pole B?
- _____
- _____
- _____

Pole A   and   Pole B

Negative results: What happens if we overfocus on Pole A to the detriment of Pole B?
- _____
- _____
- _____

Early warnings: What (measurable) things will happen to indicate that we are getting to the downside of Pole A?
- _____
- _____
- _____

Negative results: What happens if we overfocus on Pole B to the detriment of Pole A?
- _____
- _____
- _____

Early warnings: What (measurable) things will happen to indicate that we are getting to the downside of Pole B?
- _____
- _____
- _____

Deeper fear
What is the ultimate downside of fueling vicious cycles?

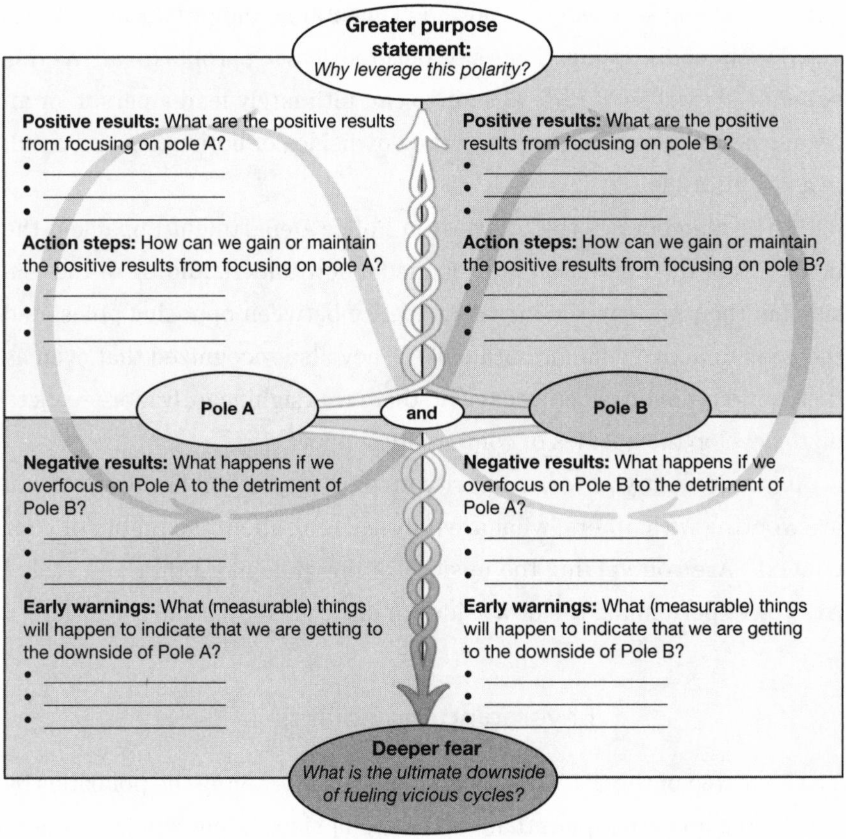

Source: Polarity map concept courtesy of Barry Johnson and Polarity Partnerships, LLC. ©2020. All rights reserved.

can end up triggering a pendulum swing, leading to a vicious cycle as we described in chapter 2. Over time, a singular emphasis on the upsides of one pole will ultimately trigger its downside, and as frustration grows with the first pole, people flip to adopt the other pole. Earlier in the book we described how LEGO got caught in this kind of pendulum swing while managing the tension between focusing on the present and planning for the future. Being so successful in the late 1990s, LEGO leaders saw no need to make changes in the organization. But soon new technologies caught up with the toymaker and the organization was left behind, stuck on an old S curve without the resources to move to a new one. In response, the leaders of LEGO shifted radically, swinging to the opposite innovation extreme. Doing so was even more detrimental as the organization innovated without discipline. Costs skyrocketed, leaving profits to fall. As this example shows, such radical swings can ultimately lead a person or an organization to oscillate between the downsides of both poles and result in a vicious cycle.

As the members of the Charleston Police Department unpacked the polarities of their situation, they gained a new understanding of the tensions in their system, the interdependence between opposing poles, and the need to actively honor both poles. They also recognized that even as their actions advanced enforcement, there was significantly more work to do to develop the upsides of community support.

As you look at your own polarity map, what are you learning? If you are working with others, what are they learning about the reality of your context? Are you valuing the upsides of one pole more than the other? Are you experiencing the downsides of one pole more than the other?

Leveraging the polarities

The final step of the SMALL process involves leveraging the polarities by developing an action plan that values the upsides of each pole and honors the synergies between them. Polarity Partnerships offers key questions that can help inform this action plan. First, what actions will increase the upsides for each pole? Second, what early-warning indicators will suggest that you may have moved too far toward the downsides of one pole and what corrections can you make to avoid doing so? These action steps offer a dynamic approach to addressing the paradoxes, encouraging people to experiment with new strategies to increase the upsides of poles while knowing how easy it is to slip into the downsides and being prepared to respond quickly when that happens. At the police department, the early conversations revealed that achieving community safety required increased efforts to rebuild trust between police officers and community members (figure 9-3). The work would advance community support and would reinforce, rather than replace, efforts in law enforcement.

You may want to take some time to build your own action steps (figure 9-4). As you continue to work through your own interpersonal tensions, consider the steps that you could take to enable the upsides of each pole. Now consider the early warning signs that would indicate that you might be heading toward the downsides and the steps you could take to avoid doing so.

The Impact of Mapping Polarities in Charleston

Seidler's workshop for the Charleston Police Department changed people's views and their approaches. The members of the police department started to appreciate that community safety required law enforcement and community support, and these employees committed to action steps to enable both. Chief Mullen made community partnerships a central strategy of the police department. Efforts included connecting with community groups, making the department's work more transparent, and advancing a trusting relationship between law enforcement and citizens.

Mullen introduced the ideas of both/and thinking and the work of Polarity Partnerships to other organizations in the community as well. Convinced of the power of creative tensions, he reached out to Charleston's chief financial officer, and together they introduced the processes to other city agencies grappling with tensions between stakeholder groups to advance the welfare of the city.

The city leaders tested both/and thinking in a contentious conflict that had emerged in the heart of the downtown business district of Charleston. The presenting dilemma involved an interest to expand the late-night culture in this area. Bar and restaurant owners valued the business from the increased night life, while surrounding residents were frustrated by the crowds, noise, and threats to public safety. City officials turned to Polarity Partnerships' SMALL process to address these opposing viewpoints and to tease out the underlying paradoxes. They convened a committee of twenty-one people with differing perspectives. Together they worked toward a goal of ensuring that Charleston remain a vibrant, and forward-looking city that would both support the nightlife businesses and address the residential neighborhoods. What could have been an ongoing conflict that tore apart the city turned into a powerful partnership that generated new opportunities. The committee developed a set of key proposals that received unanimous support from the city council.

On the night of June 17, 2015, the mass hate crime in the Mother Emanuel AME Church devastated the Charleston community, with shocks reverberating around the world. The work started by the police force several years earlier to engage with the community helped inform a powerful and positive reaction to this horrific event. People came together to grieve the tragedy—police officers and civilians, white and Black residents, city officials and other community members. Only two days later, family members of the victims stood in a courtroom and forgave Dylann Roof. Charleston became known for the compassion and connection that defined its collective grieving process. Yet Chief Mullen knew there was still more to be done:

> This horrific night changed the landscape of Charleston and me forever. It demonstrated with such clarity the power and resilience of the human spirit. It will forever signify the ability for each of us to choose between good and evil. It compelled me to take action rather than view it as another horrible situation that this time, incredibly ended without conflict, confrontation, or more violence. It would be unacceptable, because of the exceptional response, to fail to seize upon the momentum and strong relationships demonstrated between citizens and police that were manifested during this tragedy.[6]

Mullen knew that mistrust between law enforcement and citizens remained core to the challenges of advancing community safety both in Charleston and beyond. He saw how bringing divisive groups together to explore both/and possibilities helped the city progress and people heal. He saw the opportunity to move from the tragedy of the Mother Emanuel AME

Church shooting to the transformation of a community. He and Margaret Seidler, along with other members of the Charleston community and partners from Polarity Partnerships, worked to advance connections and rebuild trust between police officers and citizens. At the heart of their work was the awareness that strong communities depend on both public safety and individual rights and require the work of both law enforcement and private citizens.

In August 2017, Mullen, Seidler and others launched what they called the Illumination Project. At the heart of the project were listening sessions in which police officers and community members came together. These sessions, framed around both/and thinking and the power of paradox, invited the attendees to discuss their varied experiences with community safety. In doing so, the participants legitimized their different perspectives, increased their understanding of themselves and one another, and deepened their trust and connection.[7] As one Charleston police officer told the *Charleston Post and Courier*, he was shocked when he heard the citizens noting their fears of potential harm coming from the police. Many of the citizens felt anxious just by sitting next to him because of his police uniform: "We are coming from one dimension, and you have to look at the other side of where they are coming from. It really opened up my eyes."[8] A member of the community noted the impact of being heard while also recognizing the need for community members to take responsibility for their safety and not just to blame the police.

Between January and August 2018, the Illumination Project held thirty-three listening sessions in Charleston, generating 2,226 ideas about how to improve the safety of the community while also upholding individual rights and increasing the trust between police officers and citizens. Many of these ideas were distilled and implemented by the police department. The leaders of the Illumination Project have now spread this work to other communities across the United States.

Polarity Parternships' SMALL model is not the only way for groups to examine their tensions and paradoxes, but it is a well-structured and powerful approach that helps honor and respect competing demands and bring together opposing sides.

10

Organizational Leadership

Enabling Sustainable Impact

A visionary company doesn't seek balance between short term
and long term. A visionary company doesn't simply balance
idealism and profitability; it seeks to be highly idealistic and
highly profitable. In short, a highly visionary company doesn't
want to blend yin and yang into a grey indistinguishable circle
that is neither highly yin nor highly yang; it aims to be distinctly
yin and yang; both at the same time, all the time.

—Jim Collins and Jerry Porras

If you are leading an organization—large or small—you may be feeling
mounting pressure to navigate paradoxes. You are not alone. In 2018, Oxford
professors Michael Smets and Tim Morris teamed up with the executive
talent firm Heidrick & Struggles to interview more than 150 CEOs from
around the world about their greatest challenges. The researchers wanted
to know what kept these leaders up at night. The key finding? Paradoxes!
The CEOs struggled with ongoing tug-of-wars such as those between

adapting to ongoing change and being authentic to the organization's core mission. These leaders felt the challenges of engaging globally while competing in their local marketplaces. Each issue that the research team identified had, at its core, a paradox: "Faced with competing, yet equally valid, stakeholder demands, CEOs increasingly face paradoxical situations of choosing between 'right . . . and right.' To get the 'best of both worlds,' CEOs need to first balance their personal paradoxes so they can find balance for their companies."[1]

Recently, studies by two consulting firms amplified the importance of both/and thinking for organizational leaders. PricewaterhouseCoopers (PwC) argued that effective leaders need to successfully navigate six paradoxes, including being a globally minded localist, a humble hero, and a tech-savvy humanist.[2] Key findings from Deloitte's human capital trends survey stressed that leaders need "paradoxes as a path forward."[3]

This rising expectation of leaders to embrace and thrive with paradox invites a pressing question: How? It is one thing to label challenges as paradoxical and another to know what to do about them. These issues bring us right back to where we started on our own journeys in our research. We too wanted to move beyond the both/and label to understand how leaders effectively navigate paradoxes in their organizations.

If you have been reading along with us so far, you'll realize that the answer is not just that you need a big-brain CEO or a cadre of both/and thinking senior leaders. Nor is it just about getting the structures, mission, goals, and policies of your organization right. Rather, navigating paradoxes is about drawing on tools that create an integrated system to address both cognitive assumptions and emotional comfort and to build static boundaries and unleash dynamic practices. We have recognized that these sets of tools themselves are paradoxical—a focus on the rational and the emotional; on approaches that are static and dynamic. Again, as we have argued throughout the book—navigating paradoxes is paradoxical.

While embracing tensions is not easy, we have seen leaders from startups to *Fortune* 500 corporations succeed in doing so. In this chapter, we describe actions that leaders can take to build their organization into a paradox system. As application, we examine Paul Polman's inspiring leadership. Detailed in his recent book *Net Positive,* coauthored with Andrew Winston, Polman transformed Unilever from near failure after the 2008 financial crisis to a model of sustainable business.[4] If you are leading an organization—whether it is large or small, for-profit or nonprofit, or somewhere in between—this chapter is for you.

The Unilever Turnaround

In 2009, when Unilever hired Polman as its CEO, the company was in a death spiral. The organization experienced more than a hundred years of success, but was now facing a vicious cycle. An M&A buying spree produced more losses than gains, triggering short-term cost cutting that killed product quality, customer loyalty, and employee motivation. These losses led to even more short-term strategic decisions and more losses. The company seemed to have given up on itself and people stopped believing in their own products. As Polman observed, the "company bathrooms used competitors' soaps, and cafeterias stocked competitors' teas."[5] Was the chance to serve as Unilever's CEO at this time Polman's opportunity of a lifetime or a career-ending position?

Given his extensive experience at both Procter & Gamble and Nestlé, Polman understood the daily strains of a consumer-packaged goods company. He was also aware of the long-term challenges. It was 2009, and the world was feeling reverberations from the financial crisis. Globalization and technology offered hope for ongoing economic growth but also exposed the worldwide economy to extreme vulnerability, highlighted gaps between the Global North and the Global South, accentuated inequities across groups of people, and uncovered threats to our physical environment. As Polman repeatedly reminded his senior leaders, we now live in a VUCA world—a world of growing volatility, uncertainty, complexity, and ambiguity. The company could not ignore the challenges. The climate crisis and, eventually, the pandemic only reinforce how dependent companies are on the environment, and vice versa. The ecosystem is fragile. For Unilever to succeed for another century, Polman knew that he had to consider how the company interacted with the precarious global environment.

Many leaders were asking how their companies could weather such turbulent economic and environmental realities. Polman, however, wondered what would happen if Unilever leaders started asking different questions. Rather than ask how the company could be successful amid such global challenges, what if leaders asked how the company could positively impact these challenges? What if rather than focus solely on profits, the organization sought to solve world problems profitably? What if business could advance society rather than harm it? What if being a sustainable company meant adopting a broader approach to global sustainability? What if Unilever committed to ESG goals—environmental improvement, social advancement and sustainable governance? How could the company become, in Polman's terms, outside in—using the company to serve society—rather than inside out—using society to serve the company?

These questions eventually led Polman and his team to articulate the Unilever Sustainable Living Plan (USLP)—a bold, integrative and long-term vision in which Unilever could be a profitable company by seeking to heal the planet and advance the life it sustained. Polman knew that the USLP could do more than just rescue the organization from its current rut. The plan could position the company for a new kind of success into the future. To achieve this success, however, Polman needed to both draw on Unilever's rich traditions and transform the organization to meet modern demands. He had to rely on its successful brands in existing markets while also introducing new products and building new markets, particularly in the developing world. As Polman noted, organizational leaders would need to put sustainability at the core of their strategy. They would need to shift the company away from implementing CSR—corporate social responsibility—alongside their strategy, to focusing on being what Polman defined as becoming an RSC—a responsible social corporation—as their main strategy.

Polman's bold approach led to tremendous success. When he left the organization in 2019, he was hailed as a hero leader. He turned the company around; shareholders were rewarded with a 300 percent return over this period. He also set new standards for sustainability in companies. Doing so required that Polman lead and thrive through paradoxes.

Knotted Organizational Paradoxes

Paradoxes underpin the Unilever Sustainable Living Plan. At the heart of the plan is the tension between mission and market. Unilever sought to cut its environmental footprint in half, reducing the energy and natural resources used for its products and processes and improving the health and well-being of more than one billion people on the planet. These goals translated into projects to lower the company's water use, minimize waste, source sustainable raw materials, improve nutrition, develop a more thriving supply chain with small farmers, and many others.

What made these goals paradoxical is that Unilever senior leaders committed to achieve these environmental and social goals while doubling the company's profits. In *Net Positive*, Polman and Winston argue that adopting a purpose-driven commitment to sustainability made Unilever vulnerable to increased scrutiny by shareholders who were defensively ready to prove that ESG goals diminish business results. Unilever leaders set out to prove the opposite. "As Unilever pursued purpose, the organization felt *more* pressure to do well financially, not less."[6] These leaders recognized that failure was not an option.

The challenges at Unilever, however, went beyond the tensions leaders experienced between mission and market. In chapter 1, we introduced four types of paradoxes—paradoxes of performing, learning, belonging, and organizing. Throughout the book, we highlighted how these varied paradoxes show up across different issues in our lives. Likewise, leaders across all organizations experience these paradoxes to varying degrees. We label these organizational challenges as obligation, innovation, globalization, and coordination, and show how they reflect the four types of paradoxes.[7] As is their nature, the paradoxes associated with one challenge are knotted with paradoxes associated with other challenges to form an interwoven fabric. Pull the string of one paradox and it tugs on the others.

FIGURE 10-1

Organizational challenges associated with four types of paradoxes

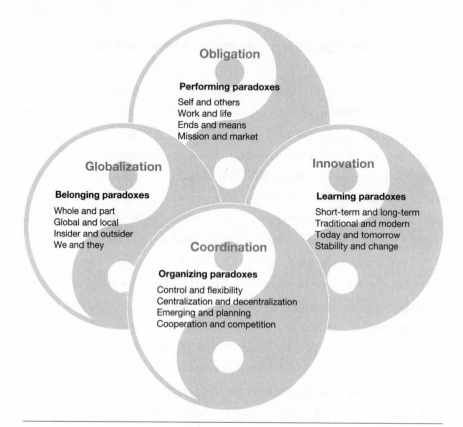

Tensions such as those between mission and market and between financial outcomes and social responsibility intensify as leaders seek to meet
their *obligations* to varying stakeholders. *Performing paradoxes* involve
opposing yet interwoven demands surrounding the organization's outcomes, goals, and expectations. Traditional strategies focus narrowly on
one set of stakeholders, typically shareholders. In contrast, Polman embedded paradoxes in the USLP by including commitments to a broader group
of stakeholders. His strategy stressed profit goals focused on market outcomes and financial shareholders. But the plan also committed to social
and environmental goals that were focused on mission-driven outcomes.

Innovation challenges involve *learning paradoxes* as they require leading for both today and tomorrow, for both short-term successes and long-

term visions, and for both stability and change. For Polman, achieving his plan for growth and sustainability meant leveraging current products for new markets in new ways. Someone living on a dollar a day in the Global South was not going to spend ten dollars on a bottle of shampoo like those sold in the Global North. Yet Polman added further criteria to Unilever's innovation strategies. He required that all efforts reduce the use of resources and lower the organization's environmental impact. His push sparked creative tensions. Tackling such problems required new processes and practices. Unilever leaders developed various means to minimize its use of palm oil, plastic packaging, extraneous paper, fossil fuels, and other resources. These innovative practices also cut expenses, which increased the company's profitability.

Addressing these varied issues creates *coordination* challenges, surfacing underlying *organizing paradoxes* such as centralization and decentralization, cooperation and competition, emergence and planning. Polman understood that his plan could only succeed with the support of an ecosystem of stakeholders. To identify new sources of growth and tackle some of their toughest problems, they needed collaboration with, rather than confrontation from, activist groups like Greenpeace, the World Wide Fund for Nature, UNICEF, the World Food Program, and others. For this reason, Polman built partnerships with both governmental and nongovernmental agencies to help set and uphold standards and create transformative change. Unilever also needed engagement from competitors especially on issues that concerned the future of humanity like deforestation or plastic pollution in oceans. Polman sought and fostered vital patience and trust, stressing that costs would drop and risks would diminish when the industry started to adopt sustainability standards. Cooperating on sustainability would allow the whole industry to be more competitive and create new opportunities.

As technology enables more and faster connections across regions, organizational leaders face increased *globalization* challenges. Embedded in these challenges are *belonging paradoxes* informed by tensions between global integration and local uniqueness, self and others, whole and parts, insiders and outsiders. Polman experienced these tensions and also purposefully intensified them. He often stressed that to advance the livelihoods of billions of people around the planet, Unilever needed to build its markets in developing countries. Again, he held a high and paradoxical bar. He called for Unilever to address unique local demands by leveraging its global brand, to use its solutions from advanced markets and power of scale while also respecting the varied tastes, cultures, and needs of distinct communities.

The more Polman explored the tensions inherent in the Unilever Sustainable Living Plan, the more he came to see paradox across the most vexing problems in any business. Polman realized something important that informed his understanding of Unilever and leadership more generally—organizations are inherently paradoxical. The challenge is to uncover those paradoxes and use them to advance novel ideas rather than get mired in conflict. Modeling both/and thinking, Polman surfaced interwoven paradoxes at Unilever, making them palpable and valued in the organization. He then created the organizational context to support people as they navigated these paradoxes. He described these challenges to us:

> In any organization, inherent complexity is built in, such as the matrix structure, where you have varied and interwoven categories and functions. At any of the intersections you have friction, because people come in with different perspectives, different needs, sometimes different performance drivers that you cannot avoid. The challenge in any organization is to turn friction into positive energy. So how do you do this? And what do you spend your time on? It is not rocket science. It is hard work. It is intensive work that you have to do all the time, and it is never perfect. At Unilever, sometimes we do not handle these tensions well, but we want to more often be on the right side of the equation.[8]

Developing Your Organization into a Paradox System

Building a sustainable corporation doesn't take rocket science. But neither is it easy, as the task is mired in paradoxes. The ability of Unilever's senior leaders to navigate paradoxes offered the organization a competitive advan-

TABLE 10-1

Leadership tasks to implement the paradox system in your organization

Build a context to enable both/and thinking	Invite people into both/and thinking
LEADERSHIP ACTIONS	
Link organizational tensions to a higher purpose (*boundaries*) • Set a long-term vision that holistically and passionately links opposing poles with one another	**Surface the underlying paradoxes (*assumptions*)** • Name the tensions • Use language to describe the paradoxical nature of the tensions
Build guardrails around paradoxical poles (*boundaries*) • Set goals and roles, and engage stakeholders who will stand up for each pole to ensure that it is represented	**Honor the discomfort (*comfort*)** • Create an environment to welcome vulnerability • Invite employees to identify underlying fears, anxieties, and discomfort with uncertainty and conflict
Diversify the stakeholders (*boundaries*) • Work with potential competitors or adversaries • Build diversity into the leadership	**Build skills for managing conflict (*comfort*)** • Model conflict-building skills and a willingness to give and receive critical feedback • Explicitly teach leaders skills for productive conflict
Encourage experimentation (*dynamism*) • Set up low-cost experiments to try out new possibilities • Use language, culture, and rewards to spur low-cost experimentation • Evaluate experiments before making a broader decision • Be willing to shut down failures	**Personalize paradoxes for employees (*assumptions*)** • Connect the competing demands with individual employees' goals • Provide training and development that fosters a paradox mindset
RESULTING IMPACT	
• Grows value from engaging opposing sides while holding tensions in relationship to one another to build connections and synergies • Enables more practices and processes for continuous learning and adaptation	• Encourages individuals to value paradox and become more adept and at ease working through tensions together

tage. In this chapter, we highlight actions you can take to create this environment in your organizations and we describe the impacts of these actions (table 10-1). The goal of these leadership tasks is to embed the various tools of the paradox system into your organization, creating opportunities for the assumptions, boundaries, comfort, and dynamism of both/and thinking to work together.

Build a Context to Enable Both/And Thinking

Developing your organization to effectively navigate paradox involves building an environment that embraces both/and thinking and then inviting people to engage with this approach. We identify some pragmatic ways that leaders can create the context to do so.

Link organizational tensions to a higher purpose

As Polman told us, "The first thing that is very important to me, which I always spend a lot of time on in the organization, is to align the organization to a higher purpose."[9]

A higher purpose—a passionate overarching vision statement—puts a stake in the ground around paradoxes, motivating and energizing people to embrace these contradictory demands.[10] In the paradox system, we note how a higher purpose offers a structural approach—a boundary—that inspires integration and connection. These overarching visions powerfully accommodate paradoxes for several reasons. First, paradoxes surface conflicts between different stakeholder groups. A higher purpose invites people to think beyond the conflict; to adopt a more holistic approach that can accommodate competing demands and blur immediate friction.[11] Warring factions for short-term resources can often find synergies when they consider long-term outcomes.[12] In chapter 5, we introduced Janet Perna, General Manager of the Data Management Division at IBM, who started each of her senior leadership meetings reminding the team of its higher purpose, setting the stage for integrative thinking. When tensions erupted between team members, as was bound to happen, she would remind the team members about their vision and invite them to think about how the opposing perspectives could work together toward that vision. As Polman told us, "The higher the purpose is, the quicker you get people to align."[13]

In crafting a higher purpose, Polman looked to the past to catapult the company into the future. Unilever started in 1885 as Lever Brothers, a soap company in the United Kingdom. Yet the Lever brothers saw their company as doing far more than just making soap; they sought to "make cleanliness commonplace and to lessen the work for women."[14] The organization became integral in building the local community of Port Sunlight, in the United Kingdom. They advanced the lives of the people who lived in the community by creating schools, health-care facilities, and art houses, while fighting for a six-day (rather than seven-day) workweek, introducing pensions and guaranteeing wages and jobs during World War I.[15] This ethos of using business to advance the social needs of the community persisted, even once Lever Brothers merged with the Dutch company Margarine Uni in 1929.

Polman brought the company back to these roots—literally. He held his first leadership meeting in Port Sunlight, inviting leaders to feel the organization's long arc and broad impact. He wanted his leaders to reconnect with the company's initial ethos—an organization that sought to have an impact beyond its bottom line. Resonating with the Lever brothers' initial thinking, Polman and his senior team developed a forward-looking higher purpose statement—"making sustainable living commonplace." With a commitment to this higher purpose, the leaders next had to align the organizational culture, structures, and practices to effectively navigate the paradoxes in this vision.

Build guardrails around paradoxical poles

Aspirational visions can motivate and unify, yet even with the boldest and most audacious vision statements, leaders still face the lure from cognitive, emotional, and behavioral traps and fall prey to either/or thinking. It is one thing to espouse goals of an innovative organization, for example, but another thing to do so when you are facing the demands of the existing world. Similarly, it is inspiring to commit to a sustainability mission, but the profit motive also poses powerful counterincentives. Leaders need to not only articulate an overarching vision that accommodates competing demands but also create the conditions for their employees to continuously engage these opposing forces.

One way to ensure that organizational leaders will continually accommodate competing demands is to build guardrails into the organization's structures. Guardrails involve people, processes, and practices that reinforce the opposing demands. Some of these structural features uphold commitments to one pole of a paradox, while others uphold commitments to the other pole. Like the guardrails on a road, these structural features serve as boundaries to keep the organization from going too far in one direction or the other. They also frame out a space, within which competing demands can surface and challenge us to find more creative and generative solutions.

Guardrails already existed to ensure that Unilever leaders would strive for financial goals, including short-term metrics and expectations from the market and shareholders. Polman and his leaders, however, needed to set up guardrails to ensure that their social and environmental goals would not be drowned out by persistent financial pressures. Key to this effort was hiring Jeff Seabright, an experienced leader, to be the chief sustainability officer to help launch the initiatives and steward the Unilever Sustainable Living Plan. Notably, while the firm initially needed to keep Seabright's role separate to ensure focus and emphasis on their sustainability initiatives, the work of sustainability eventually became embedded in everyone's roles at the company. The leadership team also set out specific goals and metrics for environmental and social impact. The USLP's three big initiatives had dozens of smaller goals, each with clear targets. These targets were challenging. Compared with using profit to measure business success, sustainability goals are often broader, more abstract, and longer term. But as the adage goes, what gets measured, gets managed. The leadership team at Unilever worked toward creating a scorecard with metrics for short-term outputs for their social and environmental goals that would keep them on track toward their longer-term goals.

Importantly, Polman committed to addressing these sustainability goals while doubling the size of the business. Even more remarkable, Polman planned to double the size of the business *through* the actions of the plan, not just alongside or in spite of it. As he and Winston note in *Net Positive*, "The plan was not a CSR-style [corporate social responsibility style] add-on, sitting to the side of the core business. It was, and is, the strategy, and it is hard-wired into the growth agenda. Because it wasn't separate, the company could not excel if the USLP was not successful, and vice versa."[16] Together, the business and sustainability goals formed the boundaries of Unilever's playing field. Within this playing field, leaders needed to find new approaches to running the business overall.

Arguably Polman's boldest and most controversial move, however, was creating guardrails to align the sustainability mission with the financial reporting. Public companies adhere to quarterly earnings, yet this kind of frequent reporting can lead to some detrimental decision making.[17] Polman knew that expecting his leaders to report profit every three months would work at cross-purposes with the USLP, diminishing considerations of long-term sustainability goals. Within his first year, he stopped offering quarterly guidance. Investors were shocked; some of them pulled their funds out of the company. It took courage, but Polman believed that making less frequent financial reports was critical to keeping the employees focused on the long term. He also understood that he needed investors who supported Unilever because of the USLP rather than despite it.

Diversify the stakeholders

People serve as a key guardrail for paradox, offering an additional boundary to support competing demands. Because people bring with them specific perspectives based on their own backgrounds, experiences, and roles, they can serve to uphold one pole of paradox. The key is to bring together people with diverse backgrounds to ensure representation of opposing poles. Diversity, however, is a double-edged sword. Done right, varied, distinct voices can come together to help reveal tensions, highlight differences, and foster more creative integration. Yet divergent perspectives can also foster discord.

Polman wanted to draw on a diversity of perspectives, skills, and experience to successfully address the varied goals of the USLP. He started with the board. Many members of the board did not understand Polman's paradoxical strategy. They questioned how sustainability could enable economic success, let alone advance a dying company. Instead, they saw sustainability as introducing unwanted risk. Polman expanded the thinking by bringing in new board members—with expertise in climate change, food insecurity, and other sustainability issues—expertise that would help guide the USLP's actions. The newcomers connected with existing board members to work through the tensions. Polman also engaged with the existing board members to ensure gender diversity on the board, knowing it was both the right thing to do and the prudent thing to do. Companies with more gender equity among senior leaders are associated with increased financial outcomes, even though such equity still remains rare.[18] Polman and his team committed to working toward increasing diversity across other dimensions as well—for example, race, sexual orientation, nationality—for both board and management. To further expand the insights and capabilities within Unilever, he then turned his attention to building partnerships with international institutions, NGOs, and environmental groups. These entities are often the nemesis of the *Fortune* 500, monitoring the social and environmental impact of for-profit corporations. The USLP goals exceeded the standards set by many watchdog organizations, and Unilever needed their collaboration, rather than their persecution, to succeed. Polman therefore forged strong ties with such environmental groups and NGOs as UNICEF, Save the Children, and the World Business Council of Sustainable Development.

Encourage experimentation

Paradoxes create ongoing change with tremendous uncertainty, as competing demands continually crash up against one another, presenting new and different dilemmas. At IBM, for example, the rate of innovation was dizzying. Just as the firm figured out how to enter the personal computing and client-server space in the 1990s, new web-based technology took over, creating a new challenge.

Navigating these paradoxes means being dynamic—staying nimble and testing out new possibilities without full information. To remain dynamic, organizations need to experiment. As Polman and Winston write in *Net Pos-*

itive, "The USLP was meant as a guiding star, but flexible enough to change as the business and the world changed."[19]

Transparency, humility, and partnerships helped Unilever ensure ongoing change. The goals embedded in the USLP were bold and aggressive, inspiring passion and intrigue. And yet the detailed plans to achieve these goals were fuzzy. For example, Unilever needed to move to sustainable raw materials, but it also had so much to learn. Polman recognized from the start that the company did not have all the answers and they would need to experiment in partnership with other organizations. "Many of the challenges we face today are just too big and complex for any one organization or sector—or even governments—to resolve alone," Polman noted. "It's only by working together in partnership that we can hope to develop the long-term solutions that are needed."[20] Polman's humility to recognize the company's limitations and his transparency in admitting any shortcomings invited others into the conversation, helping everyone better educate themselves, build connections, and be open to experimentation.

Other business leaders have adopted a variety of practices that enable dynamism. In 2014, for example, Netflix soared as an industry leader by creating HR practices that minimized their process controls on employees, enabling increased creativity and resulting in higher performance. Famously, CEO Reed Hastings posted a 125-page PowerPoint manifesto about these practices online. The manifesto recognized, for example, that "Most companies curtail freedom and become bureaucratic as they grow." Whereas other companies impose increased rules and process, which diminish creativity, Netflix leaders instead committed to, "Avoid Chaos as You Grow with Ever More High Performing People—Not with Rules."[21] With mostly words and only a few images the document quickly soared to millions of views (twenty million when we last checked). The document itself was an exercise in experimentation. Netflix leaders drafted a quick prototype of its core HR ideas without a lot of frills and then allowed the extensive feedback from people online to help them develop these ideas.

The ideas themselves were also a statement of dynamism, conveying HR practices that set out the basic boundaries and allowed for great flexibility within. For Netflix, the basic boundaries of its HR practices were a set of guiding principles: "Be honest," "Treat people like adults," and "Act in Netflix's best interest." They then allowed these principles to guide flexible work practices. Rather than count vacation days, they told employees that their vacation policy was that there was no vacation policy. People were free to take vacation as they needed. Netflix executives actually worried more about people *not* taking vacation than about people abusing the policy. The tech industry attracted hardworking people who tended to skip vacation. Worried about burnout, senior leaders modeled behaviors they wanted by taking vacations and being clear when they did. The company also let go of all formal expense and travel tracking and instead reminded people to "Act in Netflix's best interest." For the most part, cultural norms led people to be more, rather than less cost conscious, and the organizational leaders significantly reduced costs by limiting all the bureaucracy and oversight of expenses. These practices enabled Netflix to build agility into its system as it navigated the ongoing tension between freedom and responsibility.[22]

Jeremy Hockenstein embedded an experimental culture in Digital Divide Data (DDD) right from the start. Setting up a social enterprise in Cambodia in 1999 meant that the organizational leaders didn't know what they didn't know. Along the way, the leaders were willing to try all kinds of new practices that would advance its mission. They hired the most disadvantaged people to serve business technology needs. Yet sometimes the leaders would have to cancel these experiments. For example, some of the organization's leaders envisioned bringing their work out to the neediest citizens of Cambodia, the rice farmers living in mud huts and facing the lowest levels of poverty. One leader called this a "thatched-hut dream." To advance this dream, DDD leaders set up an experimental program with an NGO that provided services for these rural communities. DDD leaders soon realized that the spotty and unpredictable technological infrastructure, the challenging social norms, and the extremely limited tech skills of the farmers created such difficult obstacles that this work would ultimately kill the whole business. DDD leaders had set up guardrails—leaders who held the organization to its commitments to achieve its social mission in ways that would sustain the business. This experiment helped DDD leaders learn that the thatched-hut dream was actually a thatched-hut nightmare.

Notice that experimenting means letting go of specific ideas that just do not seem to work. Nevertheless, this experiment at DDD gave leaders new information about other ways that the organization could provide opportunities for people living in more rural areas. DDD leaders decided to instead open an office in Battambang, Cambodia, the biggest town near many rural communities. Doing so meant that DDD could still hire some people from rural towns—people who otherwise would not have had jobs, while ensuring more stable and predictable technology. This approach further allowed the company to be a bit more selective, identifying those who could develop stronger skills quicker.

In each of these examples, dynamism and change are enabled by guardrails and other structures. These boundaries help contain but also harness the creative tensions of paradox. The USLP committed to its social mission and its market goals, and both inspired and limited the practices for ongoing change. Netflix built its flexible HR practices around some clear guiding principles that articulated a plan for both freedom and responsibility. DDD's guardrails included people, external stakeholders, and practices to ensure that it succeeded in its social mission and its business purpose, and enabled flexibility for experimentation.

As these examples show, boundaries define and inspire dynamism. And dynamism creates practices to achieve goals. Truly, navigating paradoxes is paradoxical.

Invite People into Both/And Thinking

When senior leaders reach out to talk about how to embed both/and thinking in their organization, one question comes up repeatedly: "How many people in my organization need to understand and embrace paradox?" The question isn't surprising. Navigating paradoxes requires us to deal with uncertainty and irrationality. Most people do not like dealing with this kind of challenge. Employees often want their leaders to offer them concise and uncomplicated directions and feel frustrated when they perceive the complexity of paradox.

Many leaders want to protect their employees from this frustration. They aim to deliver simplified directives, acting as the captain with clear instructions to command the ship. Some leaders assume that they can keep the paradoxical tensions within their own role or among their senior team, shielding the rest of the company from the conflicts. We studied different configurations of senior leaders, classifying management teams as either leader-centric or team-centric, depending on who held the tensions.[23] The teams that engaged a broader group in both/and thinking enabled greater learning and saw more effective and lasting solutions. Yet the magic number of how many people need to practice both/and thinking to create a culture of embracing paradoxes varies. For instance, one CEO of a large corporation who we worked with estimated that she needs all the senior leaders, about 10 percent of employees, to navigate paradox. Others, like Paul Polman and Zita Cobb, created the conditions for all employees across the company to grapple with paradoxes. We explore leadership tasks that can create cultures for employees across the company to embrace paradoxes.

Surface the underlying paradoxes

Polman did not shy away from the competing demands embedded in the USLP; he called them out and embraced the tensions as paradoxical. As he told us soon after the plan launched, "The fact that you have tensions is often seen as negative, words like *compromise* or *trade-offs* are used. Obviously, this is the wrong interpretation of tensions, in my mind. If you run a company, you want to actually try to manage tensions and get to a higher place than you otherwise would be. This is what distinguishes above-average companies from the below-average companies."[24] To achieve the plan, however, he needed to help people shift their underlying assumptions and to get onboard with a paradox mindset.

Cobb, an innkeeper and the founder of Shorefast, constantly invites people to think about the paradoxes embedded in their social enterprise. Doing so is not easy. People often want a clear, direct vision. Cobb instead offers a long-term, holistic one. As one Shorefast leader told us, "We joke that Zita's name starts with Z and ends with A. She lives at Z. I live at A.

My job is to get us from A to Z. That's a tension. It is a great tension because she has so many ideas, but I have to go A to B, B to C, C to D."

Yet even as Cobb continues to engage paradoxes, she adopts a patient approach to help others do so as well, allowing people to slowly come to the ideas of paradox on their own terms. She tells stories and uses metaphors, often with poems and images that can expand people's thinking. Like an onion, stories and metaphors have layers. People can interpret the messages at the level that they are ready to engage with and can use the messages to inform their actions. Moreover, stories and metaphors are easy for people to remember and to use these ideas as mantras to remind themselves of the overarching ideas. For example, when Shorefast employees feel pulled in many directions, Cobb often shares the final stanza of "The Art of Walking Upright" by New Zealand poet Glenn Colquhoun:

> The art of walking upright here
> is the art of using both feet.
> One is for holding on.
> One is for letting go.[25]

Through such sharing, she does not tell people how to think, instead she invites them to accept and embrace the complexity of their own situation. Every senior leader at Shorefast seems to know the lines of this poem, repeating them when they face conflicts between opposing views. The organization also uses the cauliflower as its company symbol. This symbol reminds people of the ways that, like each small floret, their local community is unique but also tied to and reliant on the global stem. These rich communication tools help people gain confidence and competence to shift their assumptions from either/or thinking about competing demands to both/and thinking. When questions came up about whether the organization was trying to support the local Fogo Island community or trying to change the face of global capitalism, the leaders would go back to the cauliflower and remember that they were trying to do both.

Leaders don't always have the luxury of time to patiently wait for people to shift their mindsets. Polman was in one of those time-sensitive situations and took a swift and focused approach. Given the challenges facing Unilever, he needed some of his top leaders on board quickly. As Polman and Winston reflect in *Net Positive*, "It's okay to have productive skeptics around, but cynics are harmful."[26] Polman knew that people needed to believe in his vision and that they needed to be able to live with the complexity of paradoxes. He hired an outside firm to assess the top leaders, a move that revealed some gaps in leadership thinking, including leaders' engagement with broader systemic approaches and with the organization's purpose. Due to these gaps, Unilever let go of about seventy of the top hundred people.

Leaders' styles in shifting people's mindsets can range from a more patient approach to a bolder one. Either way, leaders consistently strive to reiterate the underlying assumptions of paradox—the shift from either/or thinking to both/and thinking. Any idea worth adopting bears repeating— and repeating. There's a reason for the huge market for swag (wall signs, key chains, bracelets, etc.) with messages to be grateful, confident, resilient, and more. Similarly, leaders need to constantly reinforce communications about paradoxes. As Zita Cobb found, communicating with evocative imagery—metaphors, stories, poems—works well. For example, in chapter 7, we noted that Terri Kelly, the CEO of W. L. Gore, used the metaphor of breathing with her leaders. To stay alive, you need to breathe in and breathe out. So too, for their organization to stay alive, she could remind Gore leaders that the organization needed to look to the past and to the future, they needed to be big and small, and they needed to be global and local. Breathe in, and breathe out.

Honor the discomfort

Emotions run deep when we are confronting paradox. Whereas assumptions address our rational thinking, emotions involve our intuitive responses. It is often these intuitions that drive our immediate reactions to competing demands. Paradoxes raise uncertainty, triggering underlying emotions of fear and anxiety, which can lead to defensive either/or thinking. To engage in paradoxical thinking, we must often honor the fear yet limit the defensiveness. We must build tools that allow us to find comfort in the discomfort. When we create virtuous cycles, our energy, enthusiasm, and passion can emerge.

For a long time, business leaders assumed that people could check their emotions at the door of work and focus only on cognitive rationality. We now know differently. Rather than assume that people can deny or repress their emotions, great leaders create environments that can recognize and help inform these reactions, welcoming people's vulnerability.

Morale was at an all-time low when Polman took over as Unilever's CEO in 2009. The company's focus on cost cutting and the loss of hundreds of thousands of employees at Unilever was no doubt emotionally taxing to everyone. Given the strain, he experienced significant resistance to many initiatives he introduced to advance the USLP. As we noted earlier, Polman's early decision to stop quarterly guidance to investors created shock waves in the market. Several angry shareholders left the organization in defiance. Meanwhile, board members argued that commitment to ESG goals over-exposed the organization to risk. Even as extensive examples and significant research proved this argument wrong, the board fought against these moves.

Polman trusted that the organization's commitment to a higher purpose would generate positive energy over time when people would see Unilever's impact on the world and could align their own sense of purpose with these goals. Yet he also needed to generate quick wins. He introduced early efforts to right the ship that included cutting non-value-generating costs while significantly investing in key businesses. Doing so enabled early successes that built some goodwill in the organization. He also organized a week-long executive education program at Harvard Business School for one hundred of his top leaders. The program was facilitated by faculty experts like Bill George, former CEO of Medtronic, and author of *Authentic Leadership*. A core focus of the week was to invite leaders to reflect deeply on their own challenges and fears, as well as their own hopes and passions. They were empowered to articulate how a "crucible" moment in their lives made them who they are. To facilitate connection and community, the leaders shared some of these moments with one another. Polman launched the program by modeling vulnerability. He shared some of his own moments where he experienced deep emotions, such as watching his father work two jobs to ensure a better life for his children, a climb to Mount Kilimanjaro with eight blind people, and being in a terrorist attack in Mumbai. Sharing his own background invited others to join him.

Other leaders have also implemented practices to address the discomfort that emerges from paradoxes. Leadership is emotional to begin with. Navigating paradoxes adds emotional intensity. We have worked with leaders who rely on personal practices of meditation, yoga, or weekly therapy sessions to be aware of, and manage, their own emotions. Some leaders have brought mindfulness training into their organization to support others. Still others have created opportunities for expressing and honoring emotions more broadly. One leader who we worked with faced ongoing conflict among members of her senior team and recognized that fear was at the heart of defensiveness and conflict. In one meeting, she invited all her senior leaders to reflect and write down their greatest fears on a piece of paper. She gave them some time to think about this, as many of us need to pause in order to tap into the deeper fears that drive our discomfort, anxiety, and anger. She then invited people to reflect on what might happen if they did not address the paradoxical tensions. To encourage people to be vulnerable and share these reflections, she started by doing so herself. The experience fostered deeper connections among the senior leaders, as well as more compassion for one another. Even as the conflicts and opposing points of view continued, the leaders on this senior team were able to more openly listen to one another and navigate conflicts that were more productive.

Leadership is an emotional challenge, exacerbated by paradoxes. If you are leading an organization, you might want to consider now how you will manage your own emotions and create opportunities for others to manage theirs. How can you honor your fears and the fears of others so you can control these fears rather than allowing them to control you? How can you trigger your passions and those of others so that they can fuel and energize you and your employees? While it may seem easier at first to sweep emotions under the rug, lumpy rugs eventually explode into dust storms.

Great leaders channel emotions toward positive outcomes rather than wait to clean up an even bigger mess.

Build skills for managing conflict

One thing that gets in the way of navigating paradoxes is the ability to manage conflict. Paradoxical leaders honor and embrace conflict. Mary Parker Follett, sometimes referred to as a prophet of management, wrote in the 1920s, "I would like to ask you to [. . .] think of conflict as neither good nor bad . . . not as warfare, but as the appearance of difference, difference of opinions, interests. . . . As conflict—difference—is here in the world, as we cannot avoid it, we should, I think, use it."[27]

Consider what happens in meetings when paradoxical tensions arise. Do people name them, or do they try to bury them? Do they take sides, picking one option and defending it, or do they honor and respect the alternatives, trying to listen, learn, and value each sides' distinct and interwoven aspects?

Effectively managing the conflicts that arise from paradoxes is a skill, one that often needs to be modeled and taught. Polman told us that he welcomes conflict. In fact, he knew that the multi-stakeholder, complex nature of the USLP would inherently create conflict, and if his leaders were not already bringing the conflict to him, he would reach out and ask for it. Kerry Ann Rockquemore, CEO of the National Center for Faculty Development and Diversity, went a step further in her organization. She invited trainers to teach her entire senior leadership team productive-conflict skills, techniques to help surface differing points of view without raising defensive reactions. The ability to engage in productive conflict became a necessary skill for anyone on her senior team. Likewise, Reed Hastings, CEO of Netflix, writes of nurturing practices of constructive criticism and open debate. In *No Rules Rules*, he stresses that nurturing a paradoxically welcoming and contentious environment must be purposeful.[28] From onboarding and socialization to annual reviews and leadership modeling, employers learn not only the value of conflict but also the expectations and practices that foster learning and collaboration.

Personalize paradoxes for employees

It is much easier to solve someone else's problems than it is to grapple with our own. So too for paradox. We can easily see a way through other people's tensions but find it harder to do so when we are in the center of the arena, with punches being thrown from all sides. Being on the sidelines can be a useful thing. With some distance, we may be able to offer some sage advice to those in the midst of the fray, but we might also act as snipers, critiquing from our favored side of the conflict. In organizations, employees sitting far from the challenges of the senior leaders might have good ideas to share, or they might offer one-sided skepticism. Paradoxes are all over the place. We have found that personalizing paradoxes—helping employees explore their personal and organizational tensions—develops their paradox mindset and awareness.

Polman sought to link the paradoxes of the USLP to the individual challenges of each employee. To do so, he applied a practice described by Larry Bossidy and Ram Charan in their book *Execution*.[29] Polman asked all 170,000 employees to write down their own goals—three business goals tied to the company strategy and one personal goal. Doing so reminded the employees of the higher purpose of the company and helped them recognize that they experienced in their own work the same kind of competing demands that senior leaders dealt with at the top of the organization. The leadership team read samples of the employees' goals, selected a handful of these answers and reached out to many employees directly to talk more about these goals. In some cases, the leaders complimented the person on their aspirations and engagement. In other cases, they asked the person for more input or even to reach for more compelling goals. For the employees, the practice invited them into the arena with the senior leaders.

Increasingly, leaders reach out to us, seeking employee training and development in navigating paradoxes. Their goals are fairly consistent: help individuals develop their own paradox mindset while fostering a shared language and understanding of paradox for the organization. We've engaged in several variations of this training. For example, we recently worked with a new CEO. He sought to lead a turnaround of his century-old risk management firm and knew he would quickly need his leadership team to help navigate the paradoxes. I (Wendy), with colleague and professor Josh Keller, worked to assist him and 150 leaders of the company's Asia division. The CEO proposed, and we implemented, a thoughtful rollout, using an initial keynote to promote open thinking. As preparation, we administered the paradox mindset inventory (see the appendix) to all the leaders so that we could present the data as scatterplots showing trends across leaders and between regional teams. We then followed up with individual and group sessions to dive into the tools of both/and thinking. What was important, however, was that the leaders move beyond just assessing paradox mindsets to truly building a culture that invited people to grapple with paradox at work.

As you consider your own organization, we encourage you to return to your competing demands and the boundaries that you set. Which competing demands are important to the organization? How do people in the organization learn about paradoxes? How are they invited to embrace their creative tensions? The context set out by leaders and the invitation to employees to engage with this context enables people to work together to ensure that their organization reflects a paradox system.

Paradox: Be Confident and Humble

We encourage all of you—as organizational leaders and individuals—to be bold and confident, yet humble and vulnerable in building a paradox system in your organizations and in your lives. As both/and thinkers, we know that an ending also marks a new beginning. We wish you success as you embrace creative tensions, and we hope you learn and thrive on your journey. We leave you with a quote that we treasure. The words of Mary C. Morrison often remind us of the power of paradox to solve our greatest challenges:

> We stand in a turmoil of contradictions without having the faintest idea of how to handle them: Law/Freedom; Rich/Poor; Right/Left;

Love/Hate—the list seems endless. Paradox lives and moves in this realm; it is the art of balancing opposites in such a way that they do not cancel each other but shoot sparks of light across their points of polarity. It looks at our desperate either/ors and tells us they are really both/ands—that life is larger than any of our concepts and can, if we let it, embrace our contractions.[30]

Paradox Mindset Inventory

Our work world is filled with multiple, often competing, demands. We need to solve problems creatively but in a timely manner, to plan yet be flexible, to learn new skills while also taking advantage of existing capabilities, to perform at our best while also helping others. Our success in the workplace depends on how we understand and manage these competing demands. The paradox mindset inventory assesses your approach to doing so.

Before you take this inventory, think about some of the competing demands that you experience. Consider these demands as you rate your agreement or disagreement with the statements presented in table A-1.

This inventory assesses how you engage competing demands. It includes two parts: (1) how you experience tensions and (2) the mindset you adopt as you engage these tensions.

Experiencing Tensions

Score: To calculate your score, average all your answers from statements 1 through 7.

Average score: An average score for a white-collar professional is 4.38.

TABLE A-1

Paradox mindset inventory

	Strongly disagree	Disagree	Slightly disagree	Neither agree nor disagree	Slightly agree	Agree	Strongly agree
Experiencing tensions							
1. I sometimes hold in mind two ideas that seem contradictory when they appear together.	1	2	3	4	5	6	7
2. I often have competing demands that need to be addressed at the same time.	1	2	3	4	5	6	7
3. I often have goals that contradict each other.	1	2	3	4	5	6	7
4. I often have to meet contradictory requirements.	1	2	3	4	5	6	7
5. My work is filled with tensions and contradictions.	1	2	3	4	5	6	7
6. I often need to decide between opposing alternatives.	1	2	3	4	5	6	7
7. When I examine a problem, the possible solutions usually seem contradictory.	1	2	3	4	5	6	7
Paradox mindset							
8. When I consider conflicting perspectives, I gain a better understanding of an issue.	1	2	3	4	5	6	7
9. I am comfortable dealing with conflicting demands at the same time.	1	2	3	4	5	6	7
10. Accepting contradictions is essential for my success.	1	2	3	4	5	6	7
11. Tension between ideas energizes me.	1	2	3	4	5	6	7
12. I enjoy it when I manage to pursue contradictory goals.	1	2	3	4	5	6	7
13. I often experience myself as simultaneously embracing conflicting demands.	1	2	3	4	5	6	7
14. I am comfortable working on tasks that contradict each other.	1	2	3	4	5	6	7
15. I feel uplifted when I realize that two opposites can be true.	1	2	3	4	5	6	7
16. I feel energized when I manage to address contradictory issues.	1	2	3	4	5	6	7

Our experience of tensions can differ across settings or across individuals. In our research, we find that people experience more tensions in settings with more (1) change—when the future more quickly becomes the present; (2) scarcity—when we have to allocate limited resources; and (3) plurality—when we face more varied perspectives. If you scored on the high end of this scale, you may work in a setting where these conditions raise greater competing demands than those faced by people on the low end of the scale. The research further shows that some people are more highly attuned to tensions, even in stable environments. If you scored high on this scale, you may be acutely aware of, and even seek out, the competing demands around you. If you scored low, you may simply ignore, avoid, or tune out competing demands.

Paradox Mindsets

Score: To calculate your score, average all your answers from questions 8 through 16.

Average score: A typical score for a white-collar professional is 4.9.

People adopt different approaches when facing competing demands. If you scored on the lower end of the scale, you tend to adopt a more dichotomous mindset in which you see competing demands as trade-offs and dilemmas, and you draw on either/or thinking. If you scored on the higher end, you tend to adopt a paradox mindset and draw on both/and thinking. You see competing demands as contradictory and interdependent—two sides of the same coin. You may address competing demands by asking "How can I do both?" and respond by finding ways that engage both demands, either by finding a creative integration or by being consistently inconsistent and frequently shifting attention and resources between alternative demands.

The Zones of Navigating Paradoxes

Our research shows that your ability to thrive with tensions depends both on whether you experience tensions and on how you approach them

FIGURE A-1

Paradox mindset inventory: zones of navigating paradoxes

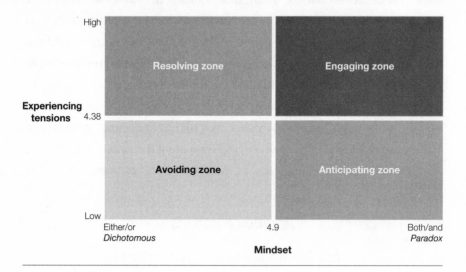

(figure A-1). Each of these factors—your experience of and approach to tensions—can be changed with awareness and training or with a move to a different environment. The interplay of these two factors determines your success in navigating paradoxes (figure A-1). Let's consider the four potential outcomes, or zones.

- Engaging zone: If your scores place you in the engaging zone, you tend to experience more tensions and accept and feel comfortable with the underlying paradoxes that lurk within dilemmas. You recognize these paradoxes as contradictory, interdependent, and persistent. You appreciate that paradoxes can never be resolved, but you still seek to engage them in a productive way. You often value how opposing forces can be interdependent and can reinforce one another. The engaging zone can be challenging, uncertain, and scary but also incredibly energizing and motivating. Our research shows that when people adopt both/and thinking to navigate paradoxes, they perform their best and are most innovative and satisfied with their work.

- Resolving zone: If your scores land in the resolving zone, you are mostly focused on resolving tensions by considering the pros and cons of alternatives and then deciding on the right option in a specific situation. You notice key tensions but generally want to come to a conclusive response. This kind of either/or thinking can often move an issue forward, but by focusing on a single choice between alternatives, you may limit more creative, generative, and integrative approaches. Moreover, when people choose between alternatives, key tensions and problems tend to resurface. Our research shows that when people try to resolve tensions quickly with either/or thinking, they are less innovative and less satisfied with their work. You can develop more creative and lasting solutions by approaching tensions as opportunities to engage opposing forces simultaneously.

- Anticipating zone: If your scores place you in the anticipating zone, you might be ready to adopt both/and thinking but are experiencing fewer tensions or simply less aware of them in your environment. However, conditions and awareness can change. Your environment can change, leaving you with greater time pressures, fewer financial resources, and more diverse perspectives—all of which may lead you to experience more tensions. You may discover conflicts that always existed but that you had ignored. When tensions arise, you are likely to reap the benefits of both/and thinking. You can become more creative and innovative by actively seeking out tensions and looking for opportunities to juxtapose opposite demands and ideas.

- Avoiding zone: If your score falls into the avoiding zone, you might simultaneously avoid tensions and want to resolve them. Or you might experience limited tensions. We have found that if you mostly adopt a dichotomous mindset and draw on either/or thinking, then you will perform better in situations with less tension. However, if the environment changes and you face greater time pressures, fewer financial resources, and more diverse perspectives, then you are likely to approach these issues as dilemmas to solve rather than as opportunities. The result is reduced performance, innovation, and satisfaction. You can become more creative and innovative by actively seeking out tensions and by reframing them as opportunities to engage opposing forces simultaneously.

People may have an initial preference toward a zone, but they can learn and change. First, we can become more aware of, and comfortable with, paradoxes. We can actively seek out these tensions, engaging them to enable more creativity. We can also learn to adopt both/and thinking when navigating paradoxes. The first step toward effectively learning these approaches is to understand our starting point.

We encourage you to take advantage of the paradox mindset inventory. You can use this tool on paper or use it online, at paradox.lerner.udel.edu. We have also used this inventory tool to aggregate scores across teams and organizations. Please feel free to reach out to us if you are interested in learning more about how we can administer the paradox mindset inventory across your team or organization and offer you aggregated results.

NOTES

Foreword

1. See A. C. Edmondson, *Teaming: How Organizations Learn, Innovate, and Compete in the Knowledge Economy* (New York: Jossey-Bass, 2012).

2. A. Edmondson, "Psychological Safety and Learning Behavior in Work Teams," *Administrative Science Quarterly* 44, no. 4 (1999): 350–383.

3. Charles Perrow, "The Bureaucratic Paradox: The Efficient Organization Centralizes in Order to Decentralize," *Organizational Dynamics* 5, no. 4 (1977): 3–14; R. E. Quinn and K. S. Cameron, eds., *Paradox and Transformation: Toward a Theory of Change in Organization and Management* (New York: Ballinger/Harper & Row, 1988); M. S. Poole and A. H. Van de Ven, "Using Paradox to Build Management and Organization Theories," *Academy of Management Review* 14, no. 4 (1988).

Introduction

1. Mary Parker Follett, in Graham (1995), 67–68.

2. We describe how factors of increased change, scarcity, and plurality expose later paradoxes and make them salient. See Smith and Lewis (2011).

3. Brené Brown, "Leadership, Family, and Service, with President Barack Obama," podcast, December 7, 2020, https://brenebrown.com/podcast/brene -with-president-barack-obama-on-leadership-family-and-service.

4. John McCain, cited in Pascal (2018).

5. "Starbucks CEO Kevin Johnson Unveils Innovation Strategy to Propel the Company's Next Decade of Growth at Starbucks 2018 Annual Meeting of Shareholders," starbucks.com, March 21, 2018, https://investor.starbucks.com /press-releases/financial-releases/press-release-details/2018/Starbucks-ceo -Kevin-Johnson-Unveils-Innovation-Strategy-to-Propel-the-Companys-Next -Decade-of-Growth-at-2018-Annual-Meeting-of-Shareholders/default .aspx downloaded January 2022.

6. Abedin (2021).

Chapter 1

1. For more on the impact of cod on the Newfoundland economy, see Kurlansky (2011).

2. Starbuck (1988), 70.

3. Our definition was developed in Smith and Lewis (2011). Modern scholars have offered varied definitions of paradox, seeking to compare and contrast paradox with other concepts, such as dualities, dichotomies, ironies, tensions, and conflicts. For more on these discussions, see Smith and Berg (1987); Quinn and Cameron (1988); Putnam, Fairhurst, and Banghart (2016); Johnson (1992, 2020, 2021). Johnson and his team at Polarity Partnerships use the term *polarities* in a way similar to how we describe paradox. He defines polarities as "interdependent pairs that need each other over time." See Johnson (2020), 11.

4. Scholars have written about the liar's paradox for centuries. For a more contemporary scholarly analysis of the liar's paradox, see Greenough (2001). For a lighter discussion of the liar's paradox, along with other similar perplexing puzzles, see Danesi (2004).

5. Schneider (1990).

6. Brown (2012).

7. Smith and Berg (1987).

8. Edmondson (2012).

9. Hill and Lineback (2011), 17–21.

10. Leonard-Barton (1992).

11. See also Miller (1992, 1993, 1994); Handy (2015).

12. Cameron and Quinn (2006).

13. Smith and Lewis (2011); Lewis (2000); Lüscher and Lewis (2008).

14. Friedman (1970).

15. Hahn et al. (2014).

16. Freeman, Martin, and Parmar (2020), 3–4.

17. March (1991), 71.

18. Festinger and Carlsmith (1959).

19. Walt Whitman, "Song of Myself," from Walt Whitman, *Song of Myself* (University of Iowa Press, 2016), 51.

20. Lowens (2018).

21. For more about the control systems in the gig economy, see Cameron (2021) and Cameron and Rahman (2021).

22. For more about knotted paradoxes, see Sheep, Fairhurst, and Khazanchi (2017).

23. For more about nested paradoxes, see Jarzabkowski, Lé, and Van de Ven (2013); Johnson (2020).

24. For this quote, see the video *Fogo Island Inn*, https://www.youtube.com/watch?v=Bqr4lHPaYDo.

25. For this quote, see www.shorefast.org (downloaded: March 2020).

Chapter 2

1. David Robertson and Bill Breen highlight the details of LEGO's rise to success and subsequent failure in Robertson and Breen (2013). See pages 39–40 for the quotes we added here.

2. Handy (2015).

3. Festinger and Carlsmith (1959).

4. Frost (1979), 105.

5. Handy (2015).

6. Handy (2015), 23.

7. See also Miller (1992, 1993, 1994).

8. Handy (1994), 53.

9. Miller (1992).

10. Grant (2021).

11. Kolb (2014).

12. Bartunek (1988).

13. Bateson (1972).

14. Simon (1947).

15. Christensen (1997).

16. Watzlawick (1993).

17. For more information about the initial study on the Pygmalian effect, see Rosenthal and Jacobson (1968). For more information about how the Pygmalian effect plays out for adults and in the workplace, see Bolman and Deal (2017); Eden (1990, 2003).

18. Smith and Berg (1987).

19. Tripsas and Gavetti (2000).

20. Cyert and March (1963).

21. Dane (2010).

22. Staw (1976).

23. We are grateful to Melinda Wheelwright Brown for introducing us to the idea that a swinging pendulum can become a wrecking ball. Wheelwright Brown (2020) describes this pattern in efforts to address issues of gender equity.

24. Robertson and Breen (2013), 63.

25. Johnson (1992); see also Polarity Partnerships, "Polarity Map," accessed January 22, 2022, www.polaritypartnerships.com.

26. Lewis (2018); Lüscher and Lewis (2008).

27. Sundaramurthy and Lewis (2003).

28. Cass Business School is now named Bayes Business School, operating within City, University of London.

29. Hampden-Turner (1981), 29.

30. Robertson and Breen (2013), 284.

31. LEGO Group, "The LEGO Group Delivered Top and Bottom Line Growth in 2019," LEGO, accessed March 2020, https://www.lego.com/en-us/aboutus/news/2020/march/annual-results/.

Chapter 3

1. Rothenberg (1979).
2. Miron-Spektor, Gino, and Argote (2011).
3. See Follett's essay "Constructive Conflict" in Graham (1995).
4. Martin (2007), 6–7.
5. Some scholars suggest that the difference between paradoxes and dialectics depends on what happens after a creative integration is found. Like paradoxes, dialectics refer to contradictory yet interdependent demands. Emerging from the work of eighteenth-century German philosopher Georg Wilhelm Friedrich Hegel, dialectics has come to suggest that a thesis and an antithesis (opposing forces) come together into a new synthesis. The new synthesis then becomes a thesis that sparks its own antithesis. The underlying tension between the initial thesis and the antithesis subsides. Debates exist whether this was actually the construction that Hegel initially meant for his dialectics. Even so, this conception of dialectics suggests that the underlying tensions morph into new and different tensions, while our depiction of paradoxes suggest that the underlying tensions persist. For more insight on the difference between paradoxes and dialectics, see Hargrave and Van de Ven (2017).
6. Schneider (1990), 140.
7. Smith (2014).
8. Quinn and Cameron (1988).

Chapter 4

1. Watzlawick, Weakland, and Fisch (1974).
2. Ellen Langer, a psychologist at Harvard University, conducted several experiments showing how mindfulness—noticing novel distinctions—changed people's behaviors and physical outcomes. As a doctoral student at Yale, she demonstrated that the health, well-being, and even life expectancy of senior citizens depended on whether they thought of themselves as important and competent (Langer, 1989; Langer and Rodin, 1976). In a more recent study, Langer worked with Alia Crum, now a professor at Stanford University, to demonstrate that the mindsets of hotel housekeeping staff influenced their physiology. The researchers told half of the housekeepers in the study that their work already satisfied the US surgeon general's recommendation for an active lifestyle. Langer and Crum said nothing to the other housekeepers. The researchers found that just adopting a mindset that their work enabled an active lifestyle led those housekeepers to improve their health as measured by their weight, blood pressure, body fat, and body mass index. More amazingly, they achieved these physiological benefits without any noticeable changes to their behaviors. See Crum and Langer (2007).

3. Smith and Lewis (2011).

4. For more information about the paradox mindset and the paradox mindset inventory, see Miron-Spektor et al. (2018).

5. We included the paradox mindset inventory in the appendix of the book. In addition, anyone can take the inventory for free at paradox.lerner.udel.edu.

6. Nisbett (2010); Spencer-Rodgers et al. (2004); Spencer-Rodgers et al. (2009).

7. A number of early philosophical traditions, including Hinduism, Buddhism, and Jainism, refer to the parable of the blind people and the elephant. For more on the parable and its varied histories, see Marcora and Goldstein (2010).

8. This stanza comes from John Godfrey Saxe's fabulous poem about the parable *The Blind Men and the Elephant,* which can be found in editions such as *The Poems of John Godfrey Saxe* (Sydney, Australia: Wentworth Press, 2016).

9. Dan Simons and Chris Chabris worked together on studies of attention and perception. More videos can be found online at Christopher Chabris and Daniel Simons, *The Invisible Gorilla,* accessed January 22, 2022, www .theinvisiblegorilla.com. See Simons and Chabris (1999); Chabris and Simons (2010).

10. For more on confirmation bias, see Lord, Ross, and Lepper (1979); Mynatt, Doherty, and Tweney (1977). For more recent work on confirmation bias, see Grant (2021).

11. *New York Times* journalist Ezra Klein examines how our confirmation biases reinforce political polarization in his book *Why We're Polarized* (Klein, 2020).

12. Dolly Chugh and Max Bazerman explore the extent to which unethical behavior often results from what they call bounded awareness—our failure to see, seek, or readily use information in our decision making. For more information on bounded awareness, see Chugh and Bazerman (2007); Chugh (2018).

13. Clay Drinko, researcher and improv actor extraordinaire who performed for Chicago's Second City, linked improv theater to neuroscience and cognition research in his *Theatrical Improvisation, Consciousness and Cognition* (Drinko, 2013). His studies so convinced him of the power of these tools that he set out to offer additional practical advice in *Play Your Way Sane* (Drinko, 2021), which offers 120 practices that allow people to engage in improv approaches.

14. Drinko (2018), 37.

15. Felsman, Gunawarden, and Seifert (2020).

16. Bazerman (1998); Fisher and Ury (1981).

17. Sonenshein (2017).

18. You can read more about Russell Maier's story and the Global Ecobrick Alliance at www.ecobricks.org.

19. Diamandis and Kotler (2012).

20. Grant (2013).

21. I (Marianne) introduced the term *workable certainty* in my research with colleague Lotte Lüscher in our study of LEGO middle managers. These managers faced ongoing tensions amid significant change at the organization. We found that the middle managers were better equipped to work through these challenges when these leaders were coached to reframe their perspectives. Rather than focus on solving these tensions, the managers did better by working to accept them and find a "workable certainty" that could help them move forward in the moment. See Lüscher and Lewis (2008).

22. Langer (1975).

23. A number of studies demonstrate the illusion of control. For example, Larwood and Whittaker (1977) found that students are willing to make riskier decisions about sales for a hypothetical firm if they think they are the sales manager of that firm. Similarly, managers are willing to make riskier decisions when they think they are in charge. More recently, Durand (2003) found that when individuals in an organization had more control over how they spent their resources, they were more likely to have a more positive forecast on their overall resources. For more on the illusion of control and its impact on decision making, see the review from Stefan and David (2013).

24. As an example, Hill and Lineback (2011) note that leaders who let go of control open themselves and their empowered subordinates to greater learning and innovation. Edmonson (2012) finds that leaders who show their vulnerability by letting go of control build psychological safety, encourage experimentation, and foster enhanced teaming.

25. Heifetz, Grashow, and Linsky (2009), 19.

26. Heifetz and Linsky (2002), 53–54.

27. Friedman (2005).

28. Kierkegaard (1962).

Chapter 5

1. "Hardware and Tear," *Economist*, December 19, 1992, 63–64.

2. For more on Gerstner's turnaround strategy, see Gerstner (2002).

3. IBM's three-horizon strategy was influenced by Baghai, Coley, and White (2000).

4. March (1991), 71–87.

5. Ibarra (1999) suggests that grappling with the authenticity paradox requires us to explore provisional selves which serve as "trials for possible but not yet fully elaborated professional identities." For more on the authenticity paradox, see Ibarra (2015a, 2015b).

6. For more about the nature of an ambidextrous organization, see Tushman and O'Reilly (1996). For more about how IBM implemented a strategy to build an ambidextrous organization, see Harreld, Tushman, and O'Reilly (2007). See also O'Reilly and Tushman (2016); Binns, O'Reilly, and Tushman (2022).

7. Frankl (1959).

8. Vozza (2014).

9. Roy West (1968), 38.

10. Translation of Saint-Exupéry quote from Quote Investigator, "Teach Them to Yearn for the Vast and Endless Sea," citing Antoine de Saint-Exupéry, *Citadelle*, section 75 (Paris: Gallimard, 1948; reprint), 687. (Reprint of text first published in 1948, https://quoteinvestigator.com/2015/08/25/sea/#note-11852-1.)

11. For more on Sinek, see Simon Sinek, "How Great Leaders Inspire Action," TEDx talk, TEDxPuget Sound, September 2009, https://www.ted.com/talks/simon_sinek_how_great_leaders_inspire_action; and Sinek (2009).

12. For more information about Seeds of Peace, see www.seedsofpeace.org.

13. Sherif et al. (1961).

14. Slawinski and Bansal (2015) discuss the role of long-term thinking to address paradoxical tensions. They find that companies in the Alberta oil sands adopted practices that were more environmental when the firms had a longer-term vision.

15. Smets et al. (2015).

16. Janet Perna, video conference interview with author, November 30, 2021.

17. In our work, we found separating and connecting activities occurred both at the level of the organization and at the level of the senior leadership team. Not only did leaders create structures that enabled their organizations, but they also built practices that allowed the senior leaders themselves to separate and connect the tensions. See Smith (2014); Tushman, Smith, and Binns (2011).

18. Tushman and O'Reilly (1996); Harreld, O'Reilly, and Tushman (2007); Gibson and Birkinshaw (2004).

19. Marya Besharov, Tiffany Darabi, and I (Wendy) compared different strategies for separating and connecting in organizations. We found that how organizations separate and connect the paradox poles depended on the types of paradoxes they were navigating. But these different approaches mattered less to their overall success than does the organizations' ensuring a balance of both separation and connection. We describe various social enterprises to offer examples of these different approaches to separating and connecting. See Besharov, Smith, and Darabi (2019).

20. For more about how stretchers use constraints to enable creativity, see Sonenshein (2017).

21. Petriglieri (2018; 2019).

22. Brown (2012).

Chapter 6

1. From Horace Mann, 12th Annual Report to the Massachusetts State Board of Education (1848).

2. Dacin, Munir, and Tracey (2010).

3. Einstein's diaries, examined by Rothenberg (1979).

4. Vince and Broussine (1996).

5. Haas and Cunningham (2014).

6. Brown (2012).

7. The Buddha's analogy of shooting the second arrow is core to his teachings. Many scholars have written about this; see, for example, Nhat Hanh (2008).

8. Stuart Manley, "First Person: 'I Am the Keep Calm and Carry on Man,'" *Independent* (London), April 25, 2009, https://www.independent.co.uk/news/people/profiles/first-person-i-am-the-keep-calm-and-carry-on-man-1672398.html.

9. Gharbo (2020).

10. Acceptance is at the heart of the clinical therapeutic practice of acceptance and commitment therapy (ACT). This approach emerges from the more traditional approaches to cognitive therapy, which suggests that changing our behavior depends on shifting our mindsets. ACT starts with an awareness and acceptance of our mindsets and emotions. For more on ACT, see Hayes, Strosahl, and Wilson (2009).

11. Brach (2004), 152. Tara Brach also has an extensive website of talks and meditations that introduce this work, at www.tarabrach.com.

12. Dostoevsky (2018), 29.

13. For more on the white bear effect, see Wegner (1989).

14. Fredrickson (2001, 2010).

15. Gharbo (2020).

16. Seligman (2012), 21–24.

17. Rothman and Northcraft (2015).

Chapter 7

1. Maslow (1968); McGregor (1960).

2. Bill Gore's founding story of the company and this quote can be found at https://www.gore.com/about/culture.

3. As example, the year Terri Kelly stepped in as CEO, Gore ranked second on *Fortune*'s 100 Best Companies to Work For, dated January 24, 2005.

4. Terri Kelly, in-person conversation with authors, Newark, DE, April 17, 2016.

5. Terri Kelly, in-person conversation with authors, Newark, DE, April 17, 2016.

6. Much has been written about the unique approaches of the Toyota production system. For more on this system, in particular its underlying paradoxical nature, see Osono, Shimizu, and Takeuchi (2008); Takeuchi and Osono (2008); Eisenhardt and Westcott (1988).

7. Osono, Shimizu, and Takeuchi (2008), 9.

8. Toyota, "Toyota Production System," Toyota Motor Corporation, accessed January 22, 2021, https://global.toyota/en/company/vision-and-philosophy/production-system/.

9. Staw (1976).

10. Kelley and Kelley (2013).

11. Toyota Motor Corporation, *Team Toyota 10* (internal company publication), January–February 2004, quoted in Osono, Shimizu, and Takeuchi (2008), 67.

12. Kerry Ann Rockquemore, telephone conversation with authors, October, 8, 2018.

13. Rockquemore, telephone conversation with authors, October 8, 2018.

14. Cunha and Berti (2022); see also Cunha, Clegg, and Mendonça (2010).

15. Busch (2020).

16. Stephen Cosgrove, video call with authors, April 1, 2021.

17. For more on Stephen Cosgrove, including his books, see his website at https://www.stephencosgrove.com.

18. The Boston Consulting Group Report can be found at Boston Consulting Group, *Strategic for the British Motorcycle Industry*, Her Majesty's Stationary Office, London, July 30, 1975.

19. For more on Honda and the debate between the schools of planning and schools of emergence, see Pascale et al. (1996); quotes are from Pascale et al. (1996), 112.

20. Chris Argyris's ideas have been captured in depth by the consulting firm Action Design (www.actiondesign.com). Argyris (1977) describes his ideas of double-loop learning.

21. Grant (2021).

Chapter 8

1. Langer (1989).

2. Fisher and Ury (1981).

Chapter 9

1. We have both read and been inspired by Ezra Klein's *Why We're Polarized* (Klein, 2020), which examines the increased polarization of American politics.

2. Scholars have written extensively on intergroup conflict. Early work on this topic, by Tajfel and colleagues (Tajfel, 1970; Tajfel et al., 1979), noted that it took very little for individuals to differentiate themselves into distinct groups. Group members seek to favor other members of their own groups at the expense of members of other groups. Scholars have pointed to strategies to navigate these tensions. Early work by Sherif and colleagues (1961) points to the value of an overarching vision. Fiol, Pratt, and O'Connor (2009) describe processes of differentiating and integration—highlighting differences to advance synergies. More recently, Goldman-Wetzler (2020) drew on her work on such intractable historical and political conflicts as the tensions between Israelis and Palestinians

to identify individual-level practices for digging deeper into our own emotions and background to connect better with others.

3. For more on the work of Barry Johnson and Polarity Partnerships, see Johnson (2020, 2021) and the organization's website, www.polaritypartnerships .com. Johnson (1992) lays out the foundation of polarity mapping. He expands on these ideas, examining polarity mapping in more depth (Johnson 2020) and sharing success stories from specific cases (Johnson 2021).

4. Horowitz, Corasaniti, and Southall (2015).

5. For more information about Polarity Partnerships and to get access to a blank polarity map, see https://www.polaritypartnerships.com.

6. Gregory G. Mullen, quoted in "Who We Are," Illumination Project, accessed April 13, 2021, http://theilluminationproject.org/who-we-are/.

7. Chris Hanclosky and Glenn Smith, *From Tragedy to Trust: Can Charleston Achieve Unity after the Emanuel AME Church Shooting?*, documentary film, written by Jennifer Berry Hawes, *Charleston (SC) Post and Courier*, June 15, 2016, https://data.postandcourier.com/saga/oneyearlater/page/6.

8. Quote from Hanclosky and Smith, *From Tragedy to Trust*, 7:07.

Chapter 10

1. Heidrick & Struggles, "The CEO Report: Embracing the Paradoxes of Leadership and the Power of Doubt," accessed April 2020, https://www.sbs.ox.ac .uk/sites/default/files/2018-09/The-CEO-Report-Final.pdf, 3.

2. PwC, "Six Paradoxes of Leadership: Addressing the Crisis of Leadership," accessed April 2020, www.pwc.com/paradoxes.

3. Deloitte, "The Social Enterprise at Work: Paradox as a Path Forward," accessed April 2020, https://www2.deloitte.com/global/en/pages/human-capital /articles/sap-response-human-capital-trends.html.

4. Polman and Winston (2021).

5. Polman and Winston (2021), 102.

6. Polman and Winston (2021), 109.

7. For more information on these varied paradoxes, see Smith, Lewis, and Tushman (2016).

8. Paul Polman, interview with authors; July 13, 2021.

9. Paul Polman, interview with authors; July 13, 2021.

10. For more on the value of purpose, see Collins and Porras (2005); Mourkogiannis (2014).

11. The Robbers Cave Camp experiment, conducted by Muzafer Sherif and colleagues in the 1950s, has become a classic example of how an overarching vision can defuse conflict. In this experiment, Sherif and colleagues brought boys to a camp for several days, put them in different teams, and created ongoing competition between the teams. The researchers found that they could shift the boys' team commitment and enable collaboration when the boys were

presented with a challenge that required all of the teams' participation and an overarching vision to accomplish this challenge. See Sherif, et al. (1961). Other scholars have further found the value of an overarching vision to enable more integrative negotiations and collaborative behaviors. See Kane (2010); Sonenshein, Nault, and Obodaru (2017).

12. Our colleagues Natalie Slawinski at the University of Victoria and Pratima Bansal at the University of Western Ontario found that long-term thinking was integral for bringing together competing demands in an organization's strategy. They compared the mindsets of leading companies operating in the Alberta oil sands region, the world's third-largest producer of crude oil through the extraction of bitumen tar. Environmental activists have decried bitumen tar as "dirty oil" and have called for the dissolution of the industry. Considering the resistance, could industry leaders rethink their business model to extract the bitumen without imposing the significant deforestation, tremendous water use, and health and economic harm on nearby communities? Slawinski and Bansal wanted to understand how leaders responded to this challenge. Interviewing sixty executives in the region, they found a significant difference in leadership mindset and impact. Most organizations felt the pressure of short-term revenues. This dominant approach made it hard to invest in serious environmental innovations. But some leaders took the long view. Any solution that would propel the organization into the future had to address these important environmental concerns, and these leaders set about finding new innovations to do so. See Slawinski and Bansal (2015).

13. Paul Polman, interview with authors; July 13, 2021.

14. See Unilever's history at https://www.unileverusa.com/brands/every-day-u-does-good/.

15. For more on the history of Unilever, see Unilever UK and Ireland, "Our History," accessed April 2020, https://www.unilever.co.uk/about/who-we-are/our-history/; David Gelles, "He Ran an Empire of Soap and Mayonnaise. Now He Wants to Reinvent Capitalism," Corner Office (blog), New York Times, August 29, 2019, https://www.nytimes.com/2019/08/29/business/paul-polman-unilever-corner-office.html.

16. Polman and Winston (2021), 121.

17. Scholars have highlighted the phenomenon of managerial myopia—the extent to which leaders sacrifice success in the long term to advance short-term profits (see Stein, 1988). In one study, Fu and colleagues (2020) found that leaders were more likely to forgo innovation when they reported quarterly earnings than they were when they reported semiannual earnings.

18. McKinsey's study of gender diversity shows that companies in the top quartile for gender diversity on their executive teams were 25 percent more likely to experience above-average profitability than companies in the fourth quartile. For more information, see Diversity Wins: How Inclusion Matters

(May 19, 2020), https://www.mckinsey.com/featured-insights/diversity-and
-inclusion/diversity-wins-how-inclusion-matters.

19. Polman and Winston (2021), 121.

20. Dan Schawbel, "Unilever's Paul Polman: Why Today's Leaders Need to
Commit to a Purpose," Forbes.com, November 21, 2017, https://www.forbes.com
/sites/danschawbel/2017/11/21/paul-polman-why-todays-leaders-need-to-commit
-to-a-purpose/?sh=8e7284212761.

21. The Netflix culture and HR practices can be found at Reed Hastings,
"Culture," PowerPoint presentation, August 1, 2009, https://www.slideshare.net
/reed2001/culture-1798664?from_action=save; see pp. 45 and 55.

22. For more on the Netflix's description of its culture see, "Netflix Culture,"
Netflix Jobs page, accessed January 22, 2022, https://jobs.netflix.com/culture.
See also McCord (2014).

23. I (Wendy) described how senior leadership teams hold paradox at the top
of the organization in Tushman, Smith, and Binns (2011). See also Smith and
Tushman (2005).

24. Paul Polman, phone interview with authors; July 13, 2021.

25. Colquhoun (1999), 33.

26. Polman and Winston (2021), 109.

27. Graham (1995), 67 (bracketed ellipsis ours). Mary Parker Follett offers
deep wisdom about how to manage conflict. Our more modern-day reading of
her ideas suggests that she is talking about navigating paradoxes. For more on
Follett, see her biography at Tonn (2008).

28. Hastings and Meyer (2020).

29. Bossidy, Charan, and Burck (2011).

30. We first read Morrison's memorable words in the inspiring work of
Kenwyn K. Smith and David N. Berg (Smith and Berg, 1987). The original
quotation is from Mary C. Morrison, "In Praise of Paradox," *Episcopalian*,
January 1983.

BIBLIOGRAPHY

Abedin, H. (2021). *Both/And: A Memoir*. New York: Scribner.

Andriopoulos, C., and M. W. Lewis (2009). "Exploitation-Exploration Tensions and Organizational Ambidexterity: Managing Paradoxes of Innovation." *Organization Science* 20(4): 696–717.

——— (2010). "Managing Innovation Paradoxes: Ambidexterity Lessons from Leading Product Design Companies." *Long Range Planning* 43(1): 104–122.

Argyris, C. (1977). "Double Loop Learning in Organizations." *Harvard Business Review*, September: 115–125.

Baghai, M., S. Coley, and D. White (2000). *The Alchemy of Growth*. Boulder, CO: Perseus Books.

Bartunek, J. (1988). "The Dynamics of Personal and Organizational Reframing." In *Paradox and Transformation: Toward a Theory of Change in Organization and Management*, edited by R. Quinn and K. Cameron, 127–162. Cambridge, MA: Ballinger.

Bateson, G. (1972). *Steps to an Ecology of Mind: Collected Essays in Anthropology, Psychiatry, Evolution, and Epistemology*. New York: Ballantine Books.

——— (1979). *Mind and Nature: A Necessary Unity*. New York: Bantam Books.

Bazerman, M. (1998). *Judgment in Managerial Decision Making*. New York: Wiley.

Bennis, W. (2003). *On Becoming a Leader*, rev. ed. Cambridge, MA: Perseus.

Berti, M., and A. V. Simpson (2021). "The Dark Side of Organizational Paradoxes: The Dynamics of Disempowerment." *Academy of Management Review* 46(2): 252–274.

Besharov, M., W. Smith, and T. Darabi (2019). "A Framework for Sustaining Hybridity in Social Enterprises: Combining Differentiating and Integrating." In *Handbook of Inclusive Innovation*, edited by G. George, T. Baker, P. Tracey, and H. Joshi. Cheltenham, UK: Edward Elgar Publishing: 394–416.

Binns, A., C. O'Reilly, and M. Tushman (2022). *Corporate Explorer: How Corporations Beat Entrepreneurs at the Innovation Game*. Hoboken, NJ: Wiley.

Bolman, L. G., and T. E. Deal (2017). *Reframing Organizations: Artistry, Choice, and Leadership*. Hoboken, NJ: Jossey-Bass.

Bossidy, L., Charan, R., and Burck, C. (2011). *Execution: The Discipline of Getting Things Done*. New York: Random House.

Brach, Tara (2004). *Radical Acceptance: Embracing Your Life with the Heart of a Buddha*. New York: Bantam Books.

Brandenburger, A. M., and B. J. Nalebuff (1996). *Co-opetition*. New York: Doubleday.

Brown, B. (2012). *Daring Greatly: How the Courage to Be Vulnerable Transforms the Way We Live, Love, Parent, and Lead*. New York: Penguin.

Busch, C. (2020). *The Serendipity Mindset*. New York: Riverhead Books.

Cameron, K., and R. Quinn (2006). *Diagnosing and Changing Culture: Based on the Competing Values Framework*. San Francisco: Jossey-Bass.

Cameron, L. D. (2021). "Making Out while Driving: Relational and Efficiency Games in the Gig Economy." *Organization Science* 33(1). https://doi.org/10.1287/orsc.2021.1547.

Cameron, L. D., and H. Rahman (2021). "Expanding the Locus of Resistance: Understanding the Co-constitution of Control and Resistance in the Gig Economy." *Organization Science* 33(1). https://doi.org/10.1287/orsc.2021.1557.

Capra, F. (1975). *The Tao of Physics: An Exploration of the Parallels between Modern Physics and Eastern Mysticism*. Boulder, CO: Shambhala Publications.

Chabris, C., and D. Simons (2010). *The Invisible Gorilla: And Other Ways Our Intuition Deceives Us*. New York: HarperCollins.

Cheng-Yih, C. (1996). *Early Chinese Work in Natural Science: A Reexamination of the Physics of Motion, Acoustics, Astronomy, and Scientific Thoughts*. Hong Kong: Hong Kong University Press.

Christensen, C. (1997). *The Innovator's Dilemma*. New York: HarperCollins.

Chugh, D., and M. H. Bazerman (2007). "Bounded Awareness: What You Fail to See Can Hurt You." *Mind & Society* 6(1): 1–18.

Chugh, D. (2018). *The Person You Mean to Be: How Good People Fight Bias*. New York: HarperBusiness.

Cohen, B., J. Greenfield, and M. Maran (1998). *Ben & Jerry's Double Dip: How to Run a Values-Led Business and Make Money, Too*. New York: Simon & Schuster.

Collins, J., and J. Porras (2005). *Built to Last: Successful Habits of Visionary Companies*. New York: Random House.

Colquhoun, G. (1999). *The Art of Walking Upright*. Wellington: Aotearoa New Zealand: Steele Roberts.

Cronin, T. E., and M. A. Genovese (2012). *Leadership Matters: Unleashing the Power of Paradox*. London: Paradigm Publishers.

Crum, A. J., and E. J. Langer (2007). "Mindset Matters: Exercise and the Placebo Effect." *Psychological Science* 18(2): 165–171.

Cunha, M. P., and M. Berti (2022). "Serendipity in Management and Organization Studies." In *Serendipity Science*, edited by S. Copeland, W. Ross, and M. Sand. London: Springer Nature.

Cunha, M. P., S. R. Clegg, and S. Mendonça (2010). "On Serendipity and Organizing." *European Management Journal* 28(5): 319–330.

Cyert, R. M., and J. G. March (1963). *A Behavioral Theory of the Firm*. Englewood Cliffs, NJ: Prentice-Hall.

Dacin, M. T., K. Munir, and P. Tracey (2010). "Formal Dining at Cambridge College: Linking Ritual Performance and Institutional Maintenance." *Academy of Management Journal* 53(6): 1393–1418.

Dane, E. (2010). "Reconsidering the Trade-Off between Expertise and Flexibility: A Cognitive Entrenchment Perspective." *Academy of Management Review* 35(4): 579–603.

Danesi, M. (2004). *The Liar Paradox and the Towers of Hanoi: The 10 Greatest Math Puzzles of All Time*. New York: Wiley.

Diamandis, P. H., and S. Kotler (2012). *Abundance: The Future Is Better Than You Think*. New York: Simon & Schuster.

Doren, C. (2019). "Is Two Too Many? Parity and Mothers' Labor Force Exit." *Journal of Marriage and Family* 81(2): 327–344.

Dostoevsky, F. (2018). *Winter Notes on Summer Impressions*. Richmond, Surrey, UK: Alma Books.

Dotlich, D. L., P. C. Cairo, and C. Cowan (2014). *The Unfinished Leader: Balancing Contradictory Answers to Unsolvable Problems*. New York: Wiley.

Drinko, C. (2013). *Theatrical Improvisation, Consciousness, and Cognition*. New York: Palgrave Macmillan.

——— (2018). "The Improv Paradigm: Three Principles That Spur Creativity in the Classroom." In *Creativity in Theatre: Creativity Theory in Action and Education*, edited by S. Burgoyne, 35–48. Cham, Switzerland: Springer.

——— (2021). *Play Your Way Sane: 120 Improv-Inspired Exercises to Help You Calm Down, Stop Spiraling, and Embrace Uncertainty*. New York: Tiller Press.

Duncker, K. (1945). *On Problem Solving*. Psychological Monographs, vol. 58. Washington, DC: American Psychological Association.

Durand, R. (2003). "Predicting a Firm's Forecasting Ability: The Roles of Organizational Illusion of Control and Organizational Attention." *Strategic Management Journal* 24(9): 821–838.

Dweck, C. (2006). *Mindset: The New Psychology of Success*. New York: Random House.

Eden, D. (1990). "Pygmalion without Interpersonal Contrast Effects: Whole Groups Gain from Raising Manager Expectations." *Journal of Applied Psychology* 75: 394–398.

——— (2003). "Self-Fulfilling Prophecies in Organizations." In *Organizational Behavior: State of the Science*, edited by J. Greenberg, 91–122. Mahwah, NJ: Erlbaum.

Edmondson, A. C. (2012). *Teaming: How Organizations Learn, Innovate, and Compete in the Knowledge Economy*. New York: Jossey-Bass.

Eisenhardt, K. M., and B. Westcott (1988). "Paradoxical Demands and the Creation of Excellence: The Case of Just in Time Manufacturing." In *Paradox and*

Transformation: Toward a Theory of Change in Organization and Management, edited by R. Quinn and K. Cameron, 19–54. Cambridge, MA: Ballinger.

Fairhurst, G. T., and L. L. Putnam (2019). "An Integrative Methodology for Organizational Oppositions: Aligning Grounded Theory and Discourse Analysis." *Organizational Research Methods* 22(4): 917–940.

Fayol, H., and C. Storrs (2013). *General and Industrial Management.* United Kingdom: Martino Publishing.

Felsman, P., S. Gunawarden, and C. M. Seifert (2020). "Improv Experience Promotes Divergent Thinking, Uncertainty Tolerance, and Affective Well-Being." *Thinking Skills and Creativity* 35.

Festinger, L., and J. Carlsmith (1959). "Cognitive Consequences of Forced Compliance." *Journal of Abnormal and Social Psychology* 58: 203–210.

Fiol, C. M., M. Pratt, and E. O'Connor (2009). "Managing Intractable Identity Conflicts." *Academy of Management Review* 34: 32–55.

Fisher, R., and W. Ury (1981). *Getting to Yes: Negotiating Agreement without Giving In.* New York: Penguin Books.

Frankl, V. (1959). *Man's Search for Meaning.* London: Hodder and Stoughton.

Fredrickson, B. L. (2001). "The Role of Positive Emotions in Positive Psychology." *American Psychologist* 56(3): 218–226.

——— (2010). *Positivity: Groundbreaking Research to Release Your Inner Optimist and Thrive.* New York: Simon & Schuster.

Freeman, R. E., K. Martin, and B. L. Parmar (2020). *The Power of and: Responsible Business without Trade-offs.* New York: Columbia University Press.

Friedman, M. (1970). "The Social Responsibility of Business Is to Increase Its Profits." *New York Times Magazine,* September 13, 122–126.

Friedman, T. L. (2005). *The World Is Flat.* New York: Farrar, Straus and Giroux.

Frost, R. (1979). *The Poetry of Robert Frost: The Collected Poems, Complete and Unabridged.* Lanthem, E. C. (ed.). New York: Henry Holt and Company.

Fu, R., A. Kraft, X. Tian, H. Zhang, and L. Zuo (2020). "Financial Reporting Frequency and Corporate Innovation." *Journal of Law and Economics* 63(3): 501–530.

Gerstner, L. (2002). *Who Says Elephants Can't Dance?* New York: Harper Collins.

Gharbo, R. S. (2020). "Autonomic Rehabilitation: Adapting to Change." *Physical Medicine and Rehabilitation Clinics* 31(4): 633–648.

Gibson, C. B., and J. Birkinshaw (2004). "The Antecedents, Consequences and Mediating Role of Organizational Ambidexterity." *Academy of Management Journal* 47(2): 209–226.

Goldman-Wetzler, J. (2020). *Optimal Outcomes: Free Yourself from Conflict at Work, at Home, and in Life.* New York: Harper Business.

Graham, D. W. (2019). "Heraclitus." In *Stanford Encyclopedia of Philosophy,* edited by Edward N. Zalta, September. https://plato.stanford.edu/archives/fall2019/entries/heraclitus.

Graham, P., ed. (1995). *Mary Parker Follett: Prophet of Management*. Boston: Harvard Business School Press.

Grant, A. M. (2013). *Give and Take*. New York: Viking.

—— (2021). *Think Again: The Power of Knowing What You Don't Know*. New York: Viking.

Grant, A. M., and J. W. Berry (2011). "The Necessity of Others Is the Mother of Invention: Intrinsic and Prosocial Motivations, Perspective Taking, and Creativity." *Academy of Management Journal* 54(1): 73–96.

Greenough, P. M. (2001). "Free Assumptions and the Liar Paradox." *American Philosophical Quarterly* 38(2): 115–135.

Haas, I. J., and W. A. Cunningham (2014). "The Uncertainty Paradox: Perceived Threat Moderates the Effect of Uncertainty on Political Tolerance." *Political Psychology* 35(2): 291–302.

Hahn, T., and E. Knight (2021). "The Ontology of Organizational Paradox: A Quantum Approach." *Academy of Management Review* 46(2): 362–384.

Hahn, T., L. Preuss, J. Pinkse, and F. Figge (2014). "Cognitive Frames in Corporate Sustainability: Managerial Sensemaking with Paradoxical and Business Case Frames." *Academy of Management Review* 39(4): 463–487.

Hampden-Turner, C. (1981). *Maps of the Mind*. New York: Macmillan.

Handy, C. (1994). *The Age of Paradox*. Boston: Harvard Business School Press.

—— (2015). *The Second Curve: Thoughts on Reinventing Society*. London: Penguin Random House UK.

Hargrave, T. J., and A. H. Van de Ven (2017). "Integrating Dialectical and Paradox Perspectives on Managing Contradictions in Organizations." *Organization Studies* 38(3–4): 319–339.

Harreld, J. B., C. O'Reilly, and M. Tushman (2007). "Dynamic Capabilities at IBM: Driving Strategy into Action." *California Management Review* 49(4): 21–43.

Harvey, J. B. (1974). "The Abilene Paradox: The Management of Agreement." *Organizational Dynamics* 3: 63–80.

Hastings, R., and E. Meyer (2020). *No Rules Rules: Netflix and the Culture of Reinvention*. New York: Penguin.

Hayes, S. C., K. D. Strosahl, and K. G. Wilson (2009). *Acceptance and Commitment Therapy*. Washington, DC: American Psychological Association.

Heifetz, R., A. Grashow, and M. Linsky (2009). *The Practice of Adaptive Leadership: Tools and Tactics for Changing Your Organization and the World*. Boston: Harvard Business Press.

Heifetz, R., and M. Linsky (2002). *Leadership on the Line: Staying Alive through the Dangers of Leading*. Boston: Harvard Business School Press.

Henrich, J., S. J. Heine, and A. Norenzayan (2010). "The Weirdest People in the World?" *Behavioral and Brain Sciences* 33(2–3): 61–83.

Hill, L. A., and K. Lineback (2011). *Being the Boss: The Three Imperatives for Becoming a Great Leader*. Boston: Harvard Business Press.

Horowitz, J., N. Corasaniti, and A. Southall (2015). "Nine Killed in Shooting at Black Church in Charleston." *New York Times*. https://www.nytimes.com /2015/06/18/us/church-attacked-in-charleston-south-carolina.html.

Ibarra, H. (1999). "Provisional Selves: Experimenting with Image and Identity in Professional Adaptation." *Administrative Science Quarterly* 44(4): 764–791.

——— (2015a). "The Authenticity Paradox." *Harvard Business Review*, January–February: 53–59.

——— (2015b). *Act Like a Leader, Think Like a Leader*. Boston: Harvard Business Review Press.

Jarzabkowski, P., J. Lé, and A. Van de Ven (2013). "Responding to Competing Strategic Demands: How Organizing, Belonging and Performing Paradoxes Co-Evolve." *Strategic Organization* 11(3): 245–280.

Jaspers, K. (1953). *The Origin and Goal of History*. New Haven, CT: Yale University Press.

Johnson, B. (1992). *Polarity Management: Identifying and Managing Unsolvable Problems*. Amherst, MA: Human Resource Development Press.

——— (2020). *Foundations*. Vol. 1 of *And . . . Making a Difference by Leveraging Polarity, Paradox or Dilemma*. Amherst, MA: Human Resource Development Press.

——— (2021) *Applications*. Vol. 2 of *And . . . Applications: Making a Difference by Leveraging Polarity, Paradox or Dilemma*. Amherst, MA: Human Resource Development Press.

Jung, Carl G. (1953). "Psychology and Alchemy," in *Collected Works*, vol. 12. Princeton, NJ: Princeton University Press.

Kane, A. (2010). "Unlocking Knowledge Transfer Potential: Knowledge Demonstrability and Superordinate Social Identity." *Organization Science* 21(3): 643–660.

Keller, J., J. Loewenstein, and J. Yan (2017). "Culture, Conditions, and Paradoxical Frames." *Organization Studies* 38(3–4): 539–560.

Kelley, T., and D. Kelley (2013). *Creative Confidence: Unleashing the Creative Potential within Us All*. New York: Crown.

Kidder, T. (2011). *The Soul of a New Machine*. London: Hachette UK.

Kierkegaard, S. (1962). *Philosophical Fragments*. Translated by David F. Swenson. Princeton, NJ: Princeton University Press.

Klein, E. (2020). *Why We're Polarized*. New York: Simon & Schuster.

Knight, E., and Hahn, T. (2021). "Paradox and Quantum Mechanics: Implications for the Management of Organizational Paradox from a Quantum Approach." In R. Bednarek, M. P. e Cunha, J. Schad, and W. K. Smith (Ed.) *Interdisciplinary Dialogues on Organizational Paradox: Learning from Belief and Science*, Part A (Research in the Sociology of Organizations, Vol. 73a). Bingley, UK: Emerald Publishing Limited. 129–150.

Kolb, D. A. (2014). *Experiential Learning: Experience as the Source of Learning and Development*. Upper Saddle River, NJ: FT Press.

Kramer, T., and L. Block (2008). "Conscious and Nonconscious Components of Superstitious Beliefs in Judgment and Decision Making." *Journal of Consumer Research* 34(6): 783–793.

Kurlansky, M. (2011). *Cod: A Biography of the Fish That Changed the World.* Toronto: Vintage Canada.

Lager, F. (2011). *Ben & Jerry's: The Inside Scoop: How Two Real Guys Built a Business with a Social Conscience and a Sense of Humor.* New York: Currency.

Langer, E. J. (1975). "The Illusion of Control." *Journal of Personality and Social Psychology* 32(2): 311–328.

——— (1989). *Mindfulness.* Reading, MA: Addison-Wesley.

Langer, E. J., and J. Rodin (1976). "The Effects of Choice and Enhanced Personal Responsibility for the Aged: A Field Experiment in an Institutional Setting." *Journal of Personality and Social Psychology* 34(2):191–198.

Larwood, L., and W. Whittaker (1977). "Managerial Myopia: Self-Serving Biases in Organizational Planning." *Journal of Applied Psychology* 62(2): 194.

Leonard-Barton, D. A. (1992). "Core Capabilities and Core Rigidities: A Paradox in Managing New Product Development." *Strategic Management Journal* 13 (summer): 111–125.

Lewis, M. W. (2018). "Vicious and Virtuous Cycles: Exploring LEGO from a Paradox Perspective." *Dualities, Dialectics, and Paradoxes of Organizational Life: Perspectives on Process Organizational Studies* 8: 106–123.

——— (2000). "Exploring Paradox: Toward a More Comprehensive Guide." *Academy of Management Review* 25(4): 760–776.

Lewis, M. W., and W. K. Smith (2014). "Paradox as a Metatheoretical Perspective: Sharpening the Focus and Widening the Scope." *Journal of Applied Behavioral Science* 50: 127–149.

Lord, C. G., L. Ross, and M. R. Lepper (1979). "Biased Assimilation and Attitude Polarization: The Effects of Prior Theories on Subsequently Considered Evidence." *Journal of Personality and Social Psychology* 37(11): 2098–2109.

Lowens, R. (2018). "How Do You Practice Intersectionalism? An Interview with bell hooks," Black Rose Anarchist Federation.

Lüscher, L., and M. W. Lewis (2008). "Organizational Change and Managerial Sensemaking: Working through Paradox." *Academy of Management Journal* 51(2): 221–240.

March, J. G. (1991). "Exploration and Exploitation in Organizational Learning." *Organization Science* 2(1): 71–87.

Marcora, S., and E. Goldstein (2010). *Encyclopedia of Perception.* Thousand Oaks, CA: SAGE.

Markus, H., and S. Kitayama (1991). "Culture and the Self: Implications for Cognition, Emotion and Motivation." *Psychological Review* 98(2): 224–253.

Martin, R. (2007). *The Opposable Mind: How Successful Leaders Win through Integrative Thinking.* Boston: Harvard Business School Press.

Maslow, A. H. (1968). *Toward a Psychology of Being*. New York: John Wiley & Sons.

McCord, P. (2014). "How Netflix Reinvented HR." *Harvard Business Review*, January–February: 71–76.

McGregor, D. M. (1960). *The Human Side of Enterprise*. New York: McGraw-Hill.

——— (1967). *The Professional Manager*. New York: McGraw-Hill.

McKenzie, J. (1996). *Paradox—The Next Strategic Dimension: Using Conflict to Re-energize Your Business*. New York: McGraw-Hill.

Miller, D. (1992). *The Icarus Paradox: How Exceptional Companies Bring about Their Own Downfall*. New York: Harper Collins.

——— (1993). "The Architecture of Simplicity." *Academy of Management Review* 18(1): 116–138.

——— (1994). "What Happens after Success: The Perils of Excellence." *Journal of Management Studies* 31(1) 325–358.

Miron-Spektor, E., F. Gino, and L. Argote (2011). "Paradoxical Frames and Creative Sparks: Enhancing Individual Creativity through Conflict and Integration." *Organizational Behavior and Human Decision Processes* 116(2): 229–240.

Miron-Spektor, E., A. S. Ingram, J. Keller, M. W. Lewis, and W. K. Smith (2018). "Microfoundations of Organizational Paradox: The Problem Is How We Think about the Problem." *Academy of Management Journal* 61(1): 26–45.

Mitchell, S. (1988). *Tao Te Ching*. New York: Harper & Row.

Mourkogiannis, N. (2014). *Purpose: The Starting Point of Great Companies*. New York: St. Martin's Press.

Mynatt, C. R., M. E. Doherty, and R. D. Tweney (1977). "Confirmation Bias in a Simulated Research Environment: An Experimental Study of Scientific Inference." *Quarterly Journal of Experimental Psychology* 29(1): 85–95.

Needham, J. (1948). *Science and Civilization in China*. Cambridge: Cambridge University Press.

Nhat Hanh, T. (2008). *The Heart of Buddha's Teaching*. New York: Random House.

Nisbett, R. (2010). *The Geography of Thought: How Asians and Westerners Think Differently . . . and Why*. New York: Simon & Schuster.

O'Neill, J. (1993). *The Paradox of Success: When Winning at Work Means Losing at Life*. New York: G.P. Putnam's Sons.

O'Reilly, C. A., and M. L. Tushman (2016). *Lead and Disrupt: How to Solve the Innovator's Dilemma*. Palo Alto, CA: Stanford University Press.

——— (2004). "The Ambidextrous Organization." *Harvard Business Review*, April: 74–83.

Osono, E., N. Shimizu, and H. Takeuchi (2008). *Extreme Toyota: Radical Contradictions That Drive Success at the World's Best Manufacturer*. Hoboken, NJ: Wiley.

Pascal, O. (2018). "John McCain's Final Letter to America." *Atlantic*, August 28, https://www.theatlantic.com/ideas/archive/2018/08/john-mccains-final-letter-to-america/568669/.

Pascale, R. T., H. Mintzberg, M. Goold, and R. Rumelt (1996). "The Honda Effect Revisited." *California Management Review* 38(4): 78–117.

Peters, T. (1987). *Thriving on Chaos*. New York: Knopf.

Peters, T., and R. Waterman (1982). *In Search of Excellence*. New York: Harper & Row.

Petriglieri, J. (2018). "Talent Management and the Dual-Career Couple." *Harvard Business Review*, May–June: 106–113.

—— (2019). *Couples That Work: How Dual-Career Couples Can Thrive in Love and Work*. Boston: Harvard Business Review Press.

Polman, P., and A. Winston (2021). *Net Positive: How Courageous Companies Thrive by Giving More Than They Take*. Boston: Harvard Business Review Press.

Poole, M. S., and A. Van de Ven (1989). "Using Paradox to Build Management and Organizational Theory." *Academy of Management Review* 14(4): 562–578.

Putnam, L. L., G. T. Fairhurst, and S. Banghart (2016). "Contradictions, Dialectics, and Paradoxes in Organizations: A Constitutive Approach." *Academy of Management Annals* 10(1).

Quinn, R., and K. Cameron (1988). *Paradox and Transformation: Toward a Theory of Change in Organization and Management*. Cambridge, MA: Ballinger.

Raza-Ullah, T., M. Bengtsson, and S. Kock (2014). "The Coopetition Paradox and Tension in Coopetition at Multiple Levels." *Industrial Marketing Management* 43(2): 189–198.

Robertson, D., and B. Breen (2013). *Brick by Brick: How LEGO Rewrote the Rules of Innovation and Conquered the Global Toy Industry*. New York: Crown Business.

Roddick, A. (2001). *Business as Unusual: The Triumph of Anita Roddick*. London: Thorsons.

Roethlisberger, F. (1977). *The Elusive Phenomena: An Autobiographical Account of My Work in the Field of Organizational Behavior at the Harvard Business School*. Boston: Division of Research, Graduate School of Business Administration, Harvard University; distributed by Harvard University Press.

Rosenthal, R., and L. Jacobson (1968). "Pygmalion in the Classroom." *The Urban Review* 3(1): 16–20.

Rothenberg, A. (1979). *The Emerging Goddess*. Chicago: University of Chicago Press.

Rothman, N. B., and G. B. Northcraft (2015). "Unlocking Integrative Potential: Expressed Emotional Ambivalence and Negotiation Outcomes." *Organizational Behavior and Human Decision Processes* 126: 65–76.

Roy West, E. (1968). *Vital Quotations.* Salt Lake City: Bookcraft.

Schad, J., M. Lewis, S. Raisch, and W. Smith (2016). "Paradox Research in Management Science: Looking Back to Move Forward." *Academy of Management Annals* 10(1): 5–64.

Schneider, K. J. (1990). *The Paradoxical Self: Toward an Understanding of Our Contradictory Nature.* New York: Insight Books.

Seligman, M. E. (2012). *Flourish: A Visionary New Understanding of Happiness and Well-Being.* New York: Simon & Schuster.

Senge, P. (1990). *The Fifth Discipline: The Art and Practice of a Learning Organization.* New York: Currency Doubleday.

Sheep, M. L., G. T. Fairhurst, and S. Khazanchi (2017). "Knots in the Discourse of Innovation: Investigating Multiple Tensions in a Re-acquired Spin-off." *Organization Studies* 38(3–4): 463–488.

Sherif, M., O. J. Harvey, et al. (1961). *The Robbers Cave Experiment: Intergroup Conflict and Cooperation.* Norman, OK: Institute of Group Relations.

Simon, H. (1947). *Administrative Behavior: A Study in the Decision Making Processes in Administrative Organizations.* New York: Macmillan.

Simons, D. J., and C. F. Chabris (1999). "Gorillas in Our Midst: Sustained Inattentional Blindness for Dynamic Events." *Perception* 28(9): 1059–1074.

Sinek, S. (2009). *Start with Why: How Great Leaders Inspire Everyone to Take Action.* New York: Portfolio/Penguin.

Slawinski, N., and P. Bansal (2015). "Short on Time: Intertemporal Tensions in Business Sustainability." *Organization Science* 26(2): 531–549.

Smets, M., P. Jarzabkowski, G. T. Burke, and P. Spee (2015). "Reinsurance Trading in Lloyd's of London: Balancing Conflicting-Yet-Complementary Logics in Practice." *Academy of Management Journal* 58(3): 932–970.

Smith, K., and D. Berg (1987). *Paradoxes of Group Life.* San Francisco: Jossey-Bass.

Smith, W. K. (2014). "Dynamic Decision Making: A Model of Senior Leaders Managing Strategic Paradoxes." *Academy of Management Journal* 57(6): 1592–1623.

Smith, W. K., and M. L. Besharov (2019). "Bowing before Dual Gods: How Structured Flexibility Sustains Organizational Hybridity." *Administrative Science Quarterly* 64(1): 1–44.

Smith, W. K., and M. W. Lewis (2011). "Toward a Theory of Paradox: A Dynamic Equilibrium Model of Organizing." *Academy of Management Review* 36(2): 381–403.

Smith, W. K., M. W. Lewis, and M. Tushman (2016). "Both/And Leadership." *Harvard Business Review,* May: 62–70.

Smith, W. K., and M. L. Tushman (2005). "Managing Strategic Contradictions: A Top Management Model for Managing Innovation Streams." *Organization Science* 16(5): 522–536.

Sonenshein, S. (2017). *Stretch: Unlock the Power of Less—and Achieve More Than You Ever Imagined.* New York: HarperBusiness.

Sonenshein, S., K. Nault, and O. Obodaru (2017). "Competition of a Different Flavor: How a Strategic Group Identity Shapes Competition and Cooperation." *Administrative Science Quarterly* 62(4): 626–656.

Spencer-Rodgers, J., H. C. Boucher, S. C. Mori, L. Wang, and K. Peng (2009). "The Dialectical Self-Concept: Contradiction, Change, and Holism in East Asian Cultures." *Personality and Social Psychology Bulletin* 35(1): 29–44.

Spencer-Rodgers, J., K. Peng, L. Wang, and Y. Hou (2004). "Dialectical Self-Esteem and East-West Differences in Psychological Well-Being." *Personality and Social Psychology Bulletin* 30(11): 1416–1432.

Starbuck, W. (1988). "Surmounting Our Human Limitations." In *Paradox and Transformation: Toward a Theory of Change in Organization and Management*, edited by R. Quinn and K. Cameron, 65–80. Cambridge, MA: Ballinger.

Staw, B. (1976). "Knee-Deep in the Big Muddy: A Study of Escalating Commitment to a Chosen Course of Action." *Organizational Behavior and Human Performance* 16(1): 27–44.

Stefan, S., and D. David (2013). "Recent Developments in the Experimental Investigation of the Illusion of Control. A Meta-analytic Review." *Journal of Applied Social Psychology* 43(2): 377–386.

Stein, J. C. (1988). "Takeover Threats and Managerial Myopia." *Journal of Political Economy* 96(1): 61–80.

Sundaramurthy, C., and M. W. Lewis (2003). "Control and Collaboration: Paradoxes of Governance." *Academy of Management Review* 28(3): 397–415.

Tajfel, H. (1970). "Experiments in Intergroup Discrimination." *Scientific American* 223(5): 96–103.

Tajfel, H., J. C. Turner, W. G. Austin, and S. Worchel (1979). "An Integrative Theory of Intergroup Conflict." *Organizational Identity: A Reader* 56(65).

Takeuchi, H., and E. Osono (2008). "The Contradictions That Drive Toyota's Success." *Harvard Business Review*, June: 96.

Taylor, F. W. (1911). *The Principles of Scientific Management*. New York: Harper.

Tonn, J. C. (2008). *Mary P. Follett: Creating Democracy, Transforming Management*. New Haven, CT: Yale University Press.

Tracey, P., N. Phillips, and O. Jarvis (2011). "Bridging Institutional Entrepreneurship and the Creation of New Organizational Forms: A Multilevel Model." *Organization Science* 22(1): 60–80.

Tripsas, M., and G. Gavetti (2000). "Capabilities, Cognition and Inertia: Evidence from Digital Imaging." *Strategic Management Journal* 18: 119–142.

Tushman, M. L., and C. A. O'Reilly (1996). "Ambidextrous Organizations: Managing Evolutionary and Revolutionary Change." *California Management Review* 38(4): 8–30.

Tushman, M. L., W. K. Smith, and A. Binns (2011). "The Ambidextrous CEO." *Harvard Business Review*, June: 74–80.

Tutu, D. (2009). *No Future without Forgiveness*. New York: Crown.

Van Vugt, M., R. Hogan, and R. Kaiser (2008). "Leadership, Followership, and Evolution: Some Lessons from the Past." *American Psychologist* 63(3): 182.

Van Vugt, M., and M. Schaller (2008). "Evolutionary Approaches to Group Dynamics: An Introduction." *Group Dynamics: Theory, Research, and Practice* 12(1): 1.

Vince, R., and M. Broussine (1996). "Paradox, Defense and Attachment: Accessing and Working with Emotions and Relations Underlying Organizational Change." *Organization Studies* 17(1): 1–21.

Vozza, S. (2014). "Personal Mission Statements of 5 Famous CEOs (and Why You Should Write One Too)." *Fast Company*, February: 25.

Watzlawick, P. (1993). *The Situation Is Hopeless but Not Serious*. Norton: New York.

Watzlawick, P., J. H. Weakland, and R. Fisch (1974). *Change: Principles of Problem Formation and Problem Resolution*. New York: Norton.

Weber, M., P. R. Baehr, and G. C. Wells (2002). *The Protestant Ethic and the "Spirit" of Capitalism and Other Writings*. New York: Penguin.

Wegner, D. (1989). *White Bears and Other Unwanted Thoughts: Suppression, Obsession, and the Psychology of Mental Control*. New York: Penguin.

Wheelwright Brown, M. (2020). *Eve and Adam: Discovering the Beautiful Balance*. Salt Lake City, UT: Deseret Books.

Winfrey, O. (2014). *What I Know for Sure*. New York: Flatiron Books.

Yunus, M. (2011). "Sacrificing Microcredit for Megaprofits." *New York Times*, January 15.

INDEX

ACKNOWLEDGMENTS

The writing of this book has been paradoxical on many fronts. The tensions we experienced and embraced in this process opened our minds and opportunities. Our gratitude to all who empowered us in this journey is overwhelming. Paradoxically, as we make special mentions here, we know we also inadvertently left people out. For that we apologize up front and we look forward to saying thank you personally!

Individual creativity arises through collective interactions. While our names are on the cover of this book, these ideas emerged from the inspiration and support of so many others. Our academic mentors and colleagues helped us engage deeply with paradox over the past twenty-five years. We are grateful to be part of such a generous and generative community of scholars. Both of us launched our careers with advisers who encouraged our seemingly rebellious dissertations. We are grateful to the mentorship of Michael Tushman, Amy Edmondson, Ellen Langer, Richard Hackman, Andy Grimes, and Keith Provan. As we developed our own ideas about paradox, we stood on the shoulders of giants who expanded insights about paradox long before us. We have vivid memories of cherished and energizing discussions with so many of these great scholars including Jean Bartunek, Michael Beer, David Berg, Kim Cameron, Stewart Clegg, Kathy Eisenhardt, Charles Hampden-Turner, Charles Handy, Barry Johnson, Ann Langley, Linda Putnam, Bob Quinn, Kenwyn Smith, Tom Peters, and Russ Vince. Paula Jarzabkowski recognized the power of studying paradox globally when we were still developing our ideas. She helped us convene our first subtrack at the European Group for Organizational Studies in 2010. This subtrack brought together an international community of scholars—a community that continues to grow and through which we developed vital relationships and deepened our research insights. We treasure our many coauthors who advanced paradox theory along with us while bringing joy and fun to the research process, including Costas Andriopoulos, Rebecca Bednarek, Marya Besharov, Ken Boyer, Gordon Dehler, Manto Gotsi, Amy Ingram, Josh Keller, Lotte Lüscher, Ella Miron-Spektor, Miguel Pina e Cunha, Sebastian Raisch, Jonathan Schad, Mathew Sheep, Natalie Slawinski, Chamu Sundaramurthy, Connie Van der Byl, and Ann Welsh. We also value those who have developed these ideas in their own research while encouraging this global community to thrive. We have connected with and learned from so many amazing people, including Ina Aust, Marco Berti, Simone Carmine, Gail Fairhurst, Medhanie Gaim, Angela Greco, Tobias Hahn, Katrin Heucher, Michael Jarrett, Eric Knight, Marc Krautzberger, Jane Lê, Valerie Michaud, Voni Pamphile, Camille Pradies, Stephanie Schrage, Garima Sharma, Harald Tuckermann, and Robert Wright. And in a call to future generations, we offer a shout out to Shay Karmatz for being a paradoxical thinker at such a young age.

A broader community of colleagues supported us along the way with advice, insights, feedback, and friendship. We connected with many of these colleagues through our home and visiting institutions, including the Lerner College of Business and Economics, University of Delaware; the Lindner College of Business, University of Cincinnati; Bayes Business School; Harvard Business School; University of Cambridge; and Nova School of Business. We are grateful to so many people in these institutions and beyond, some of whom deserve special mention for their support and friendship, including Andy Binns, Dolly Chugh, Amanda Cowen, Shasa Dobrow, Laura Empson, Erica Ariel Fox, Jennifer Goldman-Wetzler, Adam Grant, Elaine Hollensbe, Johanna Ilfeld, Adam Kleinbaum, Suzanne Masterson, Jennifer Petriglieri, Tony Silard, Jo Silvester, Scott Sonenshein, Neil Stott, Paul Tracey, and BJ Zirger.

Writing this book has been a challenge and a joy. I, Marianne, deeply value the Fulbright Scholars Program, which provided me with the time and space to launch my research and write this book. That sabbatical exposed me to greater tensions across business, academia, and my career, enabling tremendous serendipity.

During the crux of its writing, I, Wendy, came to treasure the team at University of Delaware's Women's Leadership Initiative: Amanda Bullough,

Elizabeth Calio, Lynn Evans, and Amy Stengel. You all made me realize how paradoxical the world is while helping me recognize how fun it can be to navigate these paradoxes together. Thank you also to Barbara Roche, my co-facilitator in our Women's Leadership Forum, for late-night pep talks and informal coaching to get this book written. I am also grateful to my group at the National Center for Faculty Diversity and Development— Maurice Stevens, Chrys Demetry, and Josee Johnston—as well as the wisdom of Rena Selzer, coach extraordinaire; all these colleagues helped me make sure I made the time and space to write this book. Finally, I feel blessed with varied communities of friends from Boston, Mt. Airy, Israel, and Yale University. Their periodic check-ins and ongoing friendship offered support and motivation.

The resulting book reflects synergies of academic insight and real-world experience. To that end, we feel indebted to leaders who so adeptly navigate persistent paradoxes and took the time to share with us their experiences and approaches. We are grateful to have learned from Zita Cobb, Stephen Cosgrove, Jeremy Hockenstein, Barry Johnson, Terri Kelly, Janet Perna, Paul Polman, and Kerry Ann Rockquemore. One reason that we wrote this book was to share their inspiring stories with the rest of the world. We hope we did justice to depicting the courage and wisdom of their paradoxical leadership. We are grateful for other leaders who helped extend our understanding of both/and thinking, such as Michael Chertok, Diane Eshleman, Jason Field, Jason Fox, Tammy Ganc, Stelios Haji-Ioannou, Vernon Hills, Diane Hodgins, Chandra Irvin, Jake Jacobs, Muhtar Kent, Marvin Kolodzik, Susan Kilsby, Nikos Mourkogiannis, Jeff Seabright, Dick Thornburgh, Mike Ullman, Matt Utterback, Marty Wikstrom, and Nancy Zimpher.

Ideas are only valuable when shared with a broader audience. To that end, we are grateful to fabulous people who work in publishing and who helped bring this book to the world. We knew our dream would become a reality the moment we started working with Leila Campoli as our agent. Leila deeply understands the publishing world. She also immediately grasped our vision for this book. She helped us bring our vision to life in every step of the publishing process. When we started to work with Kevin Evers as our editor, we knew that our dream could be bigger than we imagined. Kevin offered a vital blend of support and challenge. He valued our core insights while encouraging us to be clearer, stronger, and more succinct. Leila and Kevin, you proved a magical combination. Thank you! Further, we appreciate the broader "village" at Harvard Business Review Press, which continues to make this book better, including its impressive talent in design, copyediting, publishing, marketing, publicity, and other aspects of a book's life.

In the yin-yang of life, our families provide the bedrock from where we can advance our intellectual pursuits. Our personal foundations truly empowered our professional achievements.

I, Wendy, am grateful to those who led the way before me, modeling perseverance and dedication. My parents, Jewel and Larry Smith, provided me the brilliant mixture of acceptance and advancement. You are always proud of who I am in the moment while inspiring me to continually grow, learn, and achieve. My mother-in-law, Rhoda Posner Pruce, demonstrated ongoing curiosity about my work. Thank you for sending emails about both/and ideas and for editing parts of my writing with your eye for detail. I am forever grateful to my sister, Heather Martin, who is the perfect blend of pragmatic and optimistic, with an enviable sense of humor. I am so lucky to experience all of these in our daily (or multiple times a day!) conversations. I am in awe of the ways that I learn every day from my children, Yael, Jonah, and Ari. The three of you constantly point out both/ands that you see in the world while demonstrating the creativity of both/and thinking in your own ideas, actions, and relationships. I know that the world will be a better place with each of you sharing your paradoxical gifts. Finally, Michael, you have truly been the yin to my yang. You model for me new ways of thinking about the world. You challenge me to be a better version of myself. Your unwavering belief in this book, in me, and in what is possible strengthens me every day.

I, Marianne, am blessed by those who have taught me the synergistic power of high standards and unwavering values, bolstered by unconditional love and support. Kim and my kids, Jason, Samson, and Franny— words cannot express my love. You are core to my why. This book, its underlying research, and my leadership could not have developed without your encouragement and patience. Further, I cherish my parents, Steve and Margaret Wheelwright, and siblings, Melinda Brown, Kristy Taylor, Matt Wheelwright, and Spencer Wheelwright. I learn from you daily, valuing your inspiration as we nurture the next generations—Wesley, Cyrus, and beyond. And special thanks to my father, my most treasured mentor. Thank you for modeling the way. As thought leader, academic leader, and, most importantly, family leader, you have taught me to embrace love and discipline, confidence and humility, planning and innovation, the personal and the professional.

Finally, we are grateful to you, the reader. You are the ones living in and navigating paradoxes. You bring the ideas of this book to life. We hope that we can all engage with paradox to enable a more sustainable, creative, and thriving world.

ABOUT THE AUTHORS

WENDY K. SMITH is the Dana J. Johnson Professor of Management and faculty director of the Women's Leadership Initiative at the Lerner College of Business and Economics, University of Delaware. She earned her PhD in organizational behavior at Harvard Business School, where she began her intensive research on strategic paradoxes—how leaders and senior teams effectively respond to contradictory yet interdependent demands. Working with executives and scholars globally, she received the Web of Science Highly Cited Research Award (2019, 2020, and 2021) for being among the 1 percent of most-cited researchers in her field and received the Decade Award (2021) from the *Academy of Management Review* for the most cited paper in the past ten years. Her work has been published in such journals as *Academy of Management Journal*, *Administrative Science Quarterly*, *Harvard Business Review*, *Organization Science*, and *Management Science*. She has taught at the University of Delaware, Harvard University, and the University of Pennsylvania–Wharton while helping senior leaders and middle managers all over the world address issues of interpersonal dynamics, team performance, organizational change, and innovation. Wendy lives in Philadelphia with her husband, three children, and the family dog.

MARIANNE W. LEWIS is dean and professor of management at the Lindner College of Business, University of Cincinnati. She previously served as dean of Cass Business School at City, University of London, and as a Fulbright scholar. A thought leader in organizational paradoxes, she explores tensions and competing demands surrounding leadership and innovation. Collaborating with international researchers and executives, her work examines the management of paradoxes in contexts from product development and organizational change to governance and career development. Lewis has been recognized among the world's most-cited researchers in her field (Web of Science database) and received the Paper of the Year award (2000) and Decade Award (2021) from the *Academy of Management Review*. Her work also appears in such journals as *Harvard Business Review*, *Academy of Management Journal*, and *Organization Science*. Lewis earned her MBA from the Kelley School of Business at Indiana University and her PhD from the Gatton College of Business and Economics at the University of Kentucky. She enjoys her three children and two grandchildren from her home base in Cincinnati.